Some Assembly Required

Some Assembly Required

michael sorkin

University of Minnesota Press
Minneapolis / London

To George Ranalli

The University of Minnesota Press acknowledges the work of Edward Dimendberg, editorial consultant, on this project.

See pages 249–50 for information about original publication of these essays.

Published by the University of Minnesota Press
111 Third Avenue South, Suite 290
Minneapolis, MN 55401-2520
http://www.upress.umn.edu

Library of Congress Cataloging-in-Publication Data

Sorkin, Michael, 1948–
     Some assembly required / Michael Sorkin.
        p.   cm.
     ISBN 0-8166-3482-3 (HC : alk. paper) — ISBN 0-8166-3483-1 (PB : alk. paper)
     1. City planning.   2. New towns.   3. Sustainable architecture.   I. Title.
     NA9053.N4 S67 2001
     720'.47—dc21

                                                    2001002482

Printed in the United States of America on acid-free paper

The University of Minnesota is an equal-opportunity educator and employer.

12 11 10 09 08 07 06 05 04 03 02 01   10 9 8 7 6 5 4 3 2 1

Contents

Part III. Misfits

Introduction

Recently, sitting on yet another panel about architecture and globalization, I listened to the Dutchman to my right metaphorize world culture as a huge ocean wave and offer—as an architectural strategy for dealing with it—the figure of the surfer, riding the crest. Although this image has a certain détourning charm, the "wave" model is all wet, camouflaging the reality of a constructed culture as a force of nature. Confronted by the massive sameness of sprawl—the urbanism of global capital—my colleague chose not to resist but to go with the flow, to invent it as the inevitable substrate of the whole world.

Ironically, this reappropriation of the fantasy of nature as a vast autonomous web of which we are not precisely a part comes at a moment when we are busily discovering our own enormous impact on the natural environment, its fragility in the face of our own activities. Global warming, the rapid disappearance of habitats and ecosystems, worldwide pollution, and the breakneck homogenization of the built environment are all symptomatic of a world in which we can no more consider ourselves simply another of its species than we can stand raptly outside it, shivering at its majesty.

The view of my fellow panelist was deeply romantic, aspiring to a kind of post-technological sublimity. For him, the onrush of globalization was not merely irresistible, it had an aesthetic authority in its deep imprinting of power on form. Such "generic" urbanism—the architecture of the wave—represented an unavoidable default, a condition growing autonomously, throwing up its endlessness of freeways and airports, office towers and gated communities, McDonald's and KFCs. The surfer epistemology panders to this updated universality with a canny resignation of agency and, hence, responsibility.

This displaced agency, however, is also a critique of the old, modernist vision of universality, the idea that *its* own generic architecture—those serial white worker's walk-ups—was the path to world reform and happiness. We have now grown skeptical of such totalizing solutions, if only formally. But, in place of activist politics, we now prefer neural and "bio-intuitive" models, the idea of self-organizing systems and managerial protocols, the fluid dynamics of capital flows, generative strategies based on formal extrapolations of statistical data: MBArchitecture. This search for a neofunctionalist, "objective" architecture is also part of the general abjection of agency suggested by my surfer friend.

If not to such automated architecture-as-strategy, where to look for meaningful, tractable, and ethical distinctions and individualities in the fields of building and urbanism? Clearly, an acquiescent practice—an avant-garde preoccupied with irony or celebrity—does not cut it. Nor, in the light of the real power—and promise—of globalization do the melancholy "new urbanists" with their homely fetish for reductivist small-town and suburban precedents offer a serious alternative: the reality of the global tsunami means that the production of real differences can no longer simply rely on the revival of regional or cultural particularities at a remove that falls further and further from their originating contexts of meaning.

A more productive approach to making an architecture that is both resistant and relevant, critical and experimental, is to focus deeply on building's relationship to the natural environment, to reject the generic construction of the human habitat as an autonomous *second* nature. The almost complete indifference of the contemporary architectural avant-garde to questions of sustainability and planetary balm continues to be striking. Indeed, such research and practice are largely marginalized as both artistically and theoretically irrelevant, subordinated to purely visual effects.

The evasion of planetary responsibility extends to a dramatic indifference to the lived lives of people. Although architecture's theoretical cadre has devoted interesting attention to the inherence of social and sexual difference in form, neither the built production nor the visual polemics of our avant-garde have had much to say about urban life or about the way in which architecture can respond either to the dire situation of the world's poor or, for that matter, to the rapid shifts in American lifestyle, family structure, and mobility. Architecture cries out for a reinfusion of some sense of responsibility to human program as a generative basis for both its ideology and its formal and technological practices, but gets it less and less.

Ironically, this makes artistic practice even more crucial. As the local particulars of culture are winnowed by globalization, artistic strategies for the production of locality will become more and more valuable. Private eccentricity and collective invention will both become more crucial as the field of art is daily more subsumed by commerce or critique. Fresh architectures and urbanisms, however, have the potential both to stimulate new arrangements and to make relevantly concrete historic rituals now estranged by events.

The job of criticism is to advance this set of possibilities by creating a comfortable discursive territory for their celebration and analysis and to defend meaningful idiosyncrasies of taste. Architecture always represents a point of convergence between the formal and the social. This is what makes it architecture and, by extension, what makes it an important arena of struggle. But the struggle is of a particular kind: that building sits at the nexus of pleasure and necessity means that the advocacy of architecture is always—inter alia—the advocacy of enjoyment. Indeed, the contemporary rebellion against modernism—in which my own sensibilities were formed—is prompted, in great measure, by its failures of joy.

That architecture embodies both public and private components means, however, that a certain discrimination among enjoyments is required, especially from a critic: polemic always proceeds from some sense of obligation. While no one (except the Taliban) wants to be in the position of authorizing other people's pleasures, some idea of sharing enjoyment underlies any critical speculation about building, and especially about urbanism. In a time of remorseless homogenization and opinion-poll architecture—art directing for mall rats and Republicans and avant-garde arts institutions—it is crucial that criticism support a range of compacts and strategies that both lend places individuality and address the social character of inhabitation.

How to arrive at these compacts? I am no utilitarian, so the averaging function does not really work for me, too repressive and too uniform in its consequences. On the other hand, neither the narcissism of an anything-goes identity politics nor the narrowness of current avant-gardism provides satisfactory answers. While the city is an instrument for siting and accommodating difference, there is a line beyond which variety becomes a tactic of exclusion, something that cannot be deployed endlessly. In spite of their many vitalities, for example, we must still reject the planning of ghettos.

Difference, however, does provide a key. If there is an enemy, it is the idea of a correct architecture and of the one-size-fits-all thinking that is the legacy of both old-timey, architecture-as-therapy tactics and of the market with its own narcissism of trivial differences. The debate today—overwhelmingly cynical—is too couched either in purely artistic styles of production (reskinning familiar programs with "radical" forms) or in various acquiescences to the culture of consumption, yielding, ultimately, a teleology of despair. Even our feeble, post-Warholian avant-garde now declares itself for "branding."

This displacement of the discourse of effects onto the shoulders either of pure taste or—even more crudely—the operational procedures of formal or technical invention is the most notable development in architectural discourse of the past twenty or so years. This preoccupation with a priori certifications of intent, with arguments that certain theoretical constructs uniquely inhere in individual constructions, continues to dominate architectural explanation. In general, though, the translations are trivial, Derridean deconstruction leading to unstable-looking buildings, the Deleuzian fold leading to pleated buildings, and so on. Even pleasure dare not speak its name as a motive. Theory is seduced by the idea of the hidden deployment of power and meaning, trapped in a downward gyre of obscurity, carefully hiding its own meanings in a maelstrom of lines; every positive act or goal is condemned as "utopian" and therefore "dangerous." Abandoning every notion of cause, architecture has simply lost all reason.

What this surrender to the inexorability of commercial culture suggests—whether in the macho advocacy of "bigness" or its regressive nostalgia for modernist forms (a semiotic fig leaf for the cynicism)—is not only a forsaking of any meaningful idea of resistance but also a cover fiction for an ultimately narrow band of taste. Whether the Venturian tooth for kitsch or the schizy Koolhaasian love of regimentation and the Googie-esque both, an overindulgent rhetoric of form occludes any serious discussion of effects.

This is really just a back door to iconography for those who, in previous lives, would have had nothing of it. In many ways, this is unobjectionable: there is nothing evil inherent to representation and—hey—de gustibus. The conundrum comes in the way in which theory attempts to resituate the territory of representation per se. Siting their mimesis away from traditions of pictorialism and the re-representation of historical architectures, such strategies return to the hoary modernist nexus of an "abstract" representation, forcing building back on the fundamentals of purified form, on its geometry, on its structural behavior, on the capabilities of its representational techniques, and—to a very limited degree—on its use. More becomes less and less.

What has been submerged in all of this is real and progressive innovation, a willingness to speculate about alternative futures with a content beyond form. With a world population growing exponentially, billions ill-housed, and an asphyxiating planet, mainstream architecture's aggressively narrow interests are simply not helpful. Troubled about its own ir-relevance, hemmed by virtual space on the one hand and a commercial culture that finds it completely irrelevant, architecture too often chooses to opt out, to surf.

I hope this book opts in. For me, writing has always been the exten-sion of architecture by other means both polemically and as fuel for my money pit of a studio: I write because I am an architect. If this collection makes some small contribution to the reunion of architecture and ur-banism, both with their global and local responsibilities and with their eternal promise of joy, I will be a better one.

Journalistic sustainability requires—like any other kind—a certain amount of recycling. I have tried to edit out such embarrassing repeti-tions from this collection, but there are a few, including one very large one. The figure of Walter Hudson—the fattest man in history—appears twice. As a metaphor though, I have never found one more apt, not even that wave.

part i

Cities/Places

Eleven Tasks for Urban Design

Urban Design is a rump. Founded in a vacated crack between architecture and planning, its aim was to rescue physical urbanism from the humongous onus of "planning."

Not an unreasonable aim. The yoking of the roughshod therapies of urban renewal with the enervated stylings of modernism—the double culmination of the long march of a universalism that had long since lost its way—had, by the sixties, given planners a permanently bad name. Like the craven lie of Vietnam, the decimation wreaked on neighborhoods "for their own good" exposed a contradiction that could not but collapse the structures that produced it.

Ironically, the critique came simultaneously from opposing directions. Progressives—including locally based "advocacy" planners—attacked the juggernaut of command urbanism, exposed its antidemocratic, racist assumptions, and sought to empower local communities. The preservationism of the sixties and seventies was galvanized as an oppositional practice, in defense of homes and neighborhoods threatened by highways, urban renewal, and development. Its stewardship of the existing urban fabric opposed homogenizing solutions by establishing a link between life and place, defending the complex, elusive ecologies of neighborhood against the one-dimensional fantasies of the planners.

While this fight for community control was being waged politically, a second, more purely formal critique was launched from the camp of the postmodernists, who assailed modern architecture not simply as the expression of the planners' disciplinary designs but as their source. With its reflexive veneration of tradition and its preferences for historical stylings and the forms of the preindustrial city, architectural postmodernism was undergirded by a very different set of political assumptions than those of progressive preservationists. Implicitly and often explicitly, this backward-looking urbanism evoked and celebrated the putative social relations of "simpler" times, a monochrome, paternalistic vision of unalienated labor in an unpressured environment: Reaganville. But this postmodernist nostalgia participated in the same fallacy that doomed the modernism it sought to displace: conflating principles with forms, it both imputed superior virtue to particular styles and insisted that architecture was the answer. As the only vigorous and "new" argument available about the form of the city, though, this neoconservative, historicist view swept the field, rapidly becoming the default paradigm for academic urban design.

Part of the legacy of the oppositional origins of citizen participation and neighborhood preservationism is a generalized fear of physical models. Decades of well-rehearsed critiques of the Master Plan have resulted in a baby-with-the-bathwaterism, in a reticence of vision. While many fine designs have been conceived for the refitting of neighborhoods based on empowerment, sustainability, pedestrianism, or post–Daddy-Mommy-and-Me domesticity, few projects that transcend received models have been formulated. Today, the field is dominated by the rejiggered suburbanism of the so-called new urbanists. The far more promising—indeed crucial—sensibility of environmentalism is precluded by its almost complete lack of a constituency among architects, planners (and politicians) and by its corollary failure to produce a critical mass of legible urbanistic innovation.

This must be reversed. Our existing cities need gentle (and rapid) retrofitting with an elaborating apparatus of sustainability, with gardens and solar collectors, with ecological construction, with traffic-free streets and neighborhoods made over by the algorithms of walk-time. But this is not enough. Too often, green models are themselves propositions about decay, about allowing the contemporary city to decompose until it reacquires the character of the historic one, another style of preservationism. While it is crucial, of course, to nurture the best parts of our cities, the vital neighborhoods and the climax forms, these tasks cannot delimit the agenda of an urbanism that truly looks to the future. Fixated on the historical city as a source for its own inventions, urban design today both blinkers itself against the emergence of marvelous new architectures and largely resists coming to grips with urbanism's greatest crisis, the crazy, disastrous explosion of the fringe. Subject to abundant critique that never rises above itself, the edge city remains an imaginative wasteland, uncomprehended by designers who—fixated on historical patterns as both the locus and boilerplate for their research—give themselves over to monofunctional enclavism and the rarefactions of pure nostalgia.

Urban design is ready for an explosion of fresh forms, inspired by the democratic roots of the critique of modernist urbanism, by a deeply ecological sensibility, by a fond embrace of the pluralist character of our culture, and by a critical incorporation of the new and inescapably transformative technologies of electronic adjacency. This will lead not simply to the evolution of existing urban centers but must inevitably also result in the construction of many entirely new cities. A world population growing exponentially and our wounded biosphere demand no less. Urban design needs to escape the comfortable mire of mastery over forms and circumstances long ago learned: restoring existing cities to their original scales and patterns is no longer a fundamental problem for the architectural imagination, however thorny such a project may be socially, politically, or economically.

We suffer from a poverty of vision. Urban design can provide a remedy by cultivating numerous fresh fantasies of urban desirability, happy futures that exceed the mindful simplicities of both modernism and historicism to produce places of ravishing complexity. For this, we need the most dedicated and optimistic research. Without it, our cities will simply recycle themselves into increasingly ersatz locales, Disneylands of disconnect between form and meaning, scenes of architectural rituals that grow emptier and emptier. Without it, our cities will choke on their own waste, subject to ever more dire forms of collapse as they grow too far beyond comprehension and tractability.

While there can never be—should never be—a single architectural answer to the form of the city, there must be a complicit set of principles governing the urban project, principles that inform but do not finalize the myriad individuations that must become the goal of a revitalized urban design practice. Even as we revere the glorious legacies of thousands of years of successful urbanism, the struggles both of modernism *and of its critique* are simply too important to be abandoned as an invigorating, dynamic basis for thinking about the future of the city.

Here is a brief agenda for an urbanism both precedented and freely imagined:

1. Reinforce Neighborhoods

The neighborhood must be at the center. If the city is to resist the homogenization of the global culture and to nurture local cultures and participation, then the delineability and vigor of the neighborhood must be assured. The neighborhood is the means by which the social city is comprehended. Urban designers should work to create and reinforce neighborhoods that situate both the conveniences and necessities of daily life within easy walking compass of places of residence, that maximize economic, social, cultural, and ecological self-sufficiency, that assert an autonomous physical character, and that share equitably in the benefits and responsibilities of the larger metropolis. Extent—the coalescence of scale, density, dimension, and activity—is the threshold of urbanity, and we have lost the knack of its most intimate meanings.

2. Make It Sustainable

The logic of urban ecology demands a restoration of the greatest reasonable degree of self-sufficiency: local self-reliance is the lesson of global interdependence. Urban designers must become the economists of energy cycles, oxygen production, thermal regulation, agriculture, raw and reused materials—all the quiddities of the city. The issue is not invariably to begin with a fixed form and imagine how it might be improved by modest variations—a catalytic converter, an air bag, . . . —but to responsibly conjure the marvelous.

3. Add Green

The city exists as both an exception and a complement to its territory, legible only in relation to the green spaces in which it sits and which sit in it. Use of these spaces is a fundamental right of city citizens, and urban design should work to guarantee this in terms of convenience and variety, both private and public. This distribution of green should affect both the location of construction and its form. Consider, for example, the architecture that might result if the equivalent of 50 percent or 70 percent or 100 percent of the surface of a city were to be green, how building might harbor and support it. We are too caught up in an artificial dichotomy between the city and nature: the house and garden (even the city and its parks) are only the most tentative and preliminary expressions of the possibilities.

4. Secure the Edge

Cities run the risk of asphyxiating in their own extent. There is a boundary of apraxia, a point of absolute dysfunction beyond which the city simply can no longer perform coordinated actions. The urban edge secures the viability of the city both functionally and perceptually. The delineability of the city is a precondition for a sense of citizenship, therefore of urban democracy. Again, the logic of governance in a globalizing culture and economy will demand a strengthening of locality, not a progressive dissipation of the autonomy of cities into the increasingly artificial economies of nation-states. City edges—however permeable—are also formal, sets of *places*. It seems fundamental that one should be able to actually leave town. The "edge city" means one never can.

5. Make Public Places

There is simply no substitute for the physical spaces of public assembly. Increasingly imperiled by commercialization, electronification, criminality, and neglect, both the idea and the forms of gathering are a central subject for the imagination of urban design. Public space is the lever by which urban design works on the city, by which the subtle relations of public and private are nourished. A fixation on the media of production of these spaces has overcome any passion for their quality, even as a Nielsenesque resignation stupidly celebrates any gathering, however it is induced. Urban design must keep Giants Stadium from annihilating Washington Square while seeking all the alternatives in between. The Internet is great, but it ain't the Piazza Navona: free association and chance encounter still demand the meeting of bodies in space. *Embodiment* is the condition of accident, and accident is a motor of democracy.

6. Be Sure Rooms Have Views

Modernist urbanism was not all bad. Le Corbusier's three qualities—light, air, and greenery—still form a matrix for urban design. The issue is in making sure all the views are not the same. The architecture of the city is the compact of conflicting desires, continuously unfolding. If the American frontier offered a vision of absolute vision, of an untrammeled homestead unlimited by the physical presence of one's neighbor (a fantasy stoked by the sure psychical symmetry of Jefferson's infinite grid), the city is the instrument and the laboratory of adjudicated desire, in which every happy inhabitation is the marker of agreement. Here is a site for thinking architecture, for a science and art of replacing rival, hostile claims with a crafting of unvalenced difference. What is wanted is a city with an infinity of views that embody a luxury of choices, not a system of privileges.

7. Finesse the Mix

What has begun to happen to the city as locationality *really* begins to float is a saturation of the mix. As production ceases to foul the environment, as classes, races, and nationalities learn to desist in denying each other's enjoyment—enforcing segregation—and as communication becomes truly transparent, anything might appear anywhere. All the new species produced by our dizzyingly splicing culture demand a city in which they will be able to live together comfortably, not the zoning and monofunction of the planners. Urban design must keep pace by exploring the tectonics not simply of new use but of unpredictable transformation, creating

7

cities that are as malleable as lofts and as fixed as works of art. One of the main territories of this investigation will necessarily be the compatibility of sizes, likely to become the main problematic of use harmonization. Another will be the constant consideration of the *appropriateness* of various juxtapositions, questions of the deepest political and artistic import. Cities, after all, are juxtaposition engines, mutation machines. Theories of propriety, though, are necessary if we are to choose among endless possibilities and make the urban work collective.

8. Elaborate Movement

It is time for a radical shift toward human locomotion in cities. The automobile is not simply a doomed technology in its current form, it has proved fundamentally inimical to urban density. Enforcing the hydra of attenuation *and* congestion, the car usurps the spaces of production and health, of circulation and enjoyment, of greenery, of safety. Fitted to the bodies of cities that could never have anticipated it, the car is a disaster in town. We cannot again repeat the mistake of retrofitting the city with a technology that does not love it, with railway cutting or freeways. Cars must lose their priority, yielding both to the absolute privilege of pedestrians and to something else as well, something that cannot yet be described, to a skein of movement each city contours to itself. This may well involve various forms of mechanical (or biological) technology, but urban design—in considering the matter—should reject the mentality of available choices and formulate rational bases for fresh desires. If we cannot even describe the characteristics of superb urban transport— invisible? silent? small? leisurely? mobile in three axes? friendly?—this is because we have not taken the trouble to really imagine it.

9. Localize Architecture

Architecture is urban by convention, recording accumulated compacts. Climax is the key: cities are form makers, and urban design should astutely recognize indigenous forms that have reached some kind of perfection. Beautiful logics once established—whether the brownstones of Brooklyn or the labyrinths of Fez—are entitled to architectural citizenship, to a certain inalienability of rights. Climax—a term borrowed from foresters—is a condition of homeostasis, a permanent stage of growth. In cities, this must be nurtured both in use and in form. Form, after all, does enjoy a certain autonomy, originating in use and circumstances but eventually free of them. Reinforcing such character is a great task for urban design. Reproducing or simulating it is not. Fresh climaxes will not re-

8

produce those of the past but will seek out new forms of locality. This new indigenous form could come from anywhere in global culture, from the creativity of any individual, from bio-regional particulars or simply from memory. Urban design must cultivate the shoots of distinction.

10. Defend Privacy

We have probably spent a little too much time critiquing the failures of the public realm and not enough searching for alternatives to the dispirited lexicon of official public space and activity. Public space should be about choice, and choice, finally, is a private matter. Public space needs to be rethought not simply as a series of sites but as a conceptual resource out of which an infinity of private fantasies and behaviors can be drawn, a construct at once ineffable and available, a vast collective reservoir for the watering of individual activities not yet imagined and possibly secret. The range of private choices that surround the public realm define it absolutely. Urban design is a bridge between these realms.

11. Make It Beautiful

For urban *designers,* finally, there is no other goal. We are negligent in our tasks if we fail to engage deep desire, the means by which we enlarge the city of sense, the millionfold techniques of an urban erotics.

1998

Branding Space

We have been hearing for years that Times Square is becoming a theme park, and so it is. But the million and a half revelers who gather on New Year's Eve may have some difficulty—as I have—discerning exactly the theme. When their cameras flash at midnight, what will they be photographing beyond a million and a half other flashes?

A few weeks ago, I was walking by the building where JFK Jr. used to live, wrapped in this conundrum, when I noticed that a tourist in the usual knot photographing the place was carrying an "NBC Experience" plastic bag. As coincidence would have it, I had actually experienced the "Experience" (just off Times Square) the previous day, and it had perplexed me. Why, I wondered, surveying the logoed knickknacks, would someone *want* to buy an MSNBC baseball cap? Out of solidarity with the giant corporation? As a gesture of affection toward the cute Brian Williams?

Seeing the tourist completed some circuit. I realized that she was having a TV news moment. Caught up in the NBC loop, she was performing a tiny reenactment of the big media routine, authorized by the logo to intrude on the scenes of celebrity and grief, like a real reporter. The Experience, I realized, was no mere souvenir store but the setup for this. Dominating the shop, monitors were endlessly showing a clip of the Zapruder film, segueing over and over into the "I have a dream" speech—advertisements for "news," newszak. The news itself had become the word from our sponsor, NBC, and that repeated image of the presidential assassination was what gave value to those stacks of *Today Show* mugs and vice versa. This was the purpose of the place: branding everything, including experience.

For this to work efficiently, both the site of experience and the experiencer must carry the brand. Think of the teen in the Tommy tee, or the tourist in the CNBC baseball cap. A deal has been cut here. By agreeing to bear the brand, we express our willingness to be seen . . . as advertising. And in becoming vehicles for commercial speech, we simply surrender our privacy. Wearing the brand is a severely reduced version of real celebrity, of people recognizable enough to become their own trademarks.

This, I think, implies an even more generous license to stare, to admire something beyond purchase. And it is irresistible, reflexive. Last week I had a Gwyneth moment. Before I knew what I was doing, I turned in my tracks to gawk, trapped.

Times Square has become the center of all of this, a universal photo op, pure celebrity. Celebrity thrives on its own visibility, and visibility—pure exposure—is the theme of the new Times Square. In our media age, such visibility is no longer a static, space-bound, optical concept but something to be transmitted by all available means—flashing lights, sky-scrapers, coffee mugs, tee shirts, TV shows, magazines, postcards, ash-trays, margarita glasses, plastic bags, you name it. Times Square—one of the few places in America where the zoning laws *oblige* every building to advertise as intensely as possible—has become Medialand, USA.

No coincidence that among the sprouting skyscrapers of the new Times Square, media headquarters predominate, from Reuters to Bertels-mann to Condé Nast to the eponymic ex-HQ of the *Times* itself, its fine original building long gutted of inhabitants, flayed of its skin, and reclad as pure pixelated advertising space. All the networks (and MTV) now have fishbowl-style broadcast environments—stationary Popemobiles—for their morning shows, the lead disassemblers of the news/entertainment distinction. And all use the celebrity-hungry crowds as fascinated back-drops. To fully participate in the Times Square experience, we become little billboards among the big, craning to be viewed, like those football fans with their homemade, crudely logoed network banners the cameras al-ways seem to find in the stands.

Still there is a whiff of the old Times Square: those studios are not un-like peep shows. Like traditional peeps, the object is to be safely part of something unattainable, whether it is electronic fantasy architecture, a naked woman's attentions, the *Good Morning America* set, or a chat with George W. or Jewel. The new-style electronic entertainment is much the same. Visiting the ESPN Zone (not a sporting goods store, but a sports themed *experience*), playing solipsistic soccer (kick the tethered ball, miss to the taunts of the animated goalie on the screen), I felt like just another lonely guy peeping through the glass. Of course, it has been "cleaned up" for a G rating: the louche quality of the banished sex industry has been replaced by less controversial, more commercial forms of pornography: one hundred yards of Kate Moss in her Calvins, public voyeurism of the authorized celeb voyeurs in the chat show studios, the porno violence of video games, the chance of glimpsing Anna Wintour as she heads for her daily bunless burger at the Royalton.

The apotheosis of all this will come at midnight, as 1.5 million press their noses against the glass of the Y2K. They will be watching television, all eyes focused on the state-of-the-art, five-story-high, thirty-six-ton Astrovision™ screen that has been glued to the north face of the Times Tower (and that is currently blasting NBC product eighteen hours a day). As the man from the manufacturer puts it, "It's an opportunity for Panasonic to have our brand name in the middle of the crossroads of the world at one of the biggest moments in history." No mere hyperbole, this. Fifteen cameras placed around the square will feed the screen with images of the crowd, enabling it to watch itself watching itself along with another billion or so souls around the globe watching it watching itself and, in turn, watching themselves watching it, unpaid extras in the spectacle of their own amusement, hoping simply to be seen.

1999

Times Square: Status Quo Vadis

The ongoing debate over Times Square reminds me of last year's dustup over Milos Forman's bio-pic about Larry Flynt. That debate was not so much over a movie that glorified a purveyor of misogynistic smut but over the choice of a pornographer as a kind of ideal violator of public values and hence a suitable subject for a film in celebration of freedom of speech. In constructing him as an avatar of free expression, Forman foregrounded Flynt's roguishness, vulgar charm, and old-fashioned uxoriousness. And by choosing the amiable and attractive (and young) Woody Harrelson to portray Flynt, Forman was better able to conjure sympathy for his subject's struggles for self-expression. The argument against this—a telling one—is that the rhetoric of the film, in its creation of a character with whom the audience could identify, chose a pornographer in lieu of, say, a Nazi bent on marching through Skokie, and thereby implicitly suggested that pornography is—on some larger scale of public values—a more fundamentally benign violation. This is clearly a hierarchy established at the expense of women, and the objection to the film is precisely that the very possibility of making a charmer out of a truly loathsome pornographer is only possible via culture's greater willingness to tolerate this implicit denigration.

Much of the argument over Times Square is also framed as a question about the rights of the sex trade and—like the debate over Flynt—is often couched in a veneer of standard-issue liberal pieties. These include not simply the notion that the sex industry is entitled to a kind of locational freedom of the city but also the idea—as expressed, among others, by Rem Koolhaas in *Grand Street* last year—that Times Square has a special "authenticity" bred of the coupling of pornography and density and is thus entitled to absolute tolerance. Of course, this particular argument works best retrospectively, as counterpoint to the looming Disneyfication of the place. As with the Forman film, the freedom—the license—of the sex scene is to be preferred to the homogenizing repressions of the mouse. And, like the Forman film, the same fallacy is unpacked. Sex for sale—and here we are presumably meant to be drawn to the exemplary liberalism of the tolerant Dutch with their medically inspected sex workers under glass—is like Larry Flynt, a transgression sufficiently benign to be embraced as a victim of big brother rather than big brother's own m.o.

But the Forman film suggests another, even more serious consequence of current strategies toward Times Square. By choosing Flynt—whose pornographic production abounds with images of women tortured and mutilated—as a poster boy for free speech—there is a conflation of Flynt's pornography with pornography in general. This all-or-nothing approach, which refuses to make distinctions within the field of the pornographic, leads with little difficulty to an identification of the pornographic with sexuality in general. At the end of the day, this is—ironically—the problem of the film. Embraced under the shining aura of "free speech," all sexual practices become as one.

In Times Square this leads to a false choice: either celebrate the crummy and degraded sex bazaar as it is (Koolhaas's monument to his beloved laissez-faire), or bring on Disneyland. Disneyland—symbolized by that hairless, sexless mouse—is the representation of the kind of totalizing approach that is anathema to what has been best about Times Square, its complexity, unpredictability, louche charm, and—yes—its concentration of sexual energy. Disneyland is the postmodern version of urban renewal, advanced not on the theoretical grounds of a hygienic fantasy of a universal working-class subject living in circumstances of utter sameness, but on the grounds of a hygienic fantasy of a universal tourist-class subject playing in circumstances of utter sameness. Either way, the agenda is *the same.*

In making this argument, I raise one of the great and necessary difficulties of the discussion of Times Square. Times Square is burdened by the competing claims of the exemplary and the exceptional. Clearly, the "otherness" of the place and its historic role as a sanctuary for both diversity and deviance simultaneously attract liberal opinion and appall a proper bourgeois sense of urban decorum. More, in the richly coded language of urban description, Times Square has come to symbolize not simply a criminal environment but a zone in which "the criminal element"— which is to say black and gay men—is given the right of the city at the very core of the city. In New York, where "crime fighting" is the leading item on the municipal agenda, the demonization of Times Square can only presage its demolition and "cleanup," a standardization and scaling up that will dilute the mix to acceptable strength, the same hygienizing cycle that was brought to us historically by the (we thought) discredited history of exclusionary zoning and urban renewal.

History, of course, does repeat itself. First as tragedy, then as farce, then as a made-for-TV movie, then as a cartoon, then as a Broadway musical. . . . It does not seem entirely just that Times Square be made to bear the burden for the entire culture. After all, Times Square is not responsible for television, for the immaterial antimatter that has produced the circumstances for its annihilation. It bravely fights back by deploying an enormous analogue, lightbulbs like pixels, a synesthesia of luminosity, David Letterman stories high on the Jumbotron, biggest TV in the world. It may be true that the culture prefers *Beauty and the Beast,* but it is certainly true that the vast majority of both the Square's defenders and detractors have seen neither *Cats* nor the show at the Adonis. And of course, it is terribly true that the demise of Times Square, its conversion to another version of the recursion of Vegas (which has now built its own Times Square, even more pared and distilled than the vanishing "original") must be blamed squarely not simply on the energetic advocates of sanitized fun but on our own failures to propose a better idea.

1998

Round and Round

Walking around a bend in Riverside Drive a few days ago, I was startled by the sight of Donald Trump's Riverside South complex looming over the rooftops. Twice the height of the surrounding buildings, the first two of an eventual dozen towers seemed massive and alien, harbingers of a radical scale change that will forever deform the profile of Manhattan.

The vaguely deco buildings are postered with large testimonials to their superlativeness by Trump, Philip Johnson (the first building's architect), and Brendan Sexton, outgoing president of the Municipal Art Society and incoming president of the Times Square Business Improvement District. It is a telling mix of personalities, suggesting the elision of commercial advantage, architectural cachet, and civic virtue that has come to characterize so many of New York's big projects.

These same interests are behind the latest proposal for replacing the Metropolitan Transportation Authority–owned Coliseum at nearby Columbus Circle. Indeed, the night the deal was announced, Sexton, all grins, was on the local news, congratulating Mayor Giuliani for his artistry in putting together the "package." Never mind that the Coliseum scheme is essentially the same as the one proposed during an earlier round of bidding, begun in 1985, a process that finally came to grief in 1994 because of a downturn in the market and a lawsuit by . . . the Municipal Art Society. Produced by the same architect (Skidmore, Owings and Merrill's David Childs), albeit for a different developer (the Related Companies this time around instead of Boston Properties), the building—which as the result of mayoral pressure now includes a jazz theater—looks, after ten years of thought, slightly more like the New York, New York Hotel in Vegas, that Red Groomsish compendium of "New Yorkness."

The overheated rhetoric at the press conference was highly Trumpish, a bunch of white guys standing around kvelling about quant. Although Trump—a repeated contender for the Coliseum site—did not win the deal, he provided the ethic, the aesthetic, and the context for the proposal. And not only conceptually: Columbus Circle already includes Trump's hulking Gulf & Western Building, reskinned with gold glass by

Philip Johnson and renamed (what else) the Trump International Hotel and Tower.

During the endless vying for the Columbus Circle site, Trump proposed two different versions of the world's tallest building, one designed by Helmut Jahn and the other by Eli Attia. While these buildings were universally derided for their deranged phallomorphology and the eclipselike shadows they would have cast, they nevertheless created cover for equally destructive changes taking place nearby. During the past fifteen or so years, the area to the north of Columbus Circle, extending up Broadway to Seventy-second Street, has been up-zoned, a transformation concealed behind ludicrous palaver about contextualism, as if a fifty-story building could somehow be camouflaged by a low base and a few quoins. (Marisa Tomei to Joe Pesci: "Like you blend.") The result of this shift in thinking about scale is that twin seventy-one-story towers are now considered modest and appropriate.

Like Riverside South, the Columbus Circle scheme is emblematic of the way the city of New York plans and does business in the post–Robert Moses era. The homely Coliseum was itself built at the ebb tide of the legendary power broker's influence, among his last gasps. Whatever one thinks of Moses' methods (or his racism or his taste), he never hesitated to think big. While the projects at Columbus Circle and Riverside South are likewise gigantic, their architectural vision is minute, deriving from a shriveled sense of the civic.

Unfortunately, they are also a long way from the spirit of the anti-Moses movement they grew out of. Thirty-five years ago, Jane Jacobs virtually reinvented the idea of planning, switching its emphasis from wholesale demolition to a careful stewardship of urban life and the conservation of its social and physical ecologies, its neighborhoods. She popularized these ideas at a moment when community activism was on the rise across the country and the drama of new vision was being replaced by the romance of consensus. Given a general (and legitimate) concurrence that no big power, whether private or governmental, had the best interests of the public at heart, compromise emerged as the new paradigm for the planning process, creating a culture of trade-offs.

In the so-called bonus system that emerged in New York, increased building bulk was exchanged for the inclusion of some amenity—a plaza, an arcade, subsidized housing units, a jazz theater, or even an agreement to build a block or two away from zones of frenzied development, as with the Times Square special district. The irony is that amenity is always being swapped for something that is, by definition, contrary

17

to public interest: too much size. Although the huge Coliseum site allows such huge construction "as of right," the project is simply too big—a result of this bottom-line mind-set. Once conventions of size and scale, which define the shared character of a place, can be easily overturned, the door is open for every project to seek its entitlement to excess. From a developer's point of view, it becomes simply impossible to build less than the maximum that can be had.

Public agencies, on the other hand, might still be expected to take a broader view. Competing schemes for the Coliseum were supposedly judged on an aesthetic as well as an economic basis, and this put an unfamiliar pressure on the Metropolitan Transportation Authority, which ran the competitions. As anyone who has ridden on the New York subway can attest, quality design is not uppermost in the minds of the MTA leadership. It has been argued, however, that the most responsible position available to the agency is to ignore design quality and sell the property to the highest bidder to produce maximum cash for the transit system, and this appears to be what it has done.

Here, the irony is that by focusing so narrowly on money, the MTA will only increase the strain on the transport system. Like the Trump complex on the river and the Times Square redevelopment, the Columbus Circle project will dump huge numbers of riders on one of the grottiest, most disorganized, and overtaxed stations in the system. If the experience of Riverside South or Times Square is any guide, the developers will weasel out of contributions to station renovations, and the MTA will drag its feet until only the minimum improvement is made (and that years in the future).

Several months ago, a group of architects (full disclosure: myself included) were invited by the Municipal Art Society (whose good intentions and civic vigor do sometimes take strange directions) to redesign Columbus Circle itself. This was prompted by the city's decision to revise the traffic pattern around the circle by making it, well, more circular. Although the schemes varied in quality and approach, they raised a number of issues that the new building has ignored. First was the matter of considering the huge subway station below. Then there was the notion that a civic space of such consequence needed to be thought of as a piece, not simply as a collection of autonomous fragments. And, finally, there was the idea that a blockbuster project demanded the rethinking of an area far beyond its boundaries.

Unfortunately, nobody ever ran a competition to find the best architectural or programmatic idea for Columbus Circle as a whole: the two official competitions to date have been for developers, with architecture ancillary. What would such a freely imagined scheme look like? Although you know a great solution only when you see one, the concerns should be clear. To begin, it requires a formal idea at the scale of the city. Columbus Circle is an important transition point between the Upper West Side, Central Park, and Midtown. It stands at a convergence of patterns—the serpentine Olmstedian landscape, the street-walled New York grid, a collection of Ville Radieuse–style isolated elements floating in space—and it serves as a bridge between the residential north, a nearby group of campus-based cultural, educational, and medical institutions, and the commercial densities to the south. A successful scheme must commit itself to the geometry of the circle, to the building's relationship to the subway, and to managing the lateral movement between park, circle, and river.

The winning scheme does very little of this. Like every other project proposed for the site, it accepts the promulgated guidelines that call for a low circular base, as it does the maxed-out floor-area ratio offered. But why should the circular base not be high, to echo the volume and carry on the scale of Central Park West and South, where the buildings run in the twenty- to thirty-story range before setting back? Also, like a number of other schemes, this one disposes its twin towers (meant to "evoke" the twin towers of several buildings on Central Park, blah, blah, blah) on either side of what used to be Fifty-ninth Street, now blocked by the Coliseum, but it leaves the passage closed. Why not re-open Fifty-ninth Street as a grand promenade from park to river, making a visual connection that will actually be legible and useful to people on the ground?

The project has also been criticized for being too much like a shopping mall, its amenities interiorized, sucking life from the street. While there is more than enough life in the area to assure plenty of pedestrian traffic around the building, the shopping mall paradigm (the privatized version of the civic) has a deadening effect on the architecture and avoids any real urbanistic engagement. Interior shopping streets may be necessary in a building as deep as this, but why is the jazz theater up four long escalator flights? And where are the grand connections to the subway? Is everyone expected to arrive by limo? If New York has an anthem, it is Ellington's "Take the 'A' Train," whose namesake stops at Columbus Circle en route to and from 125th Street, the longest express run in the subway system. How nice to go directly from eponym to jazz.

While this project is not exactly meretricious, it represents a dramatic   **19** failure of imagination. A huge development like this, located on city-owned land, offers the opportunity to explore big issues and solve big problems. The blinkered business-as-usual approach, however, only yields big buildings and very small ideas.

1998

Cranes over TriBeCa

Today is the first day of autumn, and the city is lovely, the air crisp and clear, and the pace everywhere quickening—our best season. As I write this, I am sitting in my studio in groovy TriBeCa, rapidly become the city's most covetable neighborhood. My building—a sturdy, thirties-vintage, high-rise loft—has, until recently, been home to a wide and delightful variety of art and industrial uses (printing has a long history on lower Hudson Street) but is now largely vacant, we remaining tenants living on borrowed time. Not that no one wants the space, but the go-go regime on Wall Street is spreading new money around like manure on downtown's fertile soil, and the "demand" is for residences. My landlord, sniffing this inevitable, has decided to cash out and convert the building into deluxe multimillion-dollar condos (a million bucks no longer even gets you a conversation with a broker these days). As a result of this enormous bubble, a lovely, very mixed neighborhood is undergoing the throes of homogenization, rapidly becoming just another yuppie paradise.

Among the distinguished avatars of this transformation (over on North Moore Street—the hottest block in the city) were JFK Jr. and Carolyn Bessette. I saw them occasionally (and even writing this, I know I join the ranks of the "saw them occasionally" crowd and wanna-bes—every merchant in the neighborhood having been quoted in the media about Kennedy's buying a cup of take-out coffee, being a regular guy and a good tipper, several boasting black-framed photos of the deceased behind their cash registers) and am still halted in the street by tourists looking ("John John Junior, please?") for their doorway. This was not difficult to find in the weeks immediately after the crash, as their entire block was cordoned off by police barricades and composted shoulder deep with flowers, messages, and other tributes of celebrity grief, our own mini-bit of Princess Di madness.

More recently, there has been a proposal to rename a tiny neighborhood park in Kennedy's honor. Although I like the idea of naming local civic spaces for local heroes, I do wonder what is being commemorated in this case. To be sure, JFK was incredibly good-looking, a nice neighbor, and the author of that iconic salute at his father's funeral. Professionally, he was an indifferent lawyer and the progenitor of a not particularly interesting magazine. He was, it appears, a poor aviator. He was, however, enormously famous. Naming the park after him would certainly affirm the celebrity vibe that pervades the local sense of value. This, after all, is a neighborhood in which Robert DeNiro is a leading restaurateur, and Harvey Keitel can be spotted buying a quart of milk.

The park that is candidate for renaming sits catty-corner from another prime neighborhood site, a triangle of land that for years housed a garden shop and nursery. That plot was wonderful in its potential, its apex pointing south and its short side facing a fabulous inhabited mesa built for the phone company by Voorhees, Gmelin, and Walker, the greatest, most geological of New York's deco-era architects. To the east lies a row of small nineteenth-century commercial buildings, and to the west— along the hypotenuse—is a funky range of very low structures of somewhat more recent vintage, running down a slight grade. It was a singular space, an important moment of relief in the density, and a viewing armature across which these wonderful buildings could be seen from far away in rare perspective.

Unfortunately, the rising real estate tide is swamping all sites, and a hotel is under construction on the triangle. Recently topped out and now nearly skinned, it is a dreadful piece of work, ersatz as all get out, swaddled in phony-baloney allusions to nearby cast-iron construction. The hotel is being built by a developer who several years ago put up a much larger version a couple of blocks to the north in SoHo, which has proven highly successful commercially, but which—enormously overscaled—is a continuing affront to the fine-grained neighborhood fabric. Like the earlier flophouse, the new one can be expected to generate the queue of idling, air-fouling limousines that are the emblems of success in the current cultural regime. Although there were citizen efforts to stop both of these structures, they were to no avail, as both buildings fell within the letter of the zoning laws, which take no position on the value of such serendipitous open spaces.

Given the leading role of celebrity and entertainment in the new urbanism of downtown, there is nothing that meaningfully could have been counterposed to the hotel to attract real support on the part of the civic weal. Except perhaps a higher version of celebrity. One project that could surely have stopped the hotel in its tracks would have been a proposal to make the site into a park in honor of JFK Jr. The iconic oomph and reach of dead Kennedys are irresistibly sacred to us Americans, and even the aggressive commercialism of the new hotel would surely have been humbled by the necessity of this national project of commemoration and fraudulent grief. Kennedy, however, simply perished too late.

Open space is at a premium downtown, and we are rapidly losing all those accidental sites of uneven development—our stock of vacant lots— that have, until now, been uneconomic to build on. Nervously, I await the consumption of an impeccably scaled, might-be piazza that currently serves as a parking lot behind my building, which the landlord hopes to turn into yet another mindless condo tower. Such serendipitous space-amenity is threatened not simply by this gap-filling surge but by the opposition of the merchant class to civic improvements, even in legitimately public spaces. There has, for example, been a years-long to-do about the so-called Greening of Greenwich, a plan to convert a lane of an unusually wide stretch of Greenwich Street into a linear park space. This marginal reduction in the territory of the car is perceived as threatening to the idling limousine constituency—our hoteliers and restaurateurs—who, fearing the loss of their double-parking privileges, have opposed the project tooth and nail.

Much as I love the signs of construction and physical improvement that currently abound in the city, there are certainly days when I think that the most useful contribution to the quality of life here would be a, shall we say, five-thousand-point drop in the Dow. That should get me a decent extension on my lease and keep a few of our wonderful accidental plazas around for a while longer.

1999

Big Deal

The architectural event of early summer—the first IFCCA (International Foundation for the Canadian Centre for Architecture) Prize "competition" for the design of cities—had a certain Hillary-esque dimension. As she campaigns through the state in the guise of a "listening tour," Hillary (never having lived here) is sniped at relentlessly as a carpetbagger. And so indeed she is. I admire her frank opportunism: no one is under any illusions that Hillary Clinton is on a crusade to save New York. Phyllis Lambert on the other hand—the author of the IFCCA, its chief financier, the head of the jury, and the woman whose legendary nudge to dad produced the Seagram Building—has a slightly better claim both to locality and to mission. Still, her massive arrival on the scene disquieted many, especially those excluded from her big plans. While Lambert's project to create exemplary schemes for troubled sites around the globe is a fundamentally good one, the results of the first round, unfortunately, had more to do with mutual back-scratching than any systematic investigation of urban ideas.

The site chosen is a perennial favorite: the rail yards next to the big Javits Convention Center. For years, it has been the object of speculation by politicians, developers, and local design studios (I have probably seen two hundred projects for the place at Columbia, Cooper, and Pratt). Its immediate significance lies in its size (large) and location (near the river and the center of the city and in the proximity of all those shiny, shuttling trains and the tunnels, highways, and other "big" elements [central post office, bus terminal, Penn Station] that scream the current plannerly buzzword "infrastructure!"). Proposals for (various parts of) the site have included an expansion of the Javits Center and—most controversially— the relocation of Yankee Stadium from the Bronx, an idea favored by Mayor Giuliani and team-owner George Steinbrenner, the most loathed man in New York.

With avaricious eyes already turned to it, the site will certainly be developed, with or without a competition. The potential value of an effort like Lambert's is in demonstrating better uses and better forms than the ones that will likely be built, and—by pointing toward innovation—in exposing the truly enfeebled state of our municipal planning. But the thing was stacked toward form rather than content: the IFCCA competition brief, alas, took virtually no position on the programmatic future of the site (something strong competitors can freely invent for themselves in the absence of a client, but only if they choose to do so).

A more structural problem, however, was a confusion between the purposes of a traditional design competition and an ideas competition. This one was run as if it were a design competition—big prize, much hyping of the "winner," fantasy of definitive outcome—but with the ostensible aim of an ideas competition (i.e., producing a lot of ideas). The process was too narrow from the get-go, beginning with an open call for nominations for competitors—producing no more than a list of names, requiring jurors to be *already* familiar with them—and this attracted a big turnout. This list (again, of names, not ideas) was winnowed quickly to five, and each competitor was offered the stately sum of $50,000 to prepare a scheme. (Full disclosure: I desperately begged to be included—50K would certainly have saved my cookies this summer.)

By and large, the competitors represent a fairly standard version of the usual suspects. Both participants and procedures were a rehash of the last Phyllis-sponsored competition, held in 1998 for the design of a student center that will actually be built at the Illinois Institute of Technology in Chicago. The IFCCA prizewinner, Peter Eisenman, was a runner-up in that competition with another of his current folded schemes, which was, in fact, the most interesting submission there. For *this* competition, Eisenman was joined by Ben van Berkel and Caroline Bos from Holland (occupying the Rem slot—the actual Rem having already won the IIT competition), Jesse Reiser and Nanako Umemoto (the youth slot, the local slot), Morphosis (the Frank Gehry–California slot; the real Gehry was already a juror), and the delightful Cedric Price, who—although interest is lately reviving in some of his fab early infrastructure-based ideas—has not drawn a line in thirty years as far as anyone knows (in the out-of-left-field or the return-of-Elvis slot).

While I am friendly to the idea of affirmative action, and taken in isolation this is a pretty good list, the whole operation is an unusually succinct example of the architectural buddy system. There is an especially interesting Princeton vector that nicely deconstructs the global architectural-cultural directorate. Consider a few relationships along the six-degrees-of-separation model. Just looking at Phyllis, the organizer and chief funder of the prize, the results appear, as they say, overdetermined. Pal of Peter, sponsor of a huge show of his work at her Montreal museum, Lambert is

Eisenman's backer at IIT and part-sponsor of his magazine *ANY*. She is also a member of the board of visitors at Princeton, whence she chose Ralph Lerner (the dean) to be "prize director," Liz Diller (professor, designer of a show at CCA, recent beneficiary of Phyllis's weight on the MacArthur Award panel) as juror, and Jesse Reiser (friend of Liz from Cooper Union days) as a competitor—this at a time when Princeton was negotiating with him to take up a post (subsequently accepted). Eisenman has also taught at Princeton, and Princeton supports Eisenman's magazine. And, of course, what jury would be complete without the sparkling presence of Peter's best bud, the bionic ex-fascist Philip Johnson? Phyllis (whose tab at the Four Seasons, designed by Philip in the Seagram Building, where Liz Diller and Ric Scofidio are renovating the Brasserie at Phyllis's instigation, doubtless rivals the national economy of many a small nation-state) has known Philip for years. Philip has himself been a long-time sponsor of Eisenman, whose cogenerationalists Arata Isozaki (like Phyllis, perennially present at Peter's *ANY* conferences), Frank Gehry, and Rafael Moneo (taught at Princeton) formed the architectural core of the jury. And so it goes.

If I were inclined to an uncharitable view, I would say that this whole operation (despite Peter's modest, if premature, claim that what has been produced is "the first great urban icon of the twenty-first century"—zzzzzz) was simply an elaborate scheme to give Peter Eisenman $150,000. What is especially galling is not so much the spectacle of a friend providing welfare for a friend but the sheer waste of it all. Judging by the number of first-class airfares, the $350,000 prize pot, the acreage of glossy publicity, the high-class flacks pumping out PR, the lavish dinner, the slickly produced exhibition, and so on, it looks like at least a million dollars was spent on this affair.

The question is this: if one were *really* looking for urbanistic ideas, would this be the way to go about it? Is the big-winner mentality and the fraudulent apparatus of a "competition" the most useful means of producing innovation? What about giving $10,000 to fifty or a hundred people? What about some useful research into all the fascinating suggestions already made for the site over the years? This would not only save any number of small offices, it might actually produce a usefully broad range of proposals. After all, the hope of a great competition is that somebody will come out of nowhere with a brilliant and unexpected idea and truly change people's minds.

But what of the schemes? Although all are "big," they all fall into the trap that disables so many New York City projects: they are not big enough. For many years, planning has been in eclipse here, afraid of the physical, simply reacting to the propositions of developers or framing giveaway strategies—à la Columbus Circle or Times Square—to induce construction. This has meant that projects have been integrated into larger visions of the city (not to mention their local contexts) haphazardly and mainly after the fact. The current planning commissioner, the politically ambitious Joe Rose, has only contributed to this mentality. A man widely considered to be in the pocket of the development community and no friend of serious planning, Rose was not simply a member of the jury—his was an active ("definitive," by his account) voice in choosing the site.

Not surprisingly, then, the competition encouraged this mentality of projects seen in isolation, insufficiently attentive to broader context. Although several of the schemes give consideration to the (obvious) possibility of extending mass transit into the site, none ventures the kind of radical proposition that might transform the traffic system, a great opportunity offered by the nearby Lincoln Tunnel and the proximity of huge mass-transit resources and gateways. And although all include some kind of park within their precincts, none produces a really convincing link (Reiser and Umemoto do best) to the park now being debated and designed for the Hudson waterfront, or a strategy for a more general greening of the town. The schemes are set pieces, not goads.

Because of the big bucks on offer, competitors were intimidated into laying on special consultants up the wazoo (traffic planners, engineers, landscapers—Eisenman even teamed up with Skidmore, Owings and Merrill, just to make sure of backup in case someone had the billions to suddenly say yes). They also seemed to find it necessary to produce a kind of liminal analysis, persuaded that evidence of "process" was critical to the substance of the proposals, framing propositions according to a nonexistent reality as if to assert the schemes really were full of "ideas." The explanatory texts provided by the competitors were unusually replete with a dopey language of architectural neologisms—with "rucksacks," "crepes," and "folds"—meant to suggest real ideas in their absence. The Dutch team, in particular, provides an almost fetishistic analytical document filled with the sort of retrofitted diagrams that are so weirdly popular in Holland nowadays, part of a Rem-inspired rush to architecturalize mere datascapes. The problem with this kind of analysis is that it has no bearing on the forces that will (or should) eventually determine the uses of the site.

Despite the abundance of excitingly blobby and folded forms drawn **27** from current idiom, none of the proposals rises programmatically above the generic: media and "information" centers, convention halls, sports arenas, parks, hotels, and offices. Instead, they offer the expected, inflected only formally, fully accessible to the powers that be. Which begs the question of the choice of the big-bucks, hyper-commercial site. Phyllis, needless to say, did not ask these talents to consider Harlem or the South Bronx, and none of the competitors seriously looks at the impact of the project on the city as a whole. Eisenman, the sports fan, did provide the only stadium, and although it is called an "Olympic Stadium," it is clearly a stalking-horse for Steinbrenner. Eisenman's own position on stripping the struggling stadium neighborhood to further densify Manhattan was not articulated, but it is clearly not going to cheer the Bronx. Was this something the jurors cared about? Or did competitors simply recognize that the only people on the jury worth addressing were Joe Rose and Charles Gargano, the head of the New York State development agency, two Republican appointees and obvious conduits to the real power?

I do admire Phyllis Lambert both for the broad and generous focus of her concerns and for her activism. She is a patron in the old-fashioned way: she pays for it. With all that money, though, it is too bad she cannot act a little more independently.

1999

A Passage through India

Delhi

An indelible image of India. As I prowled the New Delhi acropolis, a truck pulled up in front of one of the Herbert Baker ministries flanking the grand, Lutyens-culminated King's Way axis. On the truck was an enormous model ship—the Indian navy's latest frigate—bristling with Plexiglas missiles and guns. Thirty men in ragged kurtas and bare feet—directed by a naval officer in crisp white uniform—shouldered the ship and shuffled, whooping and shouting, through the portal of the vast Euro-Mogul pile.

This near surrealist sense of juxtaposition is ubiquitous in the daily life of India: the cows on the highway, the bright sari-clad women hoisting baskets of concrete up webs of bamboo scaffolding to build air-con skyscrapers in the merciless haze and heat, the Coke ads on the mud huts. Like that ship, the apparatus of modernity is supported on the backs of huge numbers whose share in its benefits is marginal. India is filled with such reverberating differences, with a colonialism that both imports its own values and that co-opts sympathetic images from within the culture that are then rebroadcast in transformed guise.

Double Delhi embodies this structure of differences very directly. Old Delhi, the eight-times rebuilt capital of ancient India—most famously as Shahjahanabad, the last capital of the Moguls—is a tangle of crumbling buildings, impossible traffic, twisting lanes, warrens of life, and frenetic commerce. New Delhi, built by the British as the last capital of the Raj, inverts all of this, filled with endless tree-lined axes and round-points, stately buildings and white-washed bungalows for the white sahibs, all deployed in insane lateral hierarchy to recognize just where in the civil service their occupants sat.

While this twoness monumentally reflects the center of power of colonial India, the division was reproduced across the country and, indeed, across the empire. In town after town, the so-called civil lines were established as a parallel urbanism, a formal apartheid that left little question as to who was in charge. In a country whose Hindu tradition was

29

rooted in its own fantasies of untouchability, those revolutionaries who sought to overthrow such structures of permanent inequality must certainly have understood and reviled this division, much as the British found Indian settlements "unhealthy, noisy, and distasteful."

This repeated pattern of Indian town, military cantonment, and civil lines, each obeying its own systems of order, each imposing its own hierarchy, still resonates, embodied—if in transmogrified form—in the elements of a continuing debate about planning. On one side stands a tradition that privileges clarity, the sort of urban functionalism that remains the default mode of global urbanism and architecture. But there is another way, also tremendously "Indian": the path of synthesis, the embrace and collapse of contradiction. In much of Indian architecture the combination of motifs, the easy blending of Hindu, Muslim, Buddhist, even Christian symbols is marvelous, even transcendent. But in a country where internecine massacres remain commonplace, such blendings can be very fraught.

The architect who showed me around that day was a Delhi enthusiast, partial to Lutyens and to the calm sweep of the grand, bowered avenues. And after a couple of weeks in India, it was easy to share his appreciation for an orderly, shaded space free from the roil of typical Indian traffic. More problematic, though, was his tolerant position vis-à-vis the Lutyens style of grafted locality. Of course, the *tolerance* was admirable, but, interestingly, it had its limits, concealing a polemic repeatedly exposed in conversations with architects around India. While my friend loved Delhi, he was filled with contempt for Chandigarh, which he considered to be the real symbol of imaginative colonization. The next day, when I reported the apparent paradox to another Indian architect, he virtually exploded on hearing it, railing against Lutyens as the nadir of colonialism and racism and exalting Corbusier's city as a place that had helped to set India free, to move its architecture along a fresh and independent path.

One sees what one wants. My Delhi friend once told me a story about driving Robert Venturi on a similar tour around town. After intoning his enthusiasm for the helter-skelter signage encrusting the neoclassical buildings of Connaught Place, (and the ubiquitous layers of Indian graphic funk are amazing), he was brought to the Lutyens complex atop Raisina hill. He entered in a reverie, as to a great shrine. My colleague reported with admiration that Venturi strode through the building as if he had been there many times, pointing out details and seeking out hidden rooms with complete familiarity. He already knew—already loved—the building. Of course, such worship from afar is not simply a product of modern media but a set of choices based on criteria that both include and exclude, choices by which we structure our gazes.

The frequent reduction of the juxtaposition between Indian and European modes of urbanization and the assignment of rationality to the European side is pernicious and wrong. The rich history of Indian urbanism is filled with its own styles of rationality, which bear direct comparison with Western models. India, with its elaborately systematized spirituality and social relations, is a place in thrall to abstraction, not simply as a hedge against the awful oppressions of daily life but as a broader means of reconciliation. Consider the following passage from the late-seventeenth-century French traveler Jean-Baptiste Tavernier, who observed the self-mortification of a group of Indian ascetics, one of whom is depicted in a contemporary engraving as oblivious to a woman caressing his penis. According to Tavernier, the *sadhus* thus worshipped did not show "any sign of sensuality but, on the contrary, without regarding anyone, and rolling the eyes terribly, you would say they are absorbed in abstraction."

This penchant for abstraction pervades Indian architecture and its theory. The early Vedic architectural manual Vastu Shilpa Shastra—the Feng Shui of India—with its characteristic synthesis of spirituality and common sense—offers a strategy for harmonizing architecture with the basic forces of the universe by, in effect, building structures that absorb maximum available benefits from the character and "energies" of the site—concretizations of the abstract. Like rationalism, this measure of spirit, this rendering of one abstract system into another, works because geometry is the substance of architectural description. As with our own styles of rationality, this system is thought to aid human physical, psychical, and moral development. The urbanistic high point of its application is the eighteenth-century planned city of Jaipur, whose eponymous author, Jai Singh, was a virtual paragon of modernity. His city is based on a supple application of a nine-square plan, a symbol of order as much at home in a Palladian villa as the famous Navgraha mandala.

The urban quality that struck me most forcibly on my trip to India, however, was its traffic, the apparent antithesis of harmonization. Seething circulation occupies a space from building front to building front and—at first blush—seems to defy any rationality. Streets literally teemed with people moving with and against traffic, with cars and buses and trucks, motorcycles and rickshaws, horse carts, occasional elephants, and, of course, those ubiquitous cows. And yet, somehow, it seemed to work: from the cacophony and chaos, a harmony emerges. Indian streets are a

place of continuous negotiation over space, filled with a kind of spontaneous democracy, an extremely localized view of order subsisting within
a larger (and largely impenetrable) pattern. Indeed, one might well say
that it is the very chaos of the streets that makes them tractable. Unlike
the uncrossable motorways that are beginning to make their appearance
in India, it is precisely the congestion that makes it possible to cross the
street.

These ruminations of the character of Indian public space were deep-
ened by an experience of several days of architectural juries at the excellent architecture school in Ahmadabad. While the strictly architectural
aspects of the student projects were of a high standard, a curious quality
seemed to pervade most of them. Outside the envelope of individual
buildings, the sheets were largely blank, festooned at best with a tree or
two. There seemed to be a resistance to elaborating the spaces of public
activity, to determining the routines of public motion. As I continued to
travel and observe, I came to see this as no anomaly, and the quality of a
minimally structured shared realm continued to impress me. As a medium for mixing and sorting out seemingly impossible numbers and phe-
nomenal diversity, this lack of differentiation increasingly took on the
character of a strategy rather than an accident. Certainly, this condition
of density serves as subtext for the apparent force and contrast of the
nominal rationality of such urban schemes as New Delhi and Chandigarh.

Chandigarh

It surely helps that Chandigarh is small. Planned for five hundred thousand and now grown to around a million (although feeling like less), its
scale is tractable, in studied contrast to the impossible density and extent
of cities like Bombay or Calcutta. Compared to these, Chandigarh is far
more uniformly prosperous and extremely clean. Local industry is limited, and the city is becoming a magnet for hi-tech firms. While Bombay—
home to the largest slum in Asia (a fact some locals refer to almost
pridefully)—has a population of over twelve million, half of whom are
squatters living in appalling conditions, the utterly poor in Chandigarh
number 10 to 15 percent. And due to the rigidities of the planning and
building process and to the repeated interventions of government, the
poor (a relative term to be sure) are largely—and atypically—peripheralized, either living on the edges of town or in settlements outside its limits, made invisible.

The original plan for Chandigarh was drawn by Albert Mayer, joined
by Matthew Nowicki, who began work on individual buildings. Mayer

had been friendly with Pandit Nehru, who recommended him for the job and who remained the project's alter ego and protector to the end. More than any other, Nehru believed in the symbolic importance and necessary modernity of this first great construction project of the new nation. At the town's 1953 inaugural, Nehru declared it "the first large expression of our creative genius, flowering on our newly earned freedom . . . unfettered by traditions of the past . . . reaching beyond existing encumbrances of old towns and old traditions . . . the temple of new India." Le Corbusier's account of this collision with modernity was somewhat more jaded: "What is the significance of Indian style in the world today if you accept machines, trousers, democracy?"

While Corb retained the essential diagram of Mayer's plan—a grid of superblocks with a commercial core and a governmental precinct as its head—he obviously found the curving, Radburn-like streets too picturesque, and straightened them out into a more rationalist-feeling grid. Corb's understanding of the city was typically—and modernly—undergirded by a sense of circulation. For him, the new city was to be about clarity and speed ("the city that has speed has success"), about unimpeded flow. Famously, he had deplored the idea of a city finding its form through the meanderings of oxen but now found himself in a country in which the privileged movers were cows, enjoying complete freedom of the road. In *Urbanisme,* Corb had written, "man walks in a straight line because he has a goal and knows where he is going. The straight line is the line of man, the curved line is the line of the donkey."

Donkeys notwithstanding, Chandigarh's most fundamental physioconceptual flaw is its attempt to impose the engineer's rationality on the city universally, via a strategy of separation, erecting barriers to the typical Indian means of frustrating such hierarchies. Traffic is organized by a system that imposes too many obstacles to mingling, based on the modernist paradigm of smooth flow and separation of traffic, the seeming opposite of the indigenous condition. Designed from the position of the car, it inconveniences both the pedestrian and the bicycle, the logical means of transport in a city that is both flat and compact. Giving alpha status to the car does fulfill its own prophecy: the very generously dimensioned system *is* largely able to cope with the town's motor traffic.

The seven-fold hierarchy of street types (the famous "V" system of roadways in Chandigarh, a rationalist nightmare out of Mr. Hulot) is the medium of this strategy but has been partly sapped of its rigidity by an encrustation of improvisation, modification, and the makeshift, by bazaars in the parking lots and bikes on the motorway. But the surfeit of curbs and medians and the humongous street widths remain inconvenient. Likewise, the Delhi-style caste-colonial lexicon of housing types—fourteen categories ranked to precisely reveal status by size, elevation, and proximity to the symbolic center, the upland capitolium—is a flawed approach, certainly in a democracy. The generic architecture of the city is surely too monochrome. The commercial center remains dry.

But this having been said, Chandigarh is beautiful. Insanely generous in green space for *any* Asian city, it stands in tremendous contrast to the pollution and turmoil typical of Indian urbanism. The city has an extremely manageable scale (I did my touring on a bike), wanting only a slightly more logical and more sustainable attitude to the mix of transport means and a series of relatively minor modifications to its streets to reverse the privilege of motor traffic in favor of walkers and bikes. And the superblock system has always had the potential to be both subtle and viable, to create a richly fabricated modern Mohalla, a genuinely autonomous and coherent sense of neighborhood. What is missing are enough layers deployed in simultaneity, more of the richness of the convulsive Indian styles of compaction and the side by side. Chandigarh still needs to acquire the sense of both/and, a deeper patina.

For years I have heard the standard critique of Corb's government precinct in Chandigarh: inhuman in scale, lost in inarticulate space, a sun-parched monument to bureaucracy. In fact, the site is magnificent, slightly elevated, surrounded by green with a beautiful mountain backdrop. Clearly, the complex riffs the Lutyens acropolis at Delhi with its axial approach and formal ensemble. Like in New Delhi, the grand distances are not meant to be convenient but *impressive* and symbolic. However, if the King's Way was terminated by the palace of the Raj, Chandigarh has another iconography in mind. Approaching, the roadway leads only to emptiness, splitting in two, the court to the right and the legislature to the left. In the original plan, a governor's residence lay more or less in the axis culminating position. Compared to the other structures on the hill (or to the palace of the Raj), the building was quite small. The servant of the state was to live well but know his place, hemmed by the grandeur of the courts and the legislature. The precinct is further animated by Corb's own spray of abstract iconography, the Open Hand, the concrete-braced berm, the House of Shadows. I visited several times, and the highlight was at dusk, as the heat of the day ebbed and the plaza became the reserve of bikers and skaters and wheeling blackbirds.

Next to the Corbusian acropolis stands an astonishing anti-Chandigarh, the "Rock Garden," the town's most popular attraction. Built over many years by Nek Chand, an engineer on the Indian railways, who continues to expand the project, the garden is an explosion of folkloric construction, Simon Rodilla meets Antonio Gaudi. Where Chandigarh is geometrical, the garden is free-form and eccentric. Where Chandigarh's materiality is limited and precise, the garden's is convulsive, odd, and eclectic, from boulders to broken porcelain electrical fittings. Where Chandigarh is flat, the garden is all cliffs and gorges. Where Chandigarh is too legible, the garden's routes meander, dead-end, and double back. It is a beautiful place and easily the most brilliant and concrete critique ever rendered of the city. And yet it fits. Much as Corb's plan opposes order and nature in a familiar European way, with overgrown parkland flowing through the city, so the city assimilates the garden as a carefully enclosed icon of otherness, the order not taken.

The garden is a kind of a ghetto. Chandigarh is a monument to the prescriptive, the desire for everything in its place. One often reads, in sympathetic accounts of Chandigarh's origins, of Corb's affinity for the Indian environment, his intuitive reading of its historic architectures and spaces, emblematized by his cheery cartoons of big-horned Indian cows (although—in a familiar split—others call him superficial, his only knowledge of Indian culture coming from hobnobbing with the rich and looking out the car window). But it is also clear that Corb's rigid and antique sense of social hierarchy dovetailed precisely with an Indian mode of social division. India continues to be crippled by caste, a place where hierarchy is hereditary and inescapable. In Chandigarh's almost insane attempts to impose a hierarchical system of classification on all dwellings constructed there, the mechanizations of European rationality conjoin with the ethos of caste to produce what is in many ways a nightmare.

Any city must answer the question of who is to live there. Naturally, a democracy prefers to answer "anyone." In a poor and stratified country like India, the consequences can be Bombay, with half the city unhoused. In Chandigarh, the initial answer was to be anyone with regular employment. The question of defining the limits of population, of course, is set at the low end of the scale. But how low to go? At the city's beginning, the entire early labor population was working on construction. The intention was for workers (often with their families) to live in self-built shacks on construction sites. These shacks were meant to be self-liquidating: when the building was completed, the workers were displaced, enacting a short-cycle episode of colonial exploitation and expropriation. After it was recognized that there was no provision in the original planning for housing that these workers could afford, Corb's collaborator Jane Drew designed a house type that was buildable (in the fifties) for the equivalent of $350. Seen positively, the low end of the system was dedicated to providing people with a first step, but even this step remains too high for many seeking to make a life in the city.

Such issues of class and mobility are truly clarified at the margins, and these margins are both social and spatial. As in Brasilia, there is a large population that lives beyond the edges of what the city is able to conceive itself to be. Chandigarh supports a true underclass, excluded from the formal system of finding shelter. Because the production of housing is top-heavy with subsidy, and because the for-profit market cannot find any in sheltering these people, a diminished bureaucracy of mobility has created a set of phantom subcategories—14, 15, 16, 17. . . . To solve the problem of its homeless, the city administration created a system meant to bring people from illegal settlements into transit camps, into self-built camps with limited services, into one-room tenements, and finally into "regular" housing. Of course, most do not make it, remaining outside the system. In Chandigarh—like in Brasilia—the idea of marginalization has a particularly spatial quality: the poor are literally peripheralized in squatter colonies beyond the territory of official sanction, in a parallel city, unsusceptible to the rationales of order that shape the official zone.

All cities are shaped by social strategies for housing and income mobility. Caste or class systems in their pristine manifestations are formulas for total immobilization. In India, though, the upper caste/class's self-blinded, tolerating eye (the same blinkering that lets us step over our own homeless) allows a degree of everyday mingling—the ubiquity of the "informal" sector is an astonishing fact of life everywhere—which our political culture—which cheers the hounding of squeegee men from our streets—would not tolerate. This mingling is possible to the degree that it is unthreatening, whether of physical harm, of the deterioration of property values, of a sense of amenity, or of the displacement of the structures of privilege that dominate.

Such questions of origin, of exclusion, of mobility shape the character of space and our expectations of it. A student neighborhood may be shabby but is redeemed as the launchpad of mobility, becoming not the scene of a degraded life but of a privileged moment of bohemianism, made pleasurable by its elective and transient character. Such neighborhoods are places not of constraint but of latitude where the temporary opens up a space of freedom. The slum dweller, on the other hand, whose chances are temporary and fragile at best and whose degraded circumstances are all too permanent, will not have the same feeling of liberation.

All towns confront similar issues of order, but new towns throw them into special relief. Whether at Brasilia, Chandigarh, or Seaside, the degree of prescription can be seen with intense, schematic clarity because the accidental has been largely excluded and because—in their youth—these places continue to be largely unmodified incarnations of initiating visions. While we tend to focus on the physical aspects of these informing prescriptions, new towns also clarify the ideological constructs that undergird them, diagramming clearly a fantasy of social relations.

The character of a society can be judged by the way in which it formulates its styles of compatibility, an issue that becomes more acute the greater the degree of stratification, and all of these towns paint a precise portrait of privilege. But Chandigarh—for all its frustrations and for all its entrapment in the problems of a very poor country—is an inspiring place. Not simply as an example of willed magnificence but of that most optimistic of acts, the building of a city.

The world needs more Chandigarhs.

1998

Instrumental Cities

As Disraeli famously remarked, "The East is a career."

Indeed. China has become American architecture's wet dream. The skylines of Hong Kong, Shenzen, Guangzhou, and Shanghai map a staggering commodification of space: skyscrapers sprout like weeds in a mind-boggling volume of construction. On my first trip to China, my own reaction was salivary: how can I get a piece of this action!

Greed is always embarrassing: the spectacle of development evoked in me a colonial fantasy that was surely of a piece with the acquisitive incursions of centuries. And just as quickly the guilty liberal counterreaction set in: what business is it of mine (of ours) to help purvey this? Should we be abetting the deluge of hermetic, anticlimatic towers, of McDonald's and Haagen-Dazs and KFC, of cell phones and Audis and VCRs, the whole apparatus of multinational consumption we are so critical of back home?

The question reminded me of an incident from the early days of Gorby and glasnost. I had been invited to appear as part of a panel of Soviet and American architects to discuss peace and cooperation, or some such. As was typical at such events, an American generally took on the role of gently chiding the Soviet comrades that unabashed capitalism was not a uniformly good thing, that the promises of development had to be taken with a grain of salt.

On that particular evening, this task fell to me, and I chose as my cautionary text the recent opening of McDonald's first Soviet store on a site near Red Square. Warming to the chore, I dilated on McDonald's as an instrument of cultural imperialism and global homogenization, as a threat to the environment, and of course as everything nutritionally pernicious. When I was done, an elderly Russian rose in the audience and addressed me with infinite forbearance and a heavy accent: "Tovarich," he said, slowly shaking his head, "to you McDonald's may be a corrupting agent of cultural imperialism but to us . . . it's meat!"

The Chinese have woken up and smelled this bacon in a big way. Not only is McDonald's on seemingly every corner (and jammed!), China is building U.S.-style McCities that put L.A. or Phoenix to shame. To stimulate this great leap forward, China has decisively opted for what Deng Xiaoping has described as "one country, two systems," a far more succinct slogan than its predecessor, "socialism with a Chinese face." Now, the roar of development has largely—at least in the numerous special economic zones and regions—drowned out the Maoist pattern of antiprivatization and anticonsumption. "To get rich is glorious" is another of Deng's aphorisms, markedly contrasting to the high-flown and metaphorical inscrutabilities of the Little Red Book. The China I saw is a living monument to pent-up consumer demand, a nation on a shopping spree. Mickey has long since replaced Mao as the ubiquitous and antithetical icon. Talk about dialectical materialism!

It is, of course, equally the height of the colonial arrogance—as my chastening experience with the Moscow McDonald's should reveal—to deny people what they want or what they think they want simply because we—in our wisdom—do not think they should. As the world becomes one market, justice and the parity of nations takes on an increasingly economic cast. Ultimately, the most efficient vehicle for redress would be for Chinese architects and developers to build skyscrapers in Philadelphia and Atlanta and for Chinese franchisers to sell dim sum on every block in Chicago (which would be a true boon!). The jostling economic character of our relations with China is precisely about establishing the dimensions and rules of this reciprocity. The multinational fantasy loses its reprehensibility—at least schematically—if everyone can covet and inhabit everyone else's part of the globe.

Still, I do not want to fall into a self-serving and familiar pattern of cynicism. Globalism, after all, is another way of placing value on the idea of locality. If we understand the world from an ecological perspective, in terms of its sympathetic patterns of interdependency and its delicate husbandings of difference, then all of us have a stake in urban outcomes around the globe. This is the meaning of thinking globally and acting locally, and American architects should certainly ponder long and hard about the energy-sapping, fast-depreciating, jerry-built, carbon monoxide–laced, freeway-entangled environment they are helping the Chinese to produce, however much they may want it.

One of the hoary chestnuts of classical Marxism is the theory of the stages of development that describe society's historical trajectory to Communist nirvana. The old debate was over whether it was possible to skip stages, to accelerate, for example, directly from feudalism to socialism without going through capitalism. While the economic and ideological vectors of this construct are now thoroughly moot, it surely has bearing as a model for the environment. And it is *our* burden to report our findings and experiences to a society that is in the process of repeating our most regrettable patterns. The hope and frustration at the encounter with cities developing flat out, like Guangzhou or Shanghai, are that the opportunity to pursue the next stage of environmental management immediately is lost in the extractive frenzy of the moment.

China is, in many ways, well situated for such a stage-skipping leap. The position of the planner is nearly ideal: the state both owns *all* the land and licenses the number of residents permitted to live in a given city. This, you might say, is power. But the mind-set is not disposed to urban design. The history of postwar Chinese urbanism—like our own—embodies a high level of ambivalence both about the role of the city and about the import of modernist planning models. The new developments in the special zones repeat the arm's-length attitudes of the old concessions, the idea that these places, if useful, were fundamentally alien and had to be isolated. In the postimperial era, as the idea of planning became more identified with the project of modernization, the dominant models were themselves modernist, with influences ranging from the Garden City to the Soviet, in its later years perhaps modernism's most degenerate branch.

Postrevolutionary planning has shown radical swings in attitude toward the city and its role in building Chinese society. Initially, official ideology emphasized the city as driver and promoted urban concentration as a means for producing rapid economic results. Within a short span of years, though, attitudes changed dramatically, and policy emphasized decentralization. This was not just the consequence of a revolution that had been won by the peasants and an ethos that emphasized the countryside as the source of revolutionary virtue, but of a nuclear-war paranoia that prompted industrial dispersal and a de-emphasis of the coast. Now, however, as the dominant planning model shifts from the social to the economic, the idea of the big-city driver is again in the saddle.

My impression, both from conversations with planners and from English language sources, suggests that although an extensive professional and scholarly urban discourse exists, it remains highly subservient to primary economic models. I was unable to discover an organized critical counterforce to the rapid development paradigm that currently rules. This seems the consequence both of a long history of official strictures on free speech and of another "stages of development" issue. In the exhilaration of the shop-til-you-drop, seemingly automatic boom of the moment, the era of liberal anxiety, guilt, and independence has been further

delayed. There are stirrings on the environmental front, but clearly not enough is yet happening on the local and neighborhood levels, and—seemingly—there is no strong promotion of a longer-term vision. In this, the Chinese may have learned from us too well.

This issue of the burden to communicate our own failures becomes especially thorny in matters of culture, where we risk getting into the deepest, most spiritual forms of colonialism. The new building that I saw is not simply the same dreary multinational architecture one might see anywhere, it is rapidly destroying the historic textures of the cities in which it rises. For instance, the "longtang" is the traditional form of urban residence in old Shanghai. Developed around the beginning of the nineteenth century and passing through a complex evolution, these row houses combine both Chinese and European features and line the narrow lanes that characterize the pattern of city. This structure of houses, lanes, neighborhoods, and districts gives old Shanghai a legible and tractable sense of locality and community, however spatially, structurally, and hygienically inadequate many of the structures may be. Of course, lying at the center of town, they are tremendously vulnerable to development pressure and are being destroyed at a brisk clip. Between 1991 and 1993, over four million square meters of buildings were demolished, and three hundred thousand people moved out of the city center, and the trend is accelerating.

In a conversation with two well-placed planning officials, I wondered about the loss of this texture and heritage and asked whether there was any attempt to keep communities intact. While making all the appropriate noises about the loss of both historic social and physical textures, they told me that there was no widespread objection to displacement. Like my Soviet comrade years before, they pointed out the obvious. Offered a new apartment with a modern kitchen and bathroom and plenty of space, people leaped to leave their dilapidated old homes to move to satellite towns twenty kilometers outside the center. Indeed, the offer of an extra bedroom was strong motivation to move an additional ten kilometers out.

The problems come later. The satellite towns are regimented and unprepossessing and constructed at a scale and increment to frustrate neighborliness. Distances tremendously attenuate commuting, adding pressure for automotive solutions. And the redeveloped areas of town are scaled up and discontinuous, valuing the parcel over any sense of continuity, obliterating the qualities that make the city particular. This is a problem Shanghai shares with all older cities, the strategies for the superposition of new modes and patterns for the production of space on a body that could never have anticipated the shock. Like in our own cities, the product is sprawl without end.

Shanghai's biggest development, though, is Pudong. Since the days of Sun Yat-sen in the early part of the century, Shanghai planners have dreamed of a move across the Huangpu River to claim the territory immediately opposite the Bund and the downtown core. Following the economic liberalization of 1978 and the experience of the Shenzen Special Economic Zone, the decision was taken in 1984 to perform a similar experiment not simply in the limited area opposite the Bund but over a far greater contiguous territory stretching to the Yangtze, an area of 350 square kilometers. Planned only in a general way, flaunting the "plan before leasing" philosophy that supposedly governs, Pudong has become a remarkable urban free-fire zone, a museum of the late-twentieth-century skyscraper.

Touring Pudong, a number of truths become evident. The first is that the general, primarily land-use and infrastructure style of planning, coupled with a proclivity to global modernism yields a generic condition. One of the striking qualities of Pudong is that it looks and feels a great deal like Houston or Los Angeles (or Kuala Lumpur or Jakarta). The second evident aspect is precisely how marginal the particular differences among the dozens of skyscrapers are. Whether produced by celebrated international big offices or local big offices, the variation in quality is a matter of the narrowest connoisseurship: the formal convergence is almost total. Just as the buildings from the American firms spring from images clipped from *PA* (the current crop of buildings have been in the pipeline for a while), so the indigenous product is a synthesis of necessity and image. Chinese architectural publishing is largely devoted to either technical literature or pattern books, and I was not surprised on a visit to a large Shanghai firm to find an architect with one eye on his workstation and the other on a book opened to the curtain wall he was cribbing. Soon all differences will be gone: already the copies of *Domus* are beginning to appear on the desktops. And they are on the Net.

Pudong is an enclave both physically and legally, another concession. This instrumental view of the city yields the city as theme park. And the theme is money. The model for all of this is, of course, Hong Kong, the Ur-Concession. Its circumscribed reincorporation into China is both a "concession" to the territory's difference and the expression that these patches of otherness function, in part, because of the clarity of their isolation, like terms in a dialectic. The new concession is economic, territorial, and conceptual.

More than any other city in the world, Hong Kong produces an architecture of extraction, understands real estate strictly in terms of the production of extent. Hong Kong's endless towers are legible as bar graphs. They are already abstractions, so the details are trivial, just decorating the primary signifier. Endlessly, the city fills in its harbor, its greatest visual and public asset, to increase the availability of prime harbor-front land for yet more towers. Even the new airport, itself constructed on an artificial island and the largest construction project currently under way on the planet, may ultimately just represent a strategy for reclaiming exhilaratingly central Kai Tak for development. Hong Kong never blinks. For aviation safety, the neon signs atop the towers burn without cease, Soup Noodle and Sanyo endlessly illuminating the night.

The mesmerizing growth of Hong Kong is, at least in part, a function of shortage. Hong Kong Island, the core of the metropolis and the piece of territory originally ceded to the British in the Opium Wars, is hemmed by circumstance, harbor on one side and unbuildable peak on the other. Like Manhattan, the compressive linearity begs verticality, and Hong Kong's beautiful thicket of towers is the result. Genius loci springs from the interaction of stunning topography, lush vegetation, marvelous coastlines, and dynamic economy. This physical autonomy, though, belies the growing continuity between Hong Kong and its Pearl River Delta hinterland.

Clearly, what has mesmerized China has little to do with architecture but with the amazing economic dynamism that produces it. And it *is* breathtaking—South China is total Adam Smithland. In 1992, Deng took a much celebrated trip south to see what the new policies had wrought. One can imagine an almost giddy, Dr. Frankenstein experience at the sight of this creation. The experiment was switched on, and it worked beyond all belief, producing a city of pure accumulation. From Hong Kong to the new city of Shenzen, up the Pearl River Delta to Guangzhou, a megalopolis leaped into being. Soon the population of the Hong Kong–Guangzhou–Macau triangle will exceed thirty million. Already, one-third of Chinese exports originate in the delta. Show us the moneeeeeey!

Deng's formula simultaneously produces both a miracle and a disaster. On the one hand, truly prodigious amounts of wealth are being generated along with real improvements in the quality of life. On the other, an urban form is being produced that, while exhilarating for its dynamism, is also a formula for trouble. The marvelous intimate textures of Guangzhou with its beautiful arcaded streets, and of Shanghai with its lanes are being obliterated for a standard-issue version of progress. A culture of bicycles **43** is becoming a culture of cars. The possibility for urban limits is being swallowed up in a sea of development. And the dominant model of city building remains too abstract, focused on apparatus and icons without a rich enough fantasy of the future.

In the Pearl River Delta, ironically, what is needed is a great deal more centralized coordination. Although China is no democracy, the autonomy exercised by individual municipalities—which has resulted, among other things, in the construction of four international airports within a radius of fifty kilometers—must find a way of deferring to regional interests. The moment is ripe to create, for example, a coordinated system of parks and open space and to deal with issues of growth on a regional basis. And the time is certainly ripe to dispense with one-dimensional exaltation of size and replace it with a fantasy modeled from life.

1997

Containing Cairo

Arriving in Cairo a few months ago, the plane followed an approach from north to south over the eastern edge of the city, began a wide U-turn above the pyramids, finally descending to the north over the city's eastern side. Taken together, it was a view that encompassed all of Cairo, like looking out the window of a chariot of the gods.

What struck me was that the city did not seem large enough. Like many cities in the developing world, Cairo has a different kind of an edge than American cities. Although Cairo is huge, it does not yet exactly sprawl, cleaving in general to the line of the Nile. The combination of a delimiting desert and of a social gradient that locates wealth near the river contributes to a relatively compact area. Of course, the insane densities also help: the average in Cairo (170 souls per hectare) is close to six times that of Mexico City. A city of close to twenty million, greater Cairo occupies an area approximately twice that of Paris but holds more than four times its population. And although rates have slowed slightly, the city is growing by about 350,000 per year, a strain far beyond available resources or infrastructure.

Cairo is the mother node on a system that stretches the length of the Nile, the linear city par excellence. Egypt, in effect, is a country four hundred miles long and half a mile wide, a singular ecological entity. Settlement and cultivation occupy only 3.5 percent of the land area of the country, and one of Cairo's biggest problems is the encroachment of development on desperately scarce agricultural lands. The exacting difference between the desert and the river creates a split in character that is an indelible fact of the Egyptian environment. This extreme, bifurcated ecology defines the nation with a presence that—whether in the sand seeping through every crack or the urgent cool of the Nile banks—is all pervasive.

The character of Cairo shifted dramatically with the construction of the first Aswan dam in 1902. By stabilizing the river's banks, not simply was Egyptian agriculture rescued from the historic cycle of flood and drought, but extensive urban development along the shore was enabled, leading to a westerly shift in Cairo's center of gravity away from the medieval city to the east of the floodplain. The current character of the city, with its phalanx of high-rises straining for a view of the river, is the hyper-trophied result, the familiar Chicago syndrome. One conspicuous distortion is the insane valuation of prime riverfront sites, which fetch prices at the Tokyo or New York standard, as much as $20,000 a square meter. Indeed, Cairo is busy blowing a speculative real estate bubble of great and frightening dimension.

While it would be foolish to describe Cairo as a city flush with efficiency, there is little sense of disorder. Although the crowds are thick, the traffic legendarily grim, and the pollution ghastly (a single lead-acid battery recycling plant has apparently caused a one-point drop in the IQ of Cairene kids), the order of inconvenience does not rival, for example, Bangkok, pinioned in its paralysis of growth. Part of the reason is simply cultural. I have always been struck on visits to Cairo by both the ubiquity and the softness of the crowds. While there is a tremendous problem of underemployment in Egypt, unemployment rates are actually fairly low. Wandering commercial quarters, bazaars, and old neighborhoods, the bustle—the sense of endeavor—is tremendous but somehow calming. As anyone who has read the novels of the great Naguib Mahfouz will know, this street life is one of Cairo's historic glories, an intricate interaction of its citizens with shops, mosques, cafés, houses, and the narrow medieval pattern of streets.

There is no better place to meditate on this condition than the celebrated Al-Fishawi café—long since elevated to a tourist icon—one of the world's great institutions of urban conviviality. In the midst of the teeming Khan Khalili bazaar and near the ancient and magnificent Al Ahzar university buildings, Al-Fishawi comprises a double-deep enfilade of rooms done in the faded plush of the nineteenth century. Tables spill into the narrow pedestrian lane in front, and the opposite side of the narrow street is also lined with settees and chairs, with little tables, with a leisure of hookahs, with the comings and goings of tiny cups of murky sweet coffee and glasses of minted tea. Contained in this environment is everything an architect could possibly want to know about the relation of scale, texture, and sociability as well as an utterly exemplary and sympathetic interaction between private commerce and the space of public life.

Al-Fishawi is a reminder of the tremendous successes of the medieval pattern of the city, a pattern that still has deep relevance for contemporary planning. The Cairene "Harat"—or neighborhoods—are carefully but flexibly hierarchical. Here, density abets locality, producing a style of local self-sufficiency in cultural, religious, and commercial affairs that contemporary planning strains without success to reproduce. Part of the problem is the adoption by more and more Egyptians of the lifestyles of the global bourgeoisie, an outgrowth of the pattern produced by an economy focused on large-scale industrialization and bureaucracy rather than the smaller-scaled, more crafts-intensive pattern of the traditional city. And part of the problem is simply the lack of convincing planning models that preserve the best aspects of such traditional environments.

Egypt is one of the world's great battlegrounds between tradition and modernity. This tends to schematize politics, leaving little room for the forms of compromise, the pattern of constant giving ground between private and collective interests embodied in the traditional city. After years of a semiauthoritarian, statist view of modernization, Egyptian architecture has virtually ceased to offer useful alternatives or resistances. One of the surprises in all this—given the tense, somewhat subterranean stand-off between an essentially secular government and the network of fundamentalist institutions that oppose it—is that architecture figures so little in the elaboration of this difference, that its symbolic import seems to have so little weight in the struggle.

The best-known architect of modern Egypt, the late Hassan Fathy, embodies this contradiction precisely. Long an apostle of traditional building and town form as well an energetic investigator and advocate for traditional means of construction, Fathy followed an approach of deep cultural and environmental resonances, filled with imputations of local economy and the virtues of self-help. The resulting architecture—from the town of New Gourna to a suite of beautiful Cairene villas—is subtle, powerful, and filled with fellow feeling for the cultural and physical landscape.

But Fathy is very much a guru without a following in Egypt. Neither the architectural schools, nor the bureaucracy, nor the broad mass of citizens seem to have much concern for the relevance of Fathy's work. Part of this is due to the widely perceived failure of New Gourna, near Luxor, a town built by Fathy to rehouse a population that had made its living grave robbing in the Valley of Kings and that, ultimately, did not cotton to resettlement and reemployment, never mind how beautiful and environmentally sensitive the architecture, nor how readily available crafts training meant to reinvent the local economy.

This articulation of the relationship between Western and traditional Islamic models of urbanization as a *conflict* has long formed the major trope for discussions of the growth of Cairo, indeed of development in the Islamic world in general. Interestingly, however, although it has been replete with various strategies of segregation, Cairo never developed the **47** extreme bipolarity of other north African colonial cities, with their traditional medieval medinas twinned with the orthogonal, rationalist plans of their colonizers, most prominently the French.

Indeed, one of the abiding fascinations of Cairo is the in many ways extremely successful import of global models of urban development and their integration into the city against staggering demographic and economic odds. The large-scale grafting of European urban models began during the reign of Muhammad Ali, Egypt's first and prototypical modernizer. Confronting a city in which fewer than 8 percent of streets were wide enough to permit two-way cart traffic—and in which he was the only carriage owner—Ali removed encroachments from city streets and realigned many, with the unfortunate loss of considerable architectural texture. Large numbers of official and private structures were built, and over four hundred thousand construction workers were employed at one point on government projects.

Khedive Ismail—Muhammad Ali's grandson—deeply impressed by the Parisian Exposition Universelle of 1867 (George-Eugène Haussmann's swan song)—implemented practices of which his grandfather had only dreamed. On his return from Paris, Ismail appointed Ali Mubarak as the Haussmann of Cairo, charged with drawing up a Parisian-style master plan for the city. Spurred by the approaching festivities surrounding the opening of the Suez Canal in 1869, Ismail and Mubarak remade the face of the city, cutting a radiating system of boulevards, adding new European-style neighborhoods and buildings, even hiring Barillet-Deschamps, the landscape architect of the Bois de Boulogne, to create a local version of the Parc Monceau.

This activity had both positive and negative results. Among the latter was the wholesale destruction of much of the historic texture of the city and the bankrupting of the Egyptian economy, opening the door for British colonization in 1882. Nevertheless, the rapid growth of the city continued, much of it financed by foreign capital for speculative concessionary projects. Among these was an extensive system of streetcar lines, which set the pattern and standard for Cairene public transportation and which—retrospectively—were a highly constructive development that Cairo—unlike so many American cities—retains to this day.

Among these trolley lines was the Cairo Electric Railway built in 1906 by Baron Edouard Empain, a Belgian financier and industrialist. Empain used his trolley to leverage both the financing and development of Heliopolis, a new town in the desert to the north of the existing core. Much influenced by English garden city planning, Empain's idea was to create a largely self-sufficient town in the desert with both a lavish resort component as well as an industrial base. With this in mind, a wide range of housing types was planned, although their internal layouts were essentially European. The architecture—arcaded and elaborate—achieves a kind of orientalist sublime, and the generous apartments in the original buildings are much sought after today.

By almost any standard, Heliopolis must rank as a success. Although its initial occupants were drawn from the wealthy and foreign populations (the Brits took it over as a base during the First World War), Heliopolis was almost immediately annexed by the city of Cairo and today houses over a million people. Adjoining both the huge new development of Nasser City as well as the airport, its location continues to draw very substantial investment and to provide a fundamentally autonomous city sector. The quality of the environment—still informed by the initial picturesque—remains high.

Although there is a continuing debate over whether Heliopolis represents an alien import, involving all the usual appeals for a fictitious architecture of authenticity (what, one wonders, is the precedent for an Islamic streetcar suburb), it is clear that Cairo—a city that has added the equivalent of the population of New York to itself in the past ten years—cannot simply expand exponentially but must decentralize. And from the beginnings of the current republic, the Egyptian government has recognized this and pursued an active and in many ways exemplary policy of new town building. It was recognized early on that the uncontrolled growth of Cairo was not simply creating conditions of dysfunction for the city itself but having a distorting effect on the country as a whole. Cairo—the classic metropole—continues to draw vast numbers from the countryside, most of whom wind up either in the pattern of informal settlements within the city and its inhabited necropolis or at the urban periphery on existing agricultural land, the most genuinely valuable real estate in Egypt.

Having made the decision to try to deal with Cairo's growth as the symptom of a national problem, the government has adopted a triple approach. First, to build new cities and reinforce older centers elsewhere in Egypt in order to provide employment and residential possibilities in place. Second, to develop a group of satellite cities at the periphery of Cairo to relieve pressure on the historic city core and to manage the huge appetite of the sanctioned and the informal sectors for space. And, finally, to elaborate so-called homogeneous zones within Cairo as essentially self-sufficient communities.

This policy has developed over a number of years and has been closely tied to shifts in administration. The initial master plan was promulgated in 1956 during the Nasser period and reflected Soviet models and preoccupations. It included the city's first ring road, a massive industrial development in Helwan to the city's south, and—easily its largest component—the construction of Nasser City, the first and far and away largest of the satellites, to its northeast. Initially developed by and for the military and its suppliers and for other government facilities, Nasser City is now a very densely settled, thoroughly "modern" sector, currently housing a population of over three million, largely in high-rises. Although much derided by architects, Nasser City—with its boulevards and towers—actually approximates a city, its streets lively and the whole pervaded by a sense of completion and urban density.

The second master plan, prepared in the seventies by the new Greater Cairo Planning Commission and identified with the regime of Sadat, is called by some the "American" plan because of the sway of U.S. planners in its development. This plan included a second, outer ring road and a group of five satellite towns—Tenth of Ramadan, Sadat City, Sixth of October, Fifteenth of May, and Al Obour. The intention was that these towns, located relatively far from central Cairo, would be self-sufficient, providing both housing and employment for their populations. This however, was not to be, as industrial development lagged behind housing construction, which itself lost steam.

The third master plan—this one under the influence of French experts—was executed by the Mubarak government and took a somewhat more sophisticated, more integrated approach, moving beyond simple policies of accommodating growth to a scheme based on a plan for depopulation. This plan, prepared in 1983 and updated in 1990, included both additional work on the satellites, an attempt to redirect north-south growth into an east-west corridor, and the initiation of planning for the homogeneous zones. The plan also sought to replace the clearance policies directed at informal housing concentrations with a strategy of "upgrading in place" for informal districts and greater attention to the needs of new graduates entering the housing market.

More recently, another shift has taken place. As with so many centralized economies in the post-Soviet era, the introduction of widespread privatization of industries and institutions formerly in government hands has had a dramatic effect on the environment. In Cairo, this has entailed a revision of the new-town strategy that favors the market and its urban models and that acknowledges the great reserve of consumer demand for housing, seeking to satisfy it via the same sensibilities of consumption that help shape consumer preferences more generally, the welter of movies and advertising and multinational covetables that fill the world environment today.

The results can be both surreal and very familiar. Driving the ring road, heading east out of the city, one is almost immediately in the desert. And it is a real desert, which begins right at the edge of town, sand stretching forever, blowing across the macadam, ready to take everything back should resistance be dropped. The road passes through the vast "city of the dead"—Cairo's legendary inhabited necropolis—alongside military camps, and skirts dreary disrepaired housing blocks deployed on the global grid. Soon the city disappears, and all that remains are dunes and traffic.

Rounding a bend, though, a fantastical fata morgana heaves into view. Across the desert appears a large expanse of shimmering, apparitional emerald: a golf course, its greens manicured perfect, its flags fluttering in the breeze. Stretching along the shores of the course stands a community of large, very southern California–looking houses—roofs red-tiled, walls pale stucco, decor meant to evoke that vaguely Mediterranean feeling that is the Orange County architectural default—and presumably furnished in the style the locals call "Louis Farouk." Like Orange County, too, the community is gated and patrolled, and, like Orange County, the Beamers and Mercedes poke from the garages.

The young architect with whom I was touring took me into this development to see the site he had recently purchased and on which he was planning to build himself a house. It looked like a typical American suburb in the process of becoming: streets, curbs, and sidewalks laid in, lot lines laid out, a random pattern of houses beginning to rise. But there was more: this was not entirely virgin territory, and a portion of the site contained dozens of low slab blocks, remnants of the previous policy, many of them now designated for demolition or conversion to higher-income flats than the housing for the poor originally intended.

My friend lived in Zemalek, one of the most desirable neighborhoods in Cairo, a clutch of high-rises on an island in the Nile directly opposite the city center. I was curious why he intended to move from that very lively, very urban, very pleasant environment, a place I surely would choose to live in should I ever find myself on a extended stay in Cairo. Some of his motives—living in the same building as his parents, the desire to build—were understandable, others less so. For my friend, the suburban development on the city fringe offered, despite its lack of social and commercial activity and despite the long commute by car into town, a dream of freedom and an escape from the madding crowd of old Cairo. And the young architect simply loved the idea of a place of his own. When he spoke of the possibility of living in an environment of quiet, the idea assumed almost metaphysical overtones. Such feelings are also produced by a culture of congestion.

"New Cairo" (as it has come to be called) is the result of a planning policy that now seeks to join the partially developed new towns on the east side into a single market-driven, physical and planning entity, and similar plans are under way to the west. For the moment, though, the market is indifferent to the needs of anyone but the middle and upper classes. Despite its poverty, Egypt is awash in money—both its own as well as the cash of many from more conservative Arab states who have long used Cairo as a playground and relief valve from the dour morality back home. The government—eager to soak up as much of this cash as possible in Egypt—has encouraged privatization both in light of its own stretched resources—and for sound macroeconomic reasons. More than one progressively minded person suggested that while they were offended by the conspicuous American-style consumption, the money was, from the national standpoint, indeed better spent on a villa in the desert than an apartment in Paris or a numbered account in Zurich.

In the course of several days, I completely circumnavigated the city, looking at numerous developments on the fringe. An icon of the voyage was a roadside ad that appeared ubiquitously. Above a funky painting of Michelangelo's *David* was emblazoned the word "Concrete" (a men's clothing line, as it turned out). The signs, with their evocation of construction, strength, and the European exotic, could have just as well been advertising the buildings sprouting in the sands nearby and represented the same uneasy joining of influences. Indeed, the circumnavigation revealed the early stages of the growth of a culture of the edge that included detached fragments of the generic American exopolis—theme parks, car dealerships, shopping centers, and all the rest of the post-Disney urban apparatus.

In a sense, this style of urbanism is the indigenous form of multinationalism and reflects—like its predecessors—the most influential urban model of its time. In looking back at the history of modern Cairo, the import and modification of such models—reflected too in the shifting sensibility behind the satellite towns—have been a crucial aspect of the city's growth. What is curious—and perplexing—is the success of a number of these models and their corresponding failure to influence their successors. Cairo is a fantastic urbanistic museum, and although we tend to focus on the glories of the medieval city, there is also a city that has embraced with great success a series of paradigms of modernity, paradigms to which the city might look in describing its future.

Of course, as with all such models, the possibility for their incorporation is fraught with associations of colonialism and privilege and ancien régimes. But there is something utterly inspiring about the ongoing efforts of Cairenes to plan their city, to come to grips with its overwhelming problems. This is not simply my own pinkish nostalgia for the superior possibilities of centralized planning, but a realism that the problems confronted by the city cannot be solved any other way.

As in other megacities, Cairo's growth has been exponential and relatively recent, and the city is now home to something over a quarter of the Egyptian population, including 40 percent of the urban population. The consequence is both density and a certain familiar metropolitan distortion, a centralization of economic and cultural resources, and a magnetic attraction for success seekers of all classes. The fundamental question is whether all the despair, inequality, and failure of services that such gigantic cities produce can ever really be redressed in place.

The answer, of course, is no: there is only one solution for megacities, and that is to stop growing. This is, in the first instance, a question of redirecting investment to divert the metastasis of opportunity that accelerates the desire to come. The issue for physical planners is also a national one, the provision of housing—including especially types at the low end—in a volume of millions with the provision of a modicum of services. The issue for architects is not simply how to deal with the numbers but how to create environments that speak to both the aspirations and traditions of an extremely complex culture without prejudice for either old or new.

2001

Second Nature

Flying into Albuquerque, it is possible to see—scraped in the desert in front of the long range of hills to the east of town—the ghostly outlines of the streets of an abandoned subdivision. From the air, it is just a drawing (perhaps one of the world's largest), and the first association is with crop circles and Machu Picchu, alien artists trying to send us a message. The pattern, though, is no mystery, merely the disappearing evidence of a bubble of eighties hype, a broken promise made to a legion of visionary suckers.

The traceried subdivision may not have been built by aliens, but it surely feels like it, a form produced neither by nature nor out of any special sympathy for the desert landscape. Read two-dimensionally, however, the street pattern does look naturalistic, with its vegetable curves, leaf patterns, and clear, branching hierarchies. It is the genetic code for sprawl, expressed in cul-de-sacs, driveways, and traffic loops: another nature. This elaborate, highly evolved pattern of life is the way Americans have—through a complex set of choices and impositions—made their place on the planet.

A founding question for architecture is its relationship to some idea about nature. Building is a powerful instrument by which we situate ourselves in the world, by which we invent the very idea of nature. For modernity, nature is a construct, a cultural artifact: the moment we recognize something called "nature," we insist that we are not part of it. Even the most sympathetic of today's environmentalist metaphors—stewardship, conservation, etc.—imply a kind of detachment, putting us in the same relationship to the natural environment as a gardener is to a garden, or a zookeeper to a zoo: cultivators of the other. But in turning nature into just another human invention something is lost, the idea that there are forms and systems of life that are everywhere visible to us but that we do not control.

Still, the need to incorporate nature in architecture abides. Although we are habituated to thinking of modernism as a definitive rupture with mimetic expression, it also tried to make a portrait of nature. As the product of the materialist thinking elaborated in the eighteenth and nineteenth centuries to account "scientifically" for the nature of society and human action, modernism held a mirror to nature in all its glorious (presumptive) rationality. At the same time, though, an increasingly substantial idea of space and its flow helped to create an architecture that, in seeking to erase the difference between inside and outside, employed nature as a spectacle to be enjoyed on the other side of a protective membrane, through a glass clearly.

This is the tradition in which we continue to build, and the idea of nature enters most of our architecture through visual and representational means. The forms of the asymmetrical, unstable-looking architecture of so much fashionable building, for example, attempt to evoke nature by riffing quantum mechanics, chaos theory, or "natural" philosophy by an indirect mimesis. This approach is not exactly new but reflects a particularly contemporary obsession with the procedures of analysis, born of the uncertain position of the observer in the age of relativity. Such theoretical fantasies simply extend more literally mimetic architecture, like art nouveau, which transmuted nature into a portrait of the natural, buildings with soft curves and "naturalistic" decoration.

But modernism was born concurrently with the seeds of its undoing. The simultaneous elaboration of quantum theory and the discovery of the unconscious demanded an understanding of the natural filled with ambiguity, double meanings, and perceptual distortions, continuously modified in the eye of the observer. Nature had to be rethought: it could no longer be seen as an Edenic gift, a romantic wildness, or even a rationalist set of clockwork interdependencies. Nature had to be seen at once as an incredibly vast set of interacting mechanisms *and* our own set of ideas about what it was. Architecture today is a struggle to deal with this new nature both symbolically and in light of our new knowledge of the mechanisms of global ecology.

"Looks natural" is the primary aesthetic category in the American Southwest (think bleached colors, mock adobe, and Xeriscaped lawns), and because of the rich traditions of the region that predate our self-separation from the natural world, it is a good place to think about architecture and nature. The beauty of the southwestern landscape is deeply architectonic: those buttes and mesas and striated cliffs are already so incredibly like architecture that there is a powerful incitement to literally inhabit them (as cliff-dwelling Native Americans did for thousands of years), to imitate their forms (take a look at the mountainous massing of an art deco skyscraper), or to create an architecture that participates in the same processes—sun, wind, rain, erosion—that sculpt the cliffs.

The real founders of the Southwest aesthetic were, of course, Native Americans, especially those grouped under the rubric of the Pueblo Indians. A thousand years ago, these peoples evolved an architecture and a way of inhabiting it that remain a model response to the environment, brilliantly comprehensive, technically superb, highly complex, and very beautiful. The large, multiple dwellings of the Pueblos truly were inhabited mesas, a way of building that sought to be continuous with the larger environment through shared materiality and forms, all fitted to a system that revered the earth by subsuming architecture within a way of worship. The premise that undergirds this building was that it was *continuous* with its environment. We, on the other hand, have for the past quarter millennium or so preferred, it seems, systems of abstraction and representation to this fantasy of no difference. Indeed, the rise of landscape painting and pastoral verse, the whole romantic exaltation of nature, can be seen both as celebration and as a profound symptom of disconnection from the land.

No architecture has been more deliberately or artfully inscribed in nature than the pueblos of the Anasazi. Between the years 950 and 1100, the Anasazi developed an elaborate urban civilization and a superb architecture. Little, however, is known of their society, and their sudden disappearance around 1300 is one of America's unsolved archaeological mysteries. Perhaps the best known of the Anasazi ruins is Mesa Verde in southern Colorado, and the most famous of its over four hundred documented sites is the so-called Cliff Palace. Lodged in an alcove in a sheer south-facing cliff, the Palace contains 217 rooms and 23 kivas (circular spaces for ritual practices) and housed an estimated 200 to 250 people. It is remarkably intact, easy to imaginatively inhabit. Built of stone within the living rock, it sits in its niche as if it had grown there: its massed geometries feel like a direct translation of natural forces into the working of the hand.

Chaco Canyon, nearby in New Mexico, has a different—though no less specific—relationship to its site. A long, broad canyon dotted with large communal structures on its floor, the place is magical, without Mesa Verde's sense of defensiveness. The most magnificent of the Chaco dwellings is Pueblo Bonito, a 350-room building of beautifully dressed and laid stone—a complex unequaled in size by an American apartment house until the 1880s! The Pueblo forms a graceful, sort of semicircle, facing the sun and framing a plaza. Dotted through it are numerous half-underground, cylindrical kivas, and at the center of the plaza are three "great kivas"—larger circles, with highly elaborated and refined interior architecture.

Archaeology is the science of retrofit, matching explanations to facts.

Because so little is actually known about these places, modern reconstructions are also a record of our own desires. Pueblo Bonito and the Cliff Palace present a social architecture that suggests a nonhierarchical and collectivized physical culture, one with numerous ritual spaces, relatively uniform dwellings, a focus on public space in the form of plazas, and a continuous style of circulation and inhabitation. Highly cellular and permeable, Pueblo Bonito could be—had to be because of its passagewayless design—circulated over and through. If we are not left with much evidence of how these buildings were used, their form so completely substantiates a winning set of environmental and social propositions that its example is crucial, even if only as metaphor.

The main lines of archaeological account for Anasazi architecture are both environmental and cosmological. On the environmental side, the Anasazi builders were clearly careful of orientation, constructing buildings that were both sun scoops and windbreaks, highly efficient thermally. Their siting and structure also harbor a symbolic relationship to the landscape that includes a set of terrestrial and planetary alignments that recognized not simply seasonal events but located the structures within the geometry of both the larger pattern of Anasazi settlement and of the universe. This geomancy is very contemporary in its desire to incorporate its society's most refined physical speculations.

What lessons for the stressed American environment can be found here? Too often the issue of environmental suitability is reduced to a simple question of taste, the idea that the look of adobe (coupled with that good Native American eco-vibe) becomes the Southwest. But when we confront the phony adobe shopping mall, the limits of this approach become clear. The practices of adobe construction arose because of their clear suitability to Pueblo culture and place. Out of context, reexamination is necessary: we cannot retrieve Native American environmental relations simply by borrowing Georgia O'Keeffe-esque forms. Not that such borrowings are trivial; it is right that we express respect in our art. Indeed, architecture always asserts its relevance by tying itself to history, to social rituals and traditions, to the choreography of community: tradition is nature for architecture, its ground. But standing patterns of order cannot simply be appropriated. This kind of contextualism is a denatured approach, its authority invested simply in convention with crucial questions of use shunted aside.

Various forms of so-called green architecture have a stronger claim to reestablishing a meaningful connectedness to the natural. What distinguishes green architecture is simply this: whatever other qualities it embodies, it has a basis in an idea of quantifiable human account *to nature*. However trivial the Xeriscaped front garden may be in the larger scheme of things, the impulse is correct on at least two counts. First, it reckons directly with the balance of resources, taking a conservative, not an exploitative, approach. And it reverences the indigenous, cultivating the forms and materials of the region.

Such bioregionalism is crucial to establishing a sense of the particular within global culture, counteracting an everywhere visible trend to environmental uniformity. This particular must combine a sense of nature, region, and tradition, a synthesis for which we have lost the knack. Unfortunately, much green building is itself either freighted with the old sense of the universal—lost in the technical—or preoccupied with funk, as if nature preferred a sense of informality. But our interaction with the natural world is both physical—involving cause-and-effect relations to a series of planetary processes—and something more. In building our habitats we also construct ourselves: architecture is a point of conjunction between physical necessity and something greater, a measure of both the dimensions of our place on the planet and the spiritual, psychical, and cultural vision of what it means to us, what is means to *be* us.

Which brings us back to the Anasazi. In their religion, the earth was very much at the center, a planetary mother whose womb held humanity. Anasazi kivas are sunken into the earth in aspiration, the same impulse that stretches church steeples skyward. If one thing can be said about the Anasazi, though, it is that they were not given to making a distinction between the cosmological and the environmental but had a more integrated system of thinking, a more seamless conceptual and practical link to nature. The greatness of their architecture springs not just from its integrity but from the art with which its builders bridged between nature and culture.

1998

Millennium in Vegas

I think I will do the millennium in Vegas: The place is so *temporal.* What could be more in the moment than the intensely lit clocklessness of the casinos, than being able to eat a cheap steak at any hour, paradise for a routine-beleaguered world. In a flip of normal American life, with all its battering messages of healthy self-denial, self-indulgence is the antidote to death in Las Vegas, the *life*style. Such hyperabundance defeats time: I watched mesmerized as a man—easily 350 pounds—meticulously removed the meat from an enormous mound of crab legs (his only choice from the groaning buffet) and ate it all at once, beating the system.

The dark side of such indulgence—what in another world might be called waste—is central to the local vibe. Picture battalions of retirees with their plastic cups of quarters, pulling, pulling, pulling on the arms of the gaily tinkling, spinning bandits, kissing their savings good-bye in the vast trickle-up of the post-Reagan American economy. You have worked hard your whole life, now here is your chance to blow it all. And everyone wants to play! Not only does every municipality and tribe see gambling as salvation, but Clinton has just proposed to bet the Social Security trust fund on Wall Street.

The history of contemporary Vegas begins with the prescience of the mob and the flourishing of a culture of semi-legitimated vice in the desert. As the city grew, demanding integration into the routines of the national economy and capital market, a process of continuing mainstreaming began. Within scant years the Mafia was displaced by the multinationals in a ritual of investment that offers an ongoing object lesson on the fine line we draw between criminality and business as usual. (Interestingly, the transition was financed by an instrument that itself lay at the outer reaches of legal speculation: junk bonds. If Siegel and Lansky were the avatars of the first Vegas, Steve Wynn and Michael Milken were the geniuses behind its transformation to "legitimate" financing.)

Perhaps the most indelible marker of Vegas's evolution from mob-style to MBA-style has been the dynamiting of the "classic" hotels to make way for the gargantuan corporate models. The burial of their bricks and names surely finalizes this transition, as does the replacement of the glam Miami-esque modernist stylings of the gangster era with the banal iconographies that mark Vegas today. Whatever one thinks of the mob, their taste had legs–no Eiffel Towers, Cheops pyramids, or Venice campaniles for them.

The stirring sight of hotels coming down (Wynn throws the switch, thousands cheer, videotape at 11:00 . . .) is another celebration of temporality, of accelerated depreciation, an incitement to hurry up and bet (invest, speculate, enjoy!) lest the whole edifice crumble and crash. But the demolition of the hotels signals another cultural ritual of Vegas: potlatch, waste elevated to symbolic exchange. The whole enterprise is psychically sustained not simply by the loopy idea of the commutability of gambling and investment but by the conspicuous spectacle of waste, by blowing up a perfectly good building, by the prodigious burning of kilowatts, by throwing your money down a black hole, by (in Howard Hughes's favorite nightmare) detonating hundreds of A-bombs on your own territory, just down the road.

This spirit of waste reproduces itself in a broader urbanistic context. Las Vegas is everything an environmentally well-founded city ought not to be. Located in the heart of the desert, the city consumes over 300 percent more water than its environment provides annually. At 360 gallons a day per capita, it leads the nation in water consumption. Even L.A., the urban poster child for resource hyperindulgence, consumes a "mere" 211 gallons per capita, while Tucson, equally parched, uses 160. The rampant demand for water is largely for ornamental and symbolic purposes: 60 percent goes to watering lawns and golf courses.

The list of environmental issues facing Vegas is long and includes serious air pollution caused by a transportation network based almost entirely on cars, themselves used with the lowest level of efficiency in the country. Because of this, Las Vegas embodies a pure and powerful version of sprawl. The city's spreading periphery is a remarkably uniform low-density crust of buff-colored rancheros on quarter-acre lots, punctuated by the usual infrastructure of malls (often with casinos as anchors), schools, and tiny developer-provided green spaces. The city is classically segregated—the most segregated in America, according to some—housing its lowest rung in scraggly ghettos downtown. It is becoming enclaved and cellularized as well, with gated developments now the norm. In fact, Las Vegas has less public open space than any other major city in America.

Like casinos, the housing developments are dominated by huge corporate entities, including the Bass Brothers, Howard Hughes's Summa Corporation, and Del Webb of Sun City fame. The latter two are collaborating on Summerlin, a development at the edge of town that, when complete a few years after the millennium, will house two hundred thousand people, carefully segregated by age and income, in twenty-six elaborately designed villages.

None of that is exactly the point. Nobody looks to Las Vegas as the solution to our urban questions, but it is certainly a clear statement of the problem. Vegas is assuming the status of our designated city of the future, a place where commercial and cultural desires jockey for new form. And it continues to be the fastest growing city in the country because it offers people many things they want: low taxation, affordable housing, a growing job market for both the unskilled and professionals, a retreat from cities seen as dysfunctional (more than half of Vegas's immigrants come from California, yesterday's paradise), and, of course, that ineffable sense of possibility fostered by a city built on chance. And it is a melting pot. Here are employee name tags from my first ten minutes: Hi, I'm Debbie from Columbus; Hi, I'm Tuan from Vietnam; Hi, I'm Hilda from Germany.

There are those who take this dynamism very seriously. Hal Rothman, a historian at University of Nevada and a leading observer of the town, says that Las Vegas has become the "nation's new capital" because it offers an economic model for the next century, a postindustrial economy completely dominated by its service sector. Already, half the labor force is in "service," and the rest—including eighty thousand in the construction trades—work to service them.

Where other observers see Vegas as a nightmare, Rothman sees a postmodern Detroit, a place where a relatively high wage is paid for unskilled work, the millennial equivalent of the assembly line. To him, even the decline of the multigenerational pattern of casino employment offers a (somewhat perverse) version of the American dream, a place where hardworking parents can enable their kids to step up to white-collar work. The old Vegas was—much like the auto industry—the model of modern paternalistic capital, where fathers and daughters dealt cards down the generations. Today, the daughters go to B-school.

The increasingly corporate character of everything in Las Vegas has also had a dramatic impact on both the social and the physical feel of the place. The Bellagio, Steve Wynn's $1.6-billion replacement for the Dunes, is a conspicuous example. You enter through cool marble halls lined with Armani, Prada, and other sublime retail. The restaurants are "gourmet." There is an art collection with some very good work, and a sumptuously flower-stuffed conservatory, through which snakes a line as long as the queue outside the buffet to see the twenty-eight pictures (at $10 a pop, it is a $90 savings over Siegfried and Roy).

The new Vegas hotels are all pretty much the same. The architectural default on the Strip is now the thirty-five-story, mansardic, Dryvit old-Euro look. Across from the Bellagio, the Paris has been topped out and awaits the completion of the fifty-story Eiffel Tower that will serve as its sign. Up the street, the $2.5-billion Venetian provides an indistinguishable architectural backdrop to what will soon become a Disney version of Venice and its canals. Already up and running is the Monte Carlo, more quoined and doodadded "good taste."

Of course, the paradigm is clear: Las Vegas is being Beverly Hills'd, in homage to that other crucial cultural site, with its shared ethos of gigantic rewards for trivial accomplishments. Vegas is the free-range version of Beverly Hills, where everything is grown incredibly large, five-thousand-room hotels and gambling floors measured in football fields. As images of lifestyle become one of America's biggest exports, cities from Kuala Lumpur to Moscow hurriedly embrace this flimsy, fickle imagery, throwing up a miasma of knocked-off, cardboard, belle époque crap.

Although Las Vegas is exhibit A for the centrifugal model of urban development, it has begun—without deliberation—to challenge its own most endemic behavior. By recent count, the intersection of the Strip and Tropicana Boulevard attracts over thirty thousand pedestrians a day, an astonishing number in a town designed strictly for cars. With one hundred thousand hotel rooms clumped in a relatively small area, and with the burgeoning lure of the "attractions" offered by each hotel, Vegas is developing its own style of *flânerie,* as visitors stroll up and down the Strip, taking in the urban landscape.

Such walks can be hard-won affairs. I recently hiked the length of the Strip, from the Tropicana to Glitter Gulch, and found it a less than elevating experience. Most of the action is on the southern end, where fifty years of recycling and upscaling have created a Manhattan-style real estate market. But even here, despite billions of dollars invested in every block, throngs ready to walk from casino to casino, and generally benign weather (at least at night), you fear to tread because there is simply no place to do it.

Vegas actually lacks a continuous, negotiable sidewalk along the Strip. Constantly interrupted by parking lots, diverted around driveways, never shaded by trees, and often narrowed to no more than the width of the curb, the Strip's sidewalks are a pedestrian's nightmare. A number of explanations are offered, including the desire to discourage circulation between competing casinos and corporate contempt for the very idea of a public realm. Whichever you prefer, Las Vegas is an incredible advertisement for the selfishness of capital.

Perhaps the most interesting conflict over public space is one of free speech, paralleling the ongoing struggle over rights of private expression in shopping malls. In Vegas, though, the issue is not politics, it is sex. Although Vegas shut down its brothels at the military's behest in 1943, the sex industry is huge, and the town is awash in printed, tabloid-style come-ons for call girls, distributed from paper boxes on the Strip. Now that Vegas has remade itself as fun for the whole family, however, the casino fathers wish this traditional synergistic business would go away. Clearly, the most direct way of dealing with a problem taking place on the sidewalk is to eliminate the sidewalk. The ACLU has just won another lawsuit against a "public nuisance" law seeking to corral the news boxes.

The city has the means—both fiscal and physical—for another transformation, as dramatic as any so far. The kind of density that makes casino interiors so exciting as both place and spectacle has yet to find form in the space between interiors. But to the extent that the Stripscape is designed at all, it is done building by building, as a series of pictures to be contemplated from the window of a passing car. The streets of Vegas await the press of collectivity, something the owners—and the genius loci—continue to resist. And this horror of the public in any role but suckers is the failure of the town.

1999

Acting Urban

Robert Duvall's recent film *The Apostle* stands out for its uncanny *authenticity*. The acting, by a variety of both professional actors and everyday people, is so natural as to retreat to invisibility. And the settings, directly sampled from Texas suburban and Louisiana bayou landscapes, blend with Shakespearean connectedness into the narrative, as particular as *The Tempest*.

There is a moment when the issue of authenticity surfaces explicitly in the film. After the charismatic Duvall character has begun to preach over the radio, someone remarks admiringly that white listeners assume he is black. For a moment, the film seems to strike a familiar attitude, a standard Hollywood trope associating blacks with a special humanity, generalizing them as people of exemplary feeling and ennobling suffering. The Duvall character is able to move so easily among blacks, the film seems to say, because he is himself black at his core. But this film, I think, communicates genuine sympathy. Black and white characters—fired by the shared phantasms of faith—live together in real harmony, blind to their differences.

Compare this with the *Blues Brothers* films, their white stars—Belushi, Ackroyd, and Goodman—likewise on a "mission from god." But the pose is just a rip-off: these are clearly white people trying to be cool by acting black. And there is no mistaking the contempt: overpaid white musical mediocrities affirm their celebrity by frenziedly trying to suck vibe from great black musicians from Aretha Franklin to Muddy Waters. Of exploitation, there is no truer version.

These thoughts came to me after debating a representative of the so-called New Urbanism at a recent conference. New Urbanism has emerged over the past ten years as the leading discourse of urban design and planning in this country, and its apostles are designing and building developments all over the map. The best known are two projects in Florida, the resort community of Seaside on the panhandle coast, and the much-hyped Celebration near Disney World in Orlando. As with *The Apostle* or *The Blues Brothers,* their visual and conceptual stakes devolve on questions of "authenticity." There is something disquieting about these places, not unlike the antics of the Blues Brothers, something false.

The New Urbanist polemic grew from an attempt to join two tendencies in contemporary architecture—environmentalism and neotraditionalism—and the two coexist uneasily. Reflecting this division, New Urbanism has East and West Coast strains, the one (represented by Andres Duany, Elizabeth Platter-Zyberk, and other disciples of the ridiculous Leon Krier and Prince Charles) invested in the forms of traditional town-planning, and the other (represented by Peter Calthorpe, Dan Solomon, and Doug Kelbaugh, among others) in more dedicated mass transit, open space, growth limits, and pedestrianism.

To be sure, both approaches have something to commend them. Denser patterns of settlement instead of suburban sprawl, nonpolluting public transportation, and the revival of the life and culture of the street are all subjects of urgent importance to any conscientious urbanist. The problem, though, is both the dull homogeneity of most New Urbanist architecture and the big-brother ambiance of places like Celebration. Ironically, New Urbanism reproduces many of the worst aspects of the modernism it seeks to replace.

New Urbanism grew, in part, from the familiar critique of the planning practices of modernism, the isolated towers, the brutal urban renewal, the monoculture of the car. Undergirding modernity was the fantasy of a universal architecture girdling the globe, doing its bit to produce the socialist "new man." The basic problem of the New Urbanism is that it simply promotes another style of universality that—like modernism—is overreliant on visual cues in attempting to produce social effects. The endlessness of little clapboard houses, perfect front yards, and manicured town greens is ultimately asphyxiating in its formulaic application. While the claims of most of the practitioners of this style of urbanism stop short of the millennial palaver of someone like Leon Krier—who considers traditional architecture the manufactory of healthy yeomen—the uniformity of their production, the polemic of stylistic superiority, and the creepy corporatist lifestyles are scary.

Like modernists, New Urbanists overestimate architecture's power over behavior. Their idea is that replicating the forms of the New England town green will move citizens in the direction of the good, democratic conduct, which presumably arose from such arrangements in the past (never mind the witches being tortured just out of frame). But even as Main Street in Disneyland conceals a huge apparatus of manipulation and control behind its miniaturized, ersatz nostalgia, the towns of the New Urbanists are underpinned by a legal labyrinth of restrictive covenants, building regulations, homeowners' association codes of behavior, and engineered demographic sterility. Restrictions range from bans on children, to stipulated house colors, to limits on what is permitted to grow in the front yard, to other exclusions that cannot be placed so explicitly in writing. Robert Stern—planner for Celebration—elevates such rigid controls to the status of democratic theory with the Orwellian claim: "Regimentation can release you." What is produced, though, reminds me of the great Patrick McGoohan TV series *The Prisoner*. Behind the delightful facades of that jolly folly, Portmeirion, was jail, guarded by smiley-faced men in butler's do.

While compaction is a key antidote to the soul-deadening, landscape-ravaging pattern of traditional suburban development, the New Urbanist version reflects an even more sinister development in American culture, the enclaving of communities against the threat of genuine plurality, a new style of apartheid. At present, over thirty million Americans live in gated communities, sealed against marauders real and imagined, strategic hamlets walled against the Other. Behind the masquerade of free association and choice, we are inventing a new urbanism of exclusion. And no amount of forced cooperation can conceal this.

Not long ago, I visited Charleston, South Carolina, for the first time. I was knocked out by the languid beauty of the place, the charm and intimacy of its streets, the beauty of its buildings, the graceful situation of the town on the water. It is a wonderful town and offers many lessons about the scale, texture, and order of the good city. The New Urbanists often refer to places like Charleston as touchstones for their own plans, and their sensibility is decidedly small town: New Urbanism is largely anti-metropolitan, a fantasy of perfect small-town order that never was.

Charleston offers a cautionary tale about the limits of such grafted authenticity. To begin, it is crucial to recognize that Charleston was *historically* produced, something the New Urbanists—despite their constant invocation of the authority of history—tend to ignore. Whatever the pleasant social dynamic offered its inhabitants, then or now, this was a town built by slavery. A waterside retreat for the cotton and rice planters (down from Tara for the season), these fabulous circumstances rested on the backs of blacks. Contemporary Charleston recalls this still in a rigid pattern of residential segregation that almost completely excludes African Americans from the historic core of the city.

The real Charleston also incorporates the primary *physical* problem that the revival of historic Charleston is meant to solve. Of a population of over a million, fewer than fifty thousand actually live in the old town.

The remainder is dispersed over a huge territory in an ooze of sprawl. While endless ink has been spilled in praise of Charleston's pathbreaking efforts to keep its historic architecture intact, little notice is taken of its out-of-control periphery. The New Urbanist solution—presumably a galaxy of theme-park emulations of old Charleston—simply reinforces this difference.

As you may have detected, my own hostility to the New Urbanism is marbled by ambivalence. I certainly support the idea that the suburbs need to become more urban if we are going to protect the truly rural. Ironically, Charleston has the distinction of being the only American city to have been constructed behind a permanent medieval-style city wall: America's original gated community. While this bulwark was built to defend the city against angry Indians and from the Spanish colonists down the coast, cities today need another kind of wall, one directed inward instead of out. The countryside needs protecting from the city now, not the other way round.

If I take exception with the New Urbanism, it is for its failures of social ecology, not for its modest efforts to come to terms with the car. Harboring a single species (the white middle class) in a habitat of dulling uniformity, the New Urbanism seeks the stability of the perfectly predictable, a Prozac halcyon in which nothing can go wrong. Nature—and democracy—though, prefer more dynamic forms of stability, compounded of order and disorder both. It is just this useful disorder, this sense of contention and flux that the New Urbanism dreads. Hostile to experiment and the new, the "New" Urbanism simply produces another form of sameness. Dull as the suburbs but lacking the vivid underlying pathology, the New Urbanism is becoming the acceptable face of sprawl.

Robert Duvall is one of our greatest method actors. Stanislavski's "method" is an emotional technique for inventing a character, a style of acting by drawing on personal experience that stands in contrast to the cooler styles of traditional technique embodied by Olivier or Gielgud. The promise of the method (think Brando) is that an actor *becomes* the character, does not merely represent it. Much of the promise of the New Urbanism is tied up in a perverse version of this claim. The notion is that by embodying an array of tics and forms, a new city will not merely look like the old but will behave that way too. There is a fundamental flaw in this reasoning, though, the old behaviorist chestnut of form conducing behavior.

Like Disneyland—a "city" based purely on the value of entertainment— **67** the New Urbanism asks us to fool ourselves into thinking that a shell of a city really is a city, that appearances are enough. But cities are for real: democratic culture cannot flourish in a theme park. And the Blues Brothers are not black.

When I first wrote this essay, two extremely germane films had yet to open: *The Truman Show* (before it was a movie set, it was a *real* town . . . went the teaser on a nightly news feature about Seaside) and *Bulworth*. *The Truman Show*—a one-liner of a film starring the remorseless Jim Carey—used Seaside in the role Portmeirion played in *The Prisoner*. However, where Patrick McGoohan was explicitly a political prisoner (the classic Orwellian, modernist paranoia), Carey was a prisoner of the commercial media, of a *cultural* politics (the classic postmodern paranoia). Seaside worked perfectly, looking outstandingly creepy in the role of the perfect Stepfordesque town, a test market for consumer reality, in much the same way Leo Krier's new town for Prince Charles looks creepy: there is an apparent authenticity at first glance that evaporates at second, when the sinister stage machinery reveals itself. What is missing is depth, the patina produced by a real attitude toward difference and time. In this film, though, the same consumer culture exists both inside and outside of the bubble. Authenticity is the costume worn by contemporary styles of alienation.

This is also the issue raised by Warren Beatty's *Bulworth*. Despairing of phony Seaside-style media politics, *Bulworth* seeks authenticity in the usual spot. The film seems to be *The Blues Brothers* for grown-ups (a charge raised by various critics, including Jesse Jackson, Gary Wills, and Skip Gates), about a white liberal politician who—having lost his faith and his principles—attempts to regain them by immersing himself in ghetto culture and speaking the truth from this grafted authentic. But the film worked for me, seemed genuine. I think this was both because of a fundamentally progressive message about American politics and because the film projects such a winning, sixties-style innocence. C'mon people now, smile on your brother, everybody get together and love one another right now!

The art that sustains this message entails the over-the-top characterizations with which the film buys critical distance from its subject matter, Bulworth's artistic incompetence in his crossing over, and a gentle style of irony. There is a key scene in the film where Bulworth converts a drug dealer and his posse of gun-toting children to his political cause by buying the kids ice cream cones. The whole circumstance is so absurd—Frank

Capra gone noir—that it cannot possibly have any dramatic credibility. And yet it advertises a set of values that are so exemplary, we cannot but feel sentimental about the vision of justice and happiness that lies buried beneath.

1998

Notes on Vibe

Unlike Clinton, I inhaled.

Recently in Amsterdam for a lecture, I had bid farewell to my companions after the obligatory academic dinner. Wandering through the lively late-night streets and along the web of canals, I passed a number of "coffee shops," and smelling musky pot, I decided to check it out. Who am I kidding, I had been looking forward to it for days.

After a pleasant hour, I was ready to go. I pocketed my tiny stash, picked up the roach, and contemplated the street. There were, however, questions of etiquette to be dealt with. I wondered whether I would be able to light up a nightcap by the canal in front of my hotel and realized that although I had mastered the café scene, I had no idea whether it was cool to smoke in the street. I was obliged to ask.

Cities have vibes, and Amsterdam is an especially mellow place. The feeling in the street is one of tolerance, and the boundaries of fear are set wide. Amsterdam is not a city that provokes anxiety when asking directions or advice from strangers, and this, I think, is a hallmark of a great urban culture. Such civility—so eloquently set out by Jane Jacobs in her descriptions of the characteristics of good neighborhoods—is, of course, a product of culture, not architecture. But architecture is also a product of culture. How does architecture reinforce the good vibe?

Amsterdam is a high point in the architecture of neighborliness. Like all such architectures, it is extremely complex, constructed of the delimited vistas of winding streets and canals, of the richness, charm, and eccentricity of a texture built up by small increments—bricks, pavers, window panes, fittings—and of the careful, centuries-old patina of both careful addition and the de-symmetries of subsidence and wear. Colluding in this conviviality are also the ease of movement and the preference to walkers, bikers, boaters, and trams; the small, local scale of commerce; the density of cafés, restaurants, bars, and those "coffee" shops; and, especially, the luminous, graceful, and intimate domestic architecture. Holland is still the most densely populated country on earth, and it has produced, in its old cities, an exemplary culture, not of congestion but of density.

One of the striking qualities of Dutch domestic architecture is its transparency. Walking those Dutch streets, a passerby gains access to the whole spectacle of bourgeois domesticity. Through the big windows of the party-walled houses, people pursue daily life unself-consciously. Here is a wonderful seam between culture and architecture, a set of building practices that summarize Dutch attitudes very succinctly. A big part of this springs from a sense of openness, a productive surrender of privacy in which surveillance goes both ways. For the Dutch, this visibility works because of a kind of cultural frankness, the idea that there is nothing to hide because all is tolerated. Who cares if you smoke pot (or kill yourself).

I have noticed the same sort of casual civility in certain vacation spots, on Fire Island or the Cape. There is an implicit compact of good behavior, well beyond what one expects at home. People greet each other in passing, doors are left unlocked, merchants extend tiny amounts of credit to regular faces, who in turn make a great show of repaying the two bucks they were short for yesterday's lobster and chardonnay. Bad behavior also takes a holiday. Although there is an elective uniformity about holidays, good manners are not just the solidarity of the leisure class or the adoption of more relaxed holiday behavior: the quality of the specially designated, circumscribed "other" landscape makes it possible. A vacation always takes advantage of the opportunity to participate in another set of rules, if only those that allow you to sleep until noon and never wear shoes.

The mass market version takes place in Disneyland—the "magic" kingdom—where self-policing behavior is produced in visitors who—enjoying the hygiene and the idea of an environment dedicated to pleasure—litter less and smilingly organize themselves into orderly queues. This is not the result of a sense of literal proprietorship (the defensible space line) but stems from an implicit compact in support of a vibe, enabled by special circumstances. The knotty question, though, is whether this behavior is coerced. Ultimately, I do not think so—people are attracted to places where the deal is clear, where the possibilities are visibly established.

Vibe is produced by a combination of space and behavior, and the vibe can as easily be bad as good. For the last several years, I have been teaching urban design in Vienna, a city in which correct behavior is extolled to the point of oppression. Almost every New Yorker who visits Austria (or Germany) comes back with the same story. The street is empty, but the light is red. Of course, you cross. Standing on the curb, though, is a knot of locals waiting patiently for the light to change, their eyes boring into your back in rebuke. The behavior is all cultural: a corner where I often jaywalk has a round-the-clock cop stationed to protect the Turkish Airlines office from bomb-throwing Kurds. I have never seen him issue a jaywalking summons—perhaps he is not supposed to leave his post. Indeed—like in New York—I have *never* seen a jaywalking ticket issued in Vienna. By contrast, I am very careful in L.A. Cops are scary there: no one wants to be Rodney King.

Vibe can shift suddenly, and it can be very personal. Firearms unnerve me anywhere. I do not like hunters, and I hate those encounters with Brink's men in the city, bearing bags of dimes into the bank with their six-shooters drawn. In Vienna, although the pistols are invariably holstered, the machine guns are out. One of the more soigné bistros in town—very popular with architects—is catty-cornered from an Israeli restaurant and up the street from a synagogue that somehow managed to survive the Anschluss. Both rate twenty-four-hour police protection. Unlike their compatriots guarding the airline, though, these cops carry submachine guns. It is a sight one also sees in Germany in front of Jewish institutions. To me, this evokes feelings of fear, not security: I am made anxious by the sight of *any* Germanophone in uniform, especially carrying a gun. "Your papers please!"

In fact, Vienna is remarkably safe. Walking the city late at night, even down along the isolated quaysides of the canal that flows through the city center, I have no anxiety about crime, except an imported dread that I bring with me from New York that periodically surfaces to suggest that were I in similar circumstances at home, I would become fearful, which in turn makes me slightly afraid. This kind of grafted dread (the fear of fear itself) also strikes me from another angle. Walking those empty streets late at night, I realize that it was just over fifty years ago that the act of being seen in Vienna—erstwhile epitome of urban civilization—would have put me in far more danger than any I might face in the most crime-ridden neighborhood in America. I become aware that the eyes at any window—those beloved peepers of Jane Jacobs—could have fingered me for extermination.

This reflection—which cannot be repressed—extends, for me, to a deep suspicion of the elderly. When in Vienna, I often wake up in a jet-lagged daze in the middle of the night and go into the kitchen for some water. Out the window, I have a view of an old-age home across a wide garden, and I always see—in those wee hours—that many of the rooms across the way also have their lights burning. I wonder why, thinking first that in old age waking time becomes more precious. Then I wonder whether it is just guilty conscience. Unlike America, where urban fear is generally focused on youth, my Viennese criminals are geriatric. Where were they, I wonder? What was their complicity? White-haired old ladies become fiends. Is this the real Vienna? Nazi grannies eating strudel?

Michel Foucault's great insight into the workings of power is his close observation of the ways we internalize the means of our own repression. The appearance of surveillance—as in his celebrated metaphor of the panopticon—causes us to behave as if surveilled. Like the panoptic prisons of the early nineteenth century—circular jails in which an unseen central guard has the ability to look into every cell—culture looks remorselessly over our shoulders. As with the compact of docile behavior at traffic lights, the legal honor system in Vienna (and other European cities) extends to public transportation, a form of civility we would never be able to sustain over here. When I am in Vienna, I often take the subway to work. I always pay my fare in spite of the fact that one can simply get on the U-Bahn or a tram without either paying or passing through a turnstile. Part of my behavior may be coerced: the first week I was in Vienna, my ticket was actually "controlled" by a conductor. This early lesson may have been instrumental in shaping my behavior, although I might easily have unlearned it by now—I have not been controlled since.

Certainly, in terms of Richard Posner/Gary Becker–style arguments about what constitutes a rational choice, the low frequency of these inspections would suggest that the most economical and efficient behavior is never to buy a ticket and simply to pay the fine on the rare occasions one is caught. In my own case, the reasons I always buy a ticket are a combination of fear, honesty, a dedication to the idea of public transportation (something Vienna provides in efficient abundance), and a slightly more complicated desire not to give any Austrian a moral advantage over me. Why the Viennese pay (and why they wait on the curb) is another question. I see jaywalking and fare-beating as very different orders of transgression: the Viennese do not.

The way in which urban cultures impose their everyday morality is more complex, though, than a simple reproduction of general cultural mores. The most architectural means of teaching such urban morality is via styles of monumentalization and memory: cultures signal their values via choices about what to physically revere. Amsterdam's most popular monument is the house where Anne Frank and her family hid during the Nazi occupation. There is something typically Dutch about this memorial in its domesticity: an immense tragedy finds its legibility in a little house. The Frank family, packed into insane proximity, turns the physical character of the Dutch achievement in living together upside down. In the end, it was a failure of neighborliness that doomed them.

In Vienna and in Austria, the memory of the Nazi era is deeply repressed, the subject of an almost total national amnesia. Official remembrances are few and far between: in the city's main memorial, those murdered by the Nazis are carefully associated with residents killed in Allied bombings. But despite this official indifference, there are tremendous unofficial monuments to the times in Vienna, a truly monumental unconscious. Looming over the city are half a dozen gigantic *Flakturm*, massive concrete structures used as command posts, shelters, and gun emplacements for the wartime antiaircraft system. Enormous but unseen, these towers are arguably the largest invisible objects on the planet.

For many years, there has been an on-again, off-again debate about what to do with them, and they make frequent appearances as studio problems in the architectural schools. One has been converted into an aquarium, and another, it has just been announced, will hold a museum of coffee. In their way, they are quite beautiful: architects see them with the same fondness Paul Virilio shows for the raw, expressionistic forms of the fortresses of the Atlantic wall reproduced in his *Bunker Archaeology*. The debate in Vienna, however, always founders at the same extreme: everyone, it seems, repeats the argument that the *Flaktürme* must remain because it would simply be too expensive to tear them down. Such economic logics have the gloss of practicality and are allowed to overwhelm more fundamental truths. The case of the *Flaktürme* is especially striking because the value of a bad memory is given an exact price.

In the beginning, I was ambivalent about the *Flaktürme*. To be sure, the megalomaniac, minimalist corner of my architectural taste finds them compelling and butch. But over the years, I have come to believe that they must go and as soon as possible. The reason is simple: people have become habituated to them—they no longer carry any force of evil, an aura they *must* retain if there is any logic to their monumentalization. Without this, they simply become the pyramids, huge monuments to a vanished culture that existed way back when—tourist attractions. Stripped of evil association, they can only become monuments *to* the Nazis.

Monuments are mnemonics for the management of aura, the buzz of meanings in the environment. But the existence of the artifact is not enough: the more its originating context recedes, the more active and supplemental the work of interpretation must become. Monuments, after all, do not merely represent the past, they are containers and institutionalizers for our *fantasies* of the past. Modernism sought to overcome the necessity for reading this fluid relationship—to neutralize this problem of interpretation—by banishing history, by the idea that its meanings could be comfortably ensconced in "pure" abstraction. By making the global environment as uniform as possible, by celebrating a uniform idea of subjectivity, modernity sought to harmonize vibe. Architecture, after all, is always a form of mind control, often self-imposed.

That the aggressive, destabilized forms of so-called deconstructivist architecture have flourished particularly in Austria and Germany must certainly be connected to the desire to come to terms with a nasty sense of roots. The urgency of such in-your-face design is especially resonant in the homelands of the purveyors of orderly, criminal chaos, the builders of the *Flaktürme*. Although one has learned to resist pat psychoanalytic explanations for artistic behavior, it is clear that both the generation of creators that spent its youth under the Nazis as well as the local boomers— the generation whose parents were Nazis—have created an art that is deeply enmeshed in the anxieties of lineage. Whether in the work of the "Blut und Boden" redux of the artists of Viennese Aktionismus, with their offal-streaked, abusive art, or in that of their heirs in decon, the obvious sense of rage is not merely picturesque. Nor is it a one-dimensional response to the hackneyed maelstrom of contemporaneity. This is an art about guilt, and its fractious forms must be considered in the context of a culture that chooses to retain its Flak Towers.

A similar debate about the privileges of the past goes on in Berlin, and with far greater intensity. The most interesting current question is what is to be done with the architectural legacy of the East. One side argues that the building is cheap and dilapidated and ought to go. The other contends that this architecture is a part of German history and should, therefore, be preserved. The discussion reminds me of a clarifying (and hilarious) project that was reported in the *New York Times* a few years ago, a proposal to create a theme park based on life in the vanishing East. Fume-belching Trabants were to cruise the potholed streets among the dreary buildings. The food was to be terrible. And among the staff of the park were to be a number of informers, who would arbitrarily arrest visitors and throw them in theme-park jail.

Nazi Germany was itself perhaps the most ambitious and sinister theme park ever imagined: not simply a gated community but a gated country: Germanyland. The manipulation of history was critical to this project, and I do not simply mean the racist fantasies of Nazi ideology. The Nazis had a vision of space that has been described by many as the ultimate expression of modernity's dark side, a fantasy of a hideous uniformity. Architecture was to play a key role in producing the Nazi new man. To do so, the depraved Albert Speer theorized an architecture derived from a vague sense of historic consequence. But Speer understood that history was not place but process, and his most succinct vision of the way in which history was to inhere in this building lay in his notion that it was to be designed for picturesque ruin (although he underestimated the time span of ruination by about a millennium). Here was an idea of history that could be entirely internal to the object, projective history, a truly terrible abstraction.

The Berlin debate describes a particularly interesting divide because neither side of it advances the kind of preservationist argument that dominates our own thinking: no one argues that these buildings have *positive* architectural qualities. The reasons offered for retention are either practical (whether the crude Viennese argument or a more subtle appeal to the ethic of recycling and reuse) or didactic. History, of course, is always written by the victors, but every historian makes choices. As discussions like these make clear, the past is one of the most useful tools for controlling, even banishing, the past. By reducing the character of pastness to a bit of shriveled aura evoked by a narrow range of closely controlled, decorative signifiers, the past is captured from itself: this is the Disneyland effect. In this sense, historicist architecture carries on the task of modernity far more succinctly than modernity. Such architecture co-opts a source of authority (the putatively superior virtue of historic forms of order) while at the same time totally wresting it from its originating context of meaning. Modernity never even dreamed of such arbitrary signification, such an amazing level of abstraction. In this ironical operation, the past becomes the "past," as fantasies of harmony are directly cathected onto historical images.

If the past cannot be distinguished as being inhabited by anything but "pastness," our fantasies surely can be. Fantasies can be judged: there are good and bad, and all embody someone's desires—*every* monument is a monument to desire. Such collective fantasies of desirability always presume their own flip side: a consensus of fear. The *Flaktürme* stand because the Viennese have insufficient anxiety about the Nazis and thus see their artifacts as harmless. Not seeing themselves as opponents or victims, they have no reason to dread the victimizer. The town where I grew up had a statue of a confederate soldier, leaning on his rifle, looking south near its main intersection. This monument was not simply about acknowledgment, it was about celebration, the emblem of the town. But who was celebrating what? However many football games it waves over, the confederate flag is still the emblem of a racist culture. But it is only such a symbol to those who revile racism, and only until that meaning is lost or buried, only until the stars and bars finally become just another logo.

Like fear, vibe is a cultural construct. The neutrality of the environment is a myth. Every place—knowable only through our reading of it—produces a vibe—what used to be called a *genius loci*. But reading offers the promise of difference. Amsterdam is delightful to me both because I find the Dutch congenial and because the spaces and architecture there interact beautifully with values I see as continuous with this congeniality: openness, informality, intimacy, sensuality. But my sense of this comprehensive congeniality would probably not be so appealing to Jesse Helms or the Ayatollah. Vibe always raises the question of relativism, and relativism always risks evading the ethics of the situation.

Consumer culture obscures its project by creating empty differences, and this lack of meaningful distinction frustrates consent, which cannot genuinely be given without a sense of choice. The legibility of vibe is further complicated because different groups (and individuals) reach different forms of consensus about the meanings of different signifiers. The gated community has very different meanings for those within and without, and the *Flaktürme* only seem sinister to those who revile their builders. And this is why monuments and architecture are so important to vibe: they fix our desires where everyone can see.

1998

Phoenix Rising

Night flying into Phoenix, inky emptiness abuts the grid of lights, the desert lapping at the edges of town. As the plane circles and drops to land, the glimmer of energy seems to spread to infinity, and a paradox becomes visible: growth kills the resource that makes the city great. Climate and landscape are sunk in a miasma of development, sprawl without end. Sufferers fleeing their allergies find them again as the city urbanizes itself out of health.

The growth of Phoenix has been rapid, its settled area expanding even more rapidly than its population, the very formula for sprawl. Between 1950, when the town had one hundred thousand people, and 1980, when it hit its first million, the area of Phoenix grew from 117 square miles to 450, almost three times the rate of population growth. Today, the inhabitants of Maricopa County—Phoenix and a brace of contiguous municipalities including Mesa, Tempe, Scottsdale, Chandler, Peoria, Sun City—now number near 2.5 million, over 60 percent of the state's people. Arizona is incredibly urbanized: Phoenix is now among the ten largest American cities.

There *is* a certain perverse environmental logic to such concentrations. The fragile ecosystems of the desert have a low bearing capacity for human settlement. Concentration could be considered conservational by applying simple math: the less of the desert covered, the more of it is preserved. For all their sci-fi scale, this was the message of Paolo Soleri's daft "arcologies." Megalomaniac they may have been, but the footprint was small. This idea of balance is also the message of the spare, water-related pattern of development of the site's original inhabitants.

Because of the construction of the Salt River Project at the beginning of the century and the Central Arizona Project in the eighties, and because of enlightened restrictions on the use of ground water, Phoenix is well provided with water. And because there is little anxiety about future supply, water is not a major regulator of growth. Indeed, the region has a long history of irrigation—back to the canals of the Hohokam Indians. Phoenix's early modern character was also agricultural, dominated by a water-intensive cotton and citrus economy. Ironically, the replacement of agricultural uses by urbanization has resulted in a net *decrease* in demand for water: the requirements of even luxurious lawns do not rival the thirst of cotton. Phoenix probably has too much water: the sense of abundance induces a failure of limits.

Economy is also character. In Phoenix, growth is centered in a healthy high-tech and service sector and around those qualities of climate and culture that continue to attract waves of retirees, vacationers, and "snowbirds"—the large migratory population that arrives in the winter, swelling the city by 30 percent. The distortions of a population that is constantly increasing have economic consequences beyond simple growth. In their first year, new arrivals spend sums equivalent to six years' spending by a standing resident. The culture of immigration adds a permanent fizz to the economy that a more stable population would not, another link in the chain-letter economics of endless growth. No coincidence that S & L crook Charles Keating made his killing in Phoenix.

This economy of growth has shaped both the city's self-image and official planning practice for years. Excepting only several affluent areas, there are few curbs on either the character or the pattern of growth, and the city has expanded almost exponentially and in remarkably consistent form. Impeded by a few natural barriers and by several large Indian reservations (which have seemingly yet to get hipped to their own profitable possibilities in development), the desert is wide open for encroachment, and the city continues to give every indication of being ready to encroach.

Although the official planning philosophy has nominally changed from a simple growth formula to a strategy of "urban villages," the effects on the ground are negligible. The experience of Phoenix is of a continuous field of low-density development with few internal edges. Phoenix is filled with gaps, often the product of developer "leapfrogging" to avoid the run-up on land adjacent to existing developments. The differences among these towns are largely notional, physical fiction. Phoenix has become the dreaded polycentric automotive metropolis.

While planning styles may change, the undergirding structure seems forever: the grid, the house, the car. These found the city's urban culture. On a drive north of Phoenix, perhaps thirty miles out of town, heading for a hamlet called Carefree, the otherwise undeveloped landscape is marked with optimism, signposts hailing the "future site of 19th Avenue, future site of 20th Avenue, future site of 21st Avenue. . . ."

This vision of emptiness awaiting order fixes a historic tension. Arizona mixes opposites. The state's schizoid politics reflect the old conflict between wilderness and development, between styles of order, yielding John McCain and Bruce Babbitt and Barry Goldwater, ex-Jewish department store magnate, Air Force general, founding father of American neo-conservatism, defender of Gay rights, a liberal in the old-fashioned way. Arizona is also the state with America's first female chain gangs.

Arizona's historic immigration was comprised of people seeking not just freedom and opportunity—the standard-issue myths of the frontier—but of those seeking health and physical invigoration. If the Arizona economy grew on the fabled three C's—cotton, citrus, and copper—it was soon overtaken by a stream of health-seekers and quickly evolved a vigorous and continuing spa economy. An informal survey suggests that the service most frequently advertised on the billboards of Phoenix is chiropractic: the alleviation of psychical and physical aches and pains is the promise of the Southwest. This is everywhere. "Paradise Valley" is the city's self-designated sobriquet, and the welcome signs at the city's edges are emblazoned with the slogan: "Best Run City in America." Phoenix is a dream of order.

Grids are the leading physical expression of America's historic fantasy of paradise as order. The grid is also the primal scene for our partisan wars between density and extent. It represents the fantasy of democracy as pure extent. Jefferson's idea was not simply of a mathematical equality achieved through the continuous subdivision of an endless territory but of a citizenship guaranteed by private invisibility. After all, if the grid were large enough, each citizen could possess a private horizon, his neighbors out of sight, her own territory effectively boundless.

Reaching the coast (and building Los Angeles) naturally compromised this vision, and the big remigration from California back to places like Arizona attempts to reclaim the dream of noninterference. A sense of utopia—however devoluted—continues to shape Phoenix's take on place, a fantasy of self-realization hanging like dust in the air, often taking form as architecture. Even the rocks seem to be building in becoming. And we all know Arizona's historic affinity for utopias at the high-end, architectural experiments from Taliesin to Arcosanti to the Biosphere to Sedona. Not simply laboratories for new architecture, these have all been elective communities. Arizona is a state occupied by choice.

Of course, one person's utopia is another's forbidden gated community (or "armored cocoon" in the Faith Popcornese). The most extraordinary of such intentional community projects in Phoenix is developer Del Webb's Sun City, the famously successful retirement town at the city's northwest corner, its radial plan straight out of the eighteenth century.

Sun City embodies the fundamental conundrum of democratic space by being both elective and restrictive, limited to older people (membership in the AARP is 100 percent), forbidden to children. Sun City is also a remarkable reduction of the spatial structure of Phoenix itself. Pared of the distorting demands of employment (it is a retirement community, after all), Sun City is self-limited to residence, recreation, and consumption. The transit system is golf carts.

This is an important clue to the fate of utopia and to the current default mode of contemporary American urbanism. The leading *post*-democratic utopia is the city of segmented consumption. Phoenix is spatially organized like an inverted piece of market research. Each consumer sits in a single house on a piece of turf (there are not even dingbat apartments in Phoenix), a malleable monad, test audience for the new age, the rich here, the ghetto there. The analytic tool that unravels this organization is the advertiser's, and Phoenix—with its unconfused demographics—is a nearly ideal field of operation for contemporary consumption. Segmentation is the segregation of "choice." Sun City has reabsorbed this mode by utilizing consumer research into the preferences of its residents as a main mode of planning. Why vote?

Further ironies. If the Phoenix model is of a grid of homes focused on a series of malls, this suggests that the "urban village" may be more relevant than first blush reveals. The pattern of such local centers is quite clear within Phoenix, more so for the city's remarkable underdevelopment in freeways (or any other form of transportation save cars operating in the grid). Once more, too, the city has produced the seeds for a rational and delightful maturity. After all, the agora was also a point of purchase, and a golf course can be as green and trodden as Central Park.

How to build in such a paradise? Is it possible to look beyond developer fantasies of the city to a more popular sense of a genius loci? Is it possible to exceed the kind of creative geography in which the "Club Tribeca" is found in a shopping mall out of Georgia O'Keeffe, or eschew the hedonistic strategies of "climate control" that yield rose gardens and top-down driving with the AC blasting? The answer is surely a provisional "yes."

The choices are nowhere clearer than in Scottsdale, where I stopped one morning to acquire souvenirs. For all its raw suburbanism, Phoenix remains in love with the "look" of the Southwest. Scottsdale—with its streets of Native American tschotshkerias and its galleries of Western Art—is a crucial point of dissemination for the sensibility, source for the decor of ten million bleached-out living rooms. And people are into it: **81** one sees remarkably few of the Tudoroid or Loirish numbers one would expect in L.A. or Orange County. However tacky the expression, there is real consensus and literacy about this version of the city's visual roots.

Negotiating with such an entrenched sensibility requires astute navigation between nature and culture. As we continue in recovery from the mimetic regionalism of the Disney people, the search for a healthy architecture resumes. Which brings us back to the desert. The best desert architecture—from the Anasazi to those obsessive geometers the Navajo and Frank Lloyd Wright—treats the desert as a cause, not a trope. The Btu-guzzling ranchero with the three-car garage and the Xeriscaped front yard is the Benetton version of desert building. And yet, it is *some* version, trapped in a contradiction but game nonetheless. A meaningful desert architecture has many tough choices to make in the middle of a city of two million.

In the past few years, Phoenix has become an unexpected showcase for medium-scale modern architecture, spurred by the confident expenditures of a culturally underdeveloped city enjoying its fortunes, ornamenting itself with libraries and university buildings, museums, malls, concert halls, festive marketplaces, skyscrapers, and ball parks. The ambition can be a bit raw—the TV ads for the local opera feature a Julia Roberts look-alike in a *Pretty Woman* fantasy. Phoenix's luck is in the timing and its liberal and remarkably consistent patronage of architects of real quality. And most of this architecture takes the investigation of place very seriously.

The recent spate of publicity notwithstanding, I was unprepared for Will Bruder's superb public library. It is a confident and disciplined piece of work, imposing without being overbearing, lightly constructed with no sacrifice to solidity. After a dark blue passage to the center, space ascends through a bright, generous shaft, decompressing toward the top, blossoming into a vaulted reading room, glazed at either end, its roof supported by a graceful, ingenious, and droll system of posts and cables.

The view south frames the skyline of the Phoenix downtown. Invents it is more like it. While the downtown has a certain presence as a navigational icon (like its natural analog Camelback Mountain), it is simply ragged as a tectonic. The near vista from the library, though, gives this collection of generally mediocre buildings a presence and stature of civic dimension. This ocular contribution to the city's collection of views of itself—the foregrounded hall, the middle-distant center—is as remarkable as it is crucial to the sense of the metropolis.

From outside, the building is a big lump of corrugated copper, almost geology, formless as a lode. It has the proportions of a vertically exaggerated suburban department store, initially a little graceless, soon more challenging, and finally very satisfying. And the library does have something of the atmosphere of a hushed and hip emporium: good signage, well-lit displays, glass elevators, atrium, good access to the freeway. . . . It is a great scale, the scale of concert halls and retail, the scale of both urban and suburban monuments, dignified and big, but accessible. Bruder's library does it with no spurious clarity or denatured heft.

Another library, Scoggin, Elam, and Bray's fine law school building on a highly trafficked site at the edge of the Arizona State campus, also reflects on but does not pander to the desert, working within a narrow palette, extremely elegant. There is a seismic riff in the form of a fissure down the building's middle, and the color is sandy and pale Dryvit, the adobe of postmodernity. The building responds to the sun both optically and thermally. Its geometry—irregular but comfortable—is a fine catcher for shadows. North-drawn light floats gently into the reading rooms. Spaces are high, airy, cool-looking, though not dark. My favorite region in the building is its fish-shaped service area. From an arching roof supported by graceful composite trusses, ducts and lights are hung on a deluge of cables that streak through the low-lit room like sun rays piercing cloud.

Across the campus, Antoine Predock's art museum has an architecture at once more local and more thermally histrionic. In massing, the building evokes a traditional desert tectonics at a remove comparable to that between Le Corbusier's villas and the prismatic Mediterraneity of their origins, and recalling modernity's capacity for happiness in the heat. The building—entered via a descent underground, enjoyed climbing back up to the light—is about thickness and darkness, exclusions of the sun in its grottolike interior and in the modulations of shade that return the building's outer surfaces to use.

Down Central Avenue—the Wilshire Boulevard of Phoenix—from Bruder's library is the Phoenix Museum of Art, just expanded by Tod Williams and Billie Tsien. The Wilshire, classy boulevard of towers, comparison is not gratuitous: the museum is a kind of smaller, flattened version of the Los Angeles County Museum of Art expansion. Like the L.A. project, the Phoenix Museum conceals a bland (though not dysfunctional) original and reorganizes entry and circulation through a dramatic portal. Williams and Tsien have rehabilitated the museum's public face and then introduced another, grander range and scale of spaces. Like Bruce Goff's at LACMA, there is even to be a curvilinear excursus, an enormous concoid fiberglass baldachino for sculpture, cooled by mists in summer, a lateral displacement of a centralizing dome.

The expansion of the Phoenix Museum is a subtle yet unmistakable evocation of motifs of the region, abstracted to the border of signification. The building is almost Spanish. Massive, precast walls are battered in the load-bearing profile of adobe and topped with a metal cornice. Like roof beams through a mud wall, slabs of green glass penetrate the upper portion of the panels, transmitting not load but light—day in, night out. A frieze of circular indentations along the wall reevokes the shape of the beams. A courtyard will come.

The parti is classical: symmetrical wings on either side of an entry court. Unfenestrated elevations have a long, pueblo proportion. The precast panels, though, eschew the usual buff, colored instead with a local aggregate in a lovely green, somewhere between celadon and lime. Both Bruder's copper and William and Tsien's aggregate logically expand the local envelope of tonality without losing the color of the place.

The gap between the two wings is the museum entrance. It is overflown by a galvanized metal bridge that descends from left to right above the axis of entry, suggesting a less-classical pattern of circulation. That metal-clad ramp is part of a narrow gallery that begins in the small second-level space of the left-hand wing and gently descends across the entry, passing out and in to a small interior terrace overlooking the gallery to the right.

The right-hand wing, which contains a beautiful new auditorium as well as gallery space, also has a more complicated set of ramping galleries that combine necessary circulation with a little extra dimension, producing a composite, level-bending space "within the walls." These architects have a very refined sense of incident. Their ability to produce such complex movement within a project of relatively modest scale is by a canny, elegant plan and by beautifully developed events en route, landing sites and overlooks, changes in color and materiality, flashes of light through apertures ranging from windows to glazed form-tie holes.

Again, contrary to the expectations set up by the exterior, the two new halls of the addition are spanned *the long way* by three deep trusses that frame two remarkably graceful sections, which in turn have produced two elegant ceilings that cover two rooms of very different character. And with the most delicate inflections of material and detail.

The big room on the left is a loft, a little provisional feeling, sheetrocked and downtownish, the setting for changing shows. It has a techy movable mechanical ceiling, which adds to the raw feeling of the space as does the industrial-strength lengthwise span. The floor is wood, and finishes are plain and responsive to the cycle of sheetrock partitionings and demolitions that will support the shifting shows.

The room on the right is the museum's ceremonial great hall, site for openings and banquets. Here, the palette is richer, warmer, more local in tones. The detail is also more elaborated, more ceremonial. The floor is stone, and the folded ceiling is superb: roughed plaster, wood, paint, and a celestial spray of lights and registers. The proportion of the room is unusual—slightly wide—a space that has stayed with me. Eventually this room will connect to a new set of galleries and open onto the new courtyard.

Phoenix both newly and historically abounds with architectures that make their peace with the desert and that style local patterns for the sensitive elaboration of the landscape. But this again evokes the conundrum of the town: addition is subtraction. An answer, though, is suggested by the siting and agendas of these recent projects. Rather than colonizing new territory, each elaborates existing densities—the campus, the downtown. And surely such considered densification is both the social and the environmental key.

What will become of Phoenix? The worst fear is that it will coalesce into an endless substrate of urban nothingness somewhere between L.A. and Orange Country on the devolutionary family tree of the Western Town, solving the riddle of density and extent via totally liberated sprawl. Or perhaps there will be a drawing back from the fantasy of no limits, and the growth of a more genuinely loving relation to a place at the point of passing the boundary of its own sustainability. Perhaps this will allow Phoenix to really find its edges.

1997

Remembering the Future

I was sitting in a darkened room a couple of weeks ago in London, taking in slides at a conference on the legacy of modernist urbanism. I love those happy views of that old bright future: Nikolai Miliutin's linear cities, Radburn's greenways, Berthold Lubetkin's heroic failure at Peterlee (this was mainly a local crowd). All suggest how far we have come. Or do they? The slide that was *most* projected at the conference was that familiar perspective sketch of Corb's City of Three Million, the one with three huge cruciform slabs single pointing on down the line.

There often is a recurrent image at architectural conferences, the designated objective correlative. It figured that the Corbusian City—modern architecture's official dystopia (Pruitt-Igoe succumbing to the dynamite . . .)—would be on the screen. But as I stared at the sketch for the eighth time that afternoon, the drawing morphed: the slabs became Las Vegas, the point vanished in a blaze of light at the end of the Strip. The big new Vegas hotels—Venetian, Paris, Monte Carlo, Bellagio, Mirage—are sized, proportioned, and positioned *exactly* like the towers in the City of Three Million. Eureka!

Everybody's future, it seems, is somebody else's past. In the 1936 William Menzies film *Things to Come,* there is an interior that is a dead ringer for John Portman's Marriott Hotel in Atlanta. This image of endless tiers (never mind the glass elevators) is a recurring trope in the utopia of grandiosity. Perhaps the most sublime version of the image is from *Close Encounters of the Third Kind.* In an unusually acute marketing strategy, the film was released for a second time—several years after its debut—with a slightly elaborated ending. The original finishes with wispy Spielbergian homunculi exiting their mother ship to commune with earthlings. In the second version, we are invited indoors. And where do we wind up? At the Marriott! Tiers of adorable aliens languidly wave from their ad infinitum balconies. The whole damn hotel flies! Imagine the mini-bar!

I stray. A recent look backwards at a variety of futuristic images reveals remarkable consistency and an organization into four more or less clear categories. The first of these—the Marriott /*Close Encounters* case—

is Breathless Interiority, the world indoors. Gigantophilia is an ancient hedge against the future—think of the Egyptians, more successful than anyone so far in predicting the landscape to come by building monuments so immense they would be part of it forever. The mastery of huge *interior* spaces awaited later technological developments. If the coliseum is the source of the Portman atrium's tiers, the Gothic (the dark ages were the era of the greatest structural innovation before or since—and they did it all in *stone!*) prefigures its enclosure. Only now have we more or less caught up in construction with a physics intuitively mastered a thousand years ago.

The modernization of the Breathless Interior begins with Étienne-Louis Boullée, whose cenotaph for Newton was a spherical container for the entire universe. The nineteenth century jumped the big room in scale and added glass. Boullée's cenotaph (or Chartres) is a projection device, beaming the worshipper enthralled outward. As religion became secular—nature standing in for god—the great greenhouses (the tropics in London) flourished, beginning a line that runs through Bucky (ready to dome Manhattan), the Biosphere (the world under glass, the complete system), and all those images of space stations with self-contained, oxygen-pumping meadows and gurgling brooks in high orbit. This is the early work of virtual travel, the beginning of the end of a reliable idea of place.

Of course, every trope turns tragic. *Metropolis* depicts an entirely indoor city in the sunless underground created for nightmare culture's worker ants. *Blade Runner*'s city of the future is cast in perpetual gloom under toxic squalls. Albert Speer's monster dome wants the entire nation to stand in one room at attention. *Star Wars*—with its corps of Injection-Molded Nazis—takes an expansive view of "space" *itself* but keeps its interiors almost domestic. To be sure, Darth has a generous office with a fabulous deep-space view, but in general it is all corridors in the father ship, one of those cuts-two-ways images that depends on whether your model is the liner (glorious! modern!) or the labyrinth.

Disjunctive Technology—storm troopers, millennia hence, shooting at each other with ray-pistols—is the second category. My own first serious experience with such projective mechanics came from the film *20,000 Leagues under the Sea*, memorable for Captain Nemo's iron-plated submarine with its red plush Edwardian brothel interior. The *Nautilus* was a prescient depiction of the baseline of postmodernity, the disjunction of style and capacity. And like the best of science fiction, it is retrospectively visionary: the technology predicted (not quite possible then) has now already arrived. *Star Trek* is the B version, with its Kelvinator space-ship, toggle switches, sliding doors, and pajamas as the eternal daywear of the future, a fifties appliance moving at Warp Speed.

By the turn of the nineteenth century, transport—accelerated and multiplied by cars and trains, by flight—had assumed the role of the subject—the citizenry—of the city. The futurishness of cities began to be measured in laminations, a fantasy that reached a high point in those wonderful "King's Views" of the next Manhattan. At every level of the towering metropolis are flows of another medium: cars, aircraft, trolleys, pedestrians, bikes, you name it. . . .

Laminar Flow is the third recurring dream of modernity. From the City of Three Million to Hugh Ferris's chiaroscuro Manhattan to the tiny zooming cars at the Futurama to the three-axis-taxis in the *Fifth Element,* the little particle is in the foreground, representing both laminar flow—the multitude of means—and—by extension—their rigorous separation. Functional segregation is one of modernity's obsessions, and it is project-ed onto many a version of its dreams for future, reshaping the globe. Shanghai—to cite one example—is going through a spasm of lamina-tion, building elevated roads and subways like crazy, caught in the same brief pause between pristine vision and the law of unintended but com-pletely predictable consequences. Gravity is lamination's ultimate: once an orbit is self-sustaining, you are free of the ground. No wonder that vi-sionaries from legendary Leb Woods to Hollywood "visual futurist" Syd Meade aspire to a true hyperlamination in which gravity is brushed en-tirely aside, letting us float like angels.

Every era has its designated city of the future. Successively, New York, Los Angeles, Phoenix, Vegas, to the whole Pac Rim have held the lime-light. These images of the city are invariably (I will return to the garden city vector) about being big and being fast, but there has been a shift from the vertical to the lateral. The high modernist future was highly ver-tical, constructed in layers just like culture, producing *classes* of motion. The horizontalization of space is the "democratic" American contribu-tion, no longer measuring size in depth but in extent. But nobody's im-ages can keep up with the pace of Sprawl's need for supply. The machine is far ahead of us. No wonder there are so many movies about weird sub-urbs these days.

The last trope is the Line, the most refined version of the infinite hori-zontal, the city of meridians for which the Great Wall of China is the model, the "only man-made structure observable from space." Such line-arities have a long life in science fiction as well as in the works of such great nineteenth-century imagineers as Chambless, Borie, Soria y Mata, and—their heir—Corb. The horizontal has always struck an egalitarian, centerless equivalence based on continuous access by speed instead of the multiplying hierarchy of the vertical. This architecture of pure sinew reduces collective life to rapid motion. Such binders drew conceptual inspiration from the laying of the great transoceanic cables (using a Brunel-designed ship, but that is another subject), which limned lines of communication as world structure. The interstate is the ultimate American linear city, millions adrift in their Winnebagos (self-ownership of the particles), stopping only at the service pods at every cloverleaf, the urbanism of perfect entropy.

We like science fiction because it makes what is normal extreme. Excess perfection is extremely scary, for example, *The Truman Show,* latest in a tradition that includes *The Prisoner,* that genius TV show with Portmeirion in the Seaside role. I grew up in the suburbs, and they are still suffused with that nameless dread for me. It is a direct line to suburban high school shootings and Jon Benet Ramsey (funny that people blame this on everything but *the suburbs*). Stephen King has moved into Ozzie and Harriet's house, and although things *look* much the same, there is a strange gleam in little Ricky's eye and a funny bulge under his long black trenchcoat.

The images recirculate like the return of the repressed. We are back in the Marriott again and again.

We are condemned, it seems, endlessly to repeat the future.

1999

part ii

Architects/Buildings

Animating Space

In front of Frank Gehry's Guggenheim in Bilbao stands an enormous Jeff Koons topiary puppy. Supported by a complex but unseen armature and enabled by a fiendish system for watering and fertilizing, the floral dog dominates the museum's foreground. I wanted to hate that puppy but found myself charmed . . . sort of: once the irony was scraped off, beneath lay treacle. Thus laid bare, no longer an appropriation of kitsch, I was able to see the huge dog as pure kitsch—charming, goofy.

Architects I know who had the pleasure of visiting the Guggenheim while it was under construction raved about the beauties of its intricate armature, the rising cross-braced snakes of steel. Gehry often talks about inspiration drawn from construction sites, buildings that are at their best half done. Part of this is just the modernist aesthetic with its tooth for the forms of engineering and construction. But it also comes from a view that the unfinished version has a special innocence, clarity, authenticity, and authority. Like the childhood of the sketch, the worry is that elaboration and growth inevitably equal loss.

It is one of the many successes of the Guggenheim that it has not simply survived its transformation but has added density while retaining the vigor, kinks, and visual charm of its skeleton. In the kinetic atrium and in the picturesque tower framed beyond the preexisting bridge, the structural armature is both revealed and employed, and the exuberance and complexity of the work-in-progress is there.

For the foregrounded Koons, though, the armature remains invisible, the dog beneath the skin. Illusionistic, it depends on this invisibility, the backgrounding of its means of support. The dependence of the fuzzy hound on its concealed skeleton is ironical. The Guggenheim—equally histrionic—engages the same problematic as the pup: the elaborate unseen structure required to support the complex family of curved form. But there is no irony. And this is something that can be said about Gehry's work from the beginning: nothing is concealed, no jokes are made, no self-consciousness is exhibited, no meta-meanings are inscribed.

The Koons puppy is a cartoon. Cartooning idealizes a subject by drawing out some essence. Cartooning is an intermediary state, a subject become condensed and malleable. The cartoon prepares a subject for irony, kitsch, or critique. In the case of the Koons, the essentialized pup, stripped of detail and inflated to enormity, opens up a kind of meta-kitsch, a gigantic hyperbanality. It is this disproportion that gives the work its meaning.

Gehry also makes cartoons, forms full of pared depiction. The mimetic reading is both totally legit and unavoidable. This engages both the obvious sources (all those fish) and a certain incitement to ferret the metaphor. I have read, among others, a description in which Disney Hall is compared to a flower. It never struck me thus—I am reminded rather of those dancing hippopotamuses in Disney's *Fantasia,* improbably light of foot. And the building is ineffable in similar wise. Curvy, twisted renditions of shapes that approach familiar platonic forms but that—like cartoon houses—bulge with the energy of (incipient) animation. The building is both beautiful and incredibly apt to its patron.

The invention of the movies was transformative for architecture, paralleling and informing the invention of the idea of space. A medium that allows the continuous depiction of space, the movies goaded architecture into a new sense of flow, creating an idea of the palpability—the physics— of the space. Space was no longer just a by-product of the order of events. Animated, the rush of space could be expected to have an effect on the material conditions through which it passed. Film was able—for the first time—to capture the blur of speed much the way we—slow to process our own environment—perceive it. Interest in such distortion through attenuation has something of a history, originating in our ability to cross the landscape at increasing speeds, the view from the train or the car. (Remember all those stretched buildings in the sixties "responding" to the view from the road!)

The film conceit is useful to architecture both for its ability to capture the effects of space and for its store of techniques. I am thinking of the basic technology of filmmaking, the decomposition of a continuous kinetic activity into a series of static frames, the stills that undergird the motion. This is an uncanny metaphor for architecture, constructed via a sequence of precisely measured stabilities to produce something that finds its ultimate legibility in movement. Nothing more clearly encapsulates architecture's relationship to the idea of motion than the photographs of Eadweard Muybridge. Here the idea is not to create motion but to stop it, to decompose and deconstruct it, to add precisely the necessary stasis to open motion to analysis and—ultimately—to reconstitution.

Which brings us back to cartooning. An animated cartoon is a kind of

Gesamtkunstwerk that, like its cathedral forebears, requires the precisely coordinated assembly of a huge number of individually produced, static elements in order to construct a singularity. A single cartoon cel, then, somehow contains the implication of its successors, the idea that motion—being physical—can be created from its particles. The most revealing and intimate moment in animated cartoons is that classic image of Wiley Coyote who, having just barreled over a cliff, takes a few moments to discover that he is running through thin air, looks down, and only then plummets to earth.

The hapless coyote suggests the idea that physics is also psychical, that there is a moment of ambiguous intersection between gravity and the unconscious, true as well for architecture. In Gehry's practice, much weight is put on the sketch, on the spontaneity of impulse, and on an essence of ineffable character to which all obeisance must be paid. For Gehry's sketch (like Disney's), the next step is an inversion. The sketch—which defies conventional geometrical organization—must be translated into a system of precise coordinates and known structural properties, all of which depend on an undergirding Euclideanism. The forms are derived after the fact.

This act suggests a constant tension—constant relationship—between a system of familiar Platonic solids and a set of spontaneous forms that riff but do not ape this set of familiars, much as Mickey resembles a mouse but looks like no mouse we have ever seen. The fantasy is thus inversely symmetrical with the sketch, which distorts the unfolding reality it both exaggerates and simplifies. The Disney Hall project is also a distortion, a cartoon that inflates the unseen ideal form: those shapes in the auditorium are both dancing flowers or hippos but also dancing not-cubes and not-rectangles, distorted away from the familiar but not so far as to cease affinity.

In an interesting insight, Zaha Hadid recently described her early motivation to paint as somehow anticipating the availability of form-Z, the current Mac-based solid modeling program of choice. The observation is canny in begging the question of animation. If the current architectural avant-garde—indubitably sourced in Gehry's work—has a shared obsession, it is with the motility of architecture. The conceit—not of frozen music but of frozen motion—surely informs a myriad of fantasies of tipping facades and rotating masses, a simulation of instability that has been the hallmark of so much recent work.

Much has been made about the transformation of Gehry's practice to a computer-dominated one. Both too much and too little are implied. **95**

Too much because the computer is not used as a generative device but as an instrument of translation: thanks to computer we can—within the limits of materials and gravity—now build any shape. But the computer also provides another liberation. Secure in the knowledge that anything can be produced, drawing—sketching—is itself emboldened, offering a license that gives the sketch validity not simply as a source but as the final technical authority. The computer enables the representation and manipulation of that which cannot otherwise be drawn.

The current trend in supercomputers is to the massively parallel. Largely out of favor are the incredibly powerful single processors of older machines, and in their place hundreds of microprocessors are linked together do the job. Tasks are not performed sequentially but divided, and their components are solved separately and simultaneously. In many ways, this approach is similar to that of the traditional, pre-computer, handicraft animation studio. To produce the images necessary to inhabit the hundreds of thousands of film frames in a full-blown animated movie, cadres of artists labor for months or years to break down the sequence of animation in the freeze-frame of individual cels and then draw and paint them one by one.

Gehry's use of the computer enables the same process to take place, only backwards. Although the entire object is crunched at once, what is produced is a single model of an extremely complex form, which only the intelligence of the computer can be said to comprehend in its all-at-once. To the observer, the central model can only be constructed by observing the building through a self-propelled animation of every aspect of it, decomposing it into infinite "frozen" views.

For those actually designing the building in its detailed particulars and for those constructing it, the all-at-once is decomposed into a conventional series of working drawings. Although this is likely to change before too long, buildings are still constructed from paper plans, from individual drawings of each and every part to be assembled. However, there is a portion of the process—particularly in a case like the mechanical cutting of the doubly curved stone skin at Bilbao—in which the intermediary of a drawing is obviated by direct communication from the design computer to the machines that mill the stone to shape. There is an interesting gap between the extreme fragility of the sketch and the intense particularity of the construction documents—all of which is negotiated within the computer—that begs interesting questions about the ultimate availability of architectural "expert systems." If one thinks of the computer as no more than a sophisticated pencil, there is no issue. If it has the potential to be more. . . .

It is in this sense that Bilbao might also be described as an intermediary triumph and a harbinger of both greater freedom and license for the computer as architectural generator. Many have described the building as the first of the twenty-first century, although I prefer to think of it as the apotheosis of our own. For Gehry, the computer is a tool, not a partner—an instrument for catching the curve, not for inventing it. His design process also includes repetitive physical modeling in which the computer (in concert with laser measuring devices) becomes a notational partner. Gehry's work—full of genius—does not beg any fundamental questions for art. It is simply beautiful in the old-fashioned way, and there is no doubt as to who the artist is.

The technology used in Gehry's office—the CATIA system—began at Dassault, the French aerospace firm. CATIA enables the construction of a continuously shifting compound curvature, such as that involved in changing the camber of an aircraft wing. The Dassault system is, in fact, a machine for realizing curves, and this obsession with a "naturalistic" curvilinearity is also the culmination of an inquiry that dates back at least to Horta, Sullivan, and Gaudi, is carried on by Aalto (for whom Gehry claims special affinity), and rationalized by Bucky and the plastic Corbusier. For all of these, the mimetic drive is to recruit nature as both collaborator and source. Gehry advances the argument both by his cartooning tactics—rounding off, bloating of forms to create an image of friendliness—and by his pursuit of the limpidity of the "natural," freely drawn curve, with its legato elegance and its suggestion that nature is simply another perceptual system producing its own private styles of distortion.

Louis Kahn asked the brick what it wanted to be, and the brick confided that it was an arch. This sense of volition is the gift of functionalism to materials. Gehry's creative breakthrough has long been associated with his craftsman (in the Sears, Roebuck sense) phase. After long association with artists, Gehry turned from the depersonalized architecture of the corporate world with its abstract, immaterial air to an architecture with which he was in direct emotional contact, the sort of building you almost imagine yourself able to hand build—certainly to fully understand. For Gehry, this was an autodidactic architecture, an architecture of renewal. The funky work put an end to a functionalist lineage by refiguring the authority of materials, by offering alternative answers to the question of the inner desires of a two-by-four.

This was also the moment in which the Gehry persona—the bleeding-hearted Canadian nebbish—also began to be thoroughly mythologized, a phenomenon in which the dissembling Gehry has always artfully collaborated. Indeed, in the Woody Allen culture of wearing one's neuroses on one's sleeve, this was architecture's privilege: to reveal itself, to spill its guts. As in the work of his contemporaries Peter Eisenman (who famously used to claim to have—in the manner of Pascal's wager—both a Jungian and a Freudian shrink) and John Hejduk, the element of autobiography was returned to architecture. That Gehry's breakthrough project was a transformation of his own house is surely significant.

Most accounts of Gehry's turn to the chain-link and corrugated palette devolve on the cheap and ordinary nature of the materials. But I would suggest that the roots of the style derive not from tightfistedness but control. Control, to begin, is a question of knowledge, and these works were in a medium the newly independent practitioner could most knowledgeably and efficiently undertake. The turn to the computer as a shape maker is also a moment of conflation between liberation and control. Gehry's use of materials—in whatever register—is never eccentric. Sheet titanium, as desirous as a brick, wants to be a skin, needs to be laid on the complex curves in plates.

So much of art nowadays is forged in the techniques of observation, displaced onto the register of criticism. To this, the computer offers an interesting parallel. Like the dislocation of technique in a criticism-driven art, the computer engenders a subtle shift in the process of creation. The conceptual character of a building's prior imaginative existence—given the truly amazing modeling possibilities of computers—means that it can be observed, for the first time, in a simulacrum of the continuities of reality. The computer becomes a means of cinematizing architecture without building and may (though this is a question for another time) harbinger its eventual annihilation.

Gehry's celebrated aedicular strategy, the collage of one-room buildings to create house ensembles, also embodies a form of control. Here, the idea is to produce a transcendental diagram. A conventional tactic for getting into an architectural program is to produce a bubble diagram in which—like those Muybridge photos—a totality is reduced to a series of manageable components. The Taylorized style of mainstream modernism saw this decomposition as a physical convenience, a means of organizing circulation, hierarchy, and dimension. For Gehry, the dispersal has a more physical aura, a means not of producing hierarchy but autonomy, the instrument of what might be called architectural citizenship.

The fragmentation of Gehry's buildings takes quite a bit of interpretive heat. These building colonies have been described as either psychical or social comments on the fragmentations of modern culture (although critics have also taken the tack that what is embodied is more of an idea of the singularity of the individual). Either way, the burden of representation that this tactic of subdivision bears is clearly hermeneutic and not intentional. The fragmentation clarifies by the exposing of its programmatic parts and is, in this sense, a very modernist gambit. However, whereas traditional modernists color-coded pipes and ducts or argued for literal transparency, Gehry structures his work on a different idea of visibility. The sense of boundedness this sometimes inspires (Mike Davis has chastised Gehry's urban work as overly defensive) does not, I think, stem from a sense of hostility to the exterior world but from a devotion to the individuality of the architectural object.

While the formal lineage for Gehry's fragmenting strategy surely remembers the forms of villages and small towns—whether the rooftop collection of the Wosk penthouse, the pavilionated Simon house, the Winton guest house, the Loyola Campus, or the truly amazing and (alas) unbuilt Lewis house—there is another aspect of consequence: tinyness, the merger of difference and diminutiveness. The history of the little building is an unwritten chapter in the development of architecture but an important one. Certainly, some of the current interest in the question stems from the theory revival of the past twenty years, in the revisitation of the idea of the "primitive hut," the putative origin point of architecture. There is something biological about all this, the idea of growth via cellular division, and Gehry's projects—as they become increasingly sophisticated—seem progressively to embrace this metaphor.

This having been said, I prefer to see Gehry's aedicular tendency as more of an autoanalytical organ, a means by which Gehry has reinvented his architecture. It is instructive to look through Gehry's artistic prehistory, his twenty years before the mast at Luckman and Pereira. Search as one does for hints of things to come, there is little to recommend itself as the harbinger of genius. Acceptable corporate design, always decent, never especially innovative is the order of those days. The only hint of the future lies in Gehry's long experience with the shopping mall. The paradigmatic mall is binucleated like the family, mama and papa anchors holding up opposite ends of an enclosed family room around which cluster the lesser shops, the children of the arrangement. This mall *parti* informs many of Gehry's works, from his first big independent project—the actual mall in Santa Monica—through the Loyola Campus, and culminating, after a long voyage, with Bilbao, its specialty spaces deployed around a central "atrium" that organizes functions around it.

The autonomous courtyard is a spectacularly useful architectural device because it can effectively cut loose the surrounding elements to develop their own autonomy. The courtyard, in its voidedness, offers a take-up space, a distributor that cedes the orbiting elements enough slack to develop in an informal system, expanding unconstrained by a hemming figural space that demands that their own geometries be subservient. Strange and eccentric shapes can nose into a flexible central figure that permits them the room to retain their own eccentric integrity.

Gehry speaks frequently of his friendship for and admiration of artists. This influence is both literal—an indebtedness for representational courage to Oldenburg, an affinity for curvature to Serra—but what is probably most important is the influence of anxiety. It was art (and Los Angeles) that saved Gehry from the seemingly inescapable consequences of universalism. It may also be from this cadre that Gehry acquired the comforting (and historic) notion that politics can inhere in avant-gardism.

Gehry went to school at the height of the influence of modernism (including time served in the planning program at that Kremlin of modernist-think, Harvard's Graduate School of Design), when certain truths were held to be self-evident. The first of these was the need for generic solutions to architectural problems, for systems rather than objects. And the second was a version of minimalism—functionalism— that singular mix of liberalism and Taylorism with its creepy fantasy of mass subjectivity.

Somewhere, Frank was bridling at this. Conscience-full product of a Jewish-Canadian, liberal environment, he wanted to help. But inside, the fish of creativity was wiggling to be free. And here the metaphor may be important. Looking back at that Proustian carp alive in the tub, one reads not just animation but imprisonment, circumscribed desire: fish gotta swim, after all, and in the tub they don't get far. And what object can be said to be less vested with its own desires than the carp become part of that gray lump of gefilte fish (however tasty, not what the fish wants to be). Like a Chinese painting of a fish in which a stroke suffices to animate the shape, Gehry reanimates. He sees the orthodox formal vocabulary of most architecture as lifeless and gets to work, not with the production of an alternative system, an accidental incursion from left field produced not by surrealistic trickery nor a single imaginative leap, but with the breath of new life injected into old forms.

100   The revision starts slowly at the Davis House, in which the box under-

goes a mild, sight-line-generated skewing to produce (along with the skewed wing of Asplund's Snellman House) one of the most seminal twists in the history of architecture. With his own house, Gehry extends his palette of distortions to strategies of decomposition and second skin. Here, the box is not simply distorted geometrically, it is stripped bare. Gehry dances down the line of essence, inquiring how much can be removed and reconfigured before the house disappears. The crummy material palette is, to be sure, a part of this, but there is nothing in the materials Gehry introduces that really stands outside the standard-issue materiality of stick-built homes with their 2× construction, chain-link back fences, and asphalted drives—a large part of the point. The box has been broken, and this new energy parallels Gehry's own escape from the box of corporate practice to a circumstance in which his newly confident and increasingly articulate desires are able to directly imprint his work, to make something new from the old familiars.

Having demystified the box via distortion and dematerialization, Gehry is ready to move on to ensemble, to the ways in which uses, not simply forms, go together. The city is the ultimate architectural ensemble, and Gehry's urbanism is, at the end of the day, fundamentally respectful of the accumulated conventions of the historic. While the forms may be wild, the strategies of situation are both calm and precise. Bilbao, for example, is brilliant not just in its siting but in the way in which it resolves the primary issue of the Bilbao riverfront, the dramatic sectional drop from the main grade of the town to the riverbank. Disney Hall, for all its crazed neobaroquisms, produces an acropolis in friendly collaboration with its dreary predecessors on Bunker Hill. Santa Monica Place skillfully separates automotive and pedestrian access, a mall that both contains its own anchors and that anchors Santa Monica's Third Street pedestrian shopping street, which existed only as an idea at the time of the mall's building.

The bringing together of pieces in peaceable assembly is the most urgent creative agenda of Gehry's breakout. Although his architecture is relentlessly alleged to incorporate the genius loci of Los Angeles as one of its most fundamental inspirations, the reading is too often distorted by an identification of the city with tackiness and ephemerality—the shake, rattle, and roll of quakes and slides—and with a general celebration of the city's transient veneer. Slighted in this interpretation are certain sounder elements, especially a history of local place making. The film studio complexes, endearing shopping centers, like the Farmers Market, bungalow courts, and especially the small pedestrian cul-de-sacs, such as

101

the Crossroads of the World, are clear prototypes for the likes of Edgemar, one of Gehry's most successful ensembles.

As with any village, the crucial questions are over the limits of inclusion in community, the tolerable degrees of difference, and the nature of the public or shared spaces. For Gehry, difference is embodied in shape and material, secondarily in use. Elements express their individuality by standing free, an attitude that both de-inscribes them and that—in offering the possibility of a comprehensive, cubistic view of the element—makes the individual piece more comprehensible as such, vesting it with a kind of citizenship via the autonomy of (perceptual) wholeness.

Naturally, there is a problem with treating forms as citizens inasmuch as formalism always risks superseding the desires of users. But—with our most artistic architect—the user's desire is necessarily to inhabit Gehry's own sense of expression, largely mooting the point. Except at its periphery where collective spaces are defined—in their edges—as the residue of individual assembly. And here is the innovation. Although Gehry's collective spaces have carefully nuanced scale and detail, they are seldom recoverable as figures. This is genius, this noumenal creation of a public realm that is drawn out of the private, described in detail only by the individual spaces that define it.

The Guggenheim is the Weisman Museum rotated through 180 degrees. One side of the arc is occupied with the convulsive geometry of the stainless steel facade, the other with rectangular boxes of masonry. Bilbao gives a "functional" logic to this geometrical opposition by creating two different kinds of spaces: geometrical, stone-clad for "historic" modern art, and free-form, titanium-swaddled for contemporary work. Although there is nothing philosophically necessary in this distinction, it works very well, if only in the sense that all the work in the museum is beautifully housed. The only dysfunctional space is the largest, the huge loft room on the ground floor. Here, the issue is not architectural but the curatorial insistence of trying to display puny two-dimensional works on its 450-foot-long walls.

Gehry's work has remarkable command of direction, something—as opposed to orientation—intrinsic and internal. This begins with an acute sense of front and back. In many earlier projects, the twoness was the outgrowth of a sense of the role of building in the urban fabric, between the faces of public and private, a condition recursively explored within the working arrangements of the grouping itself. Of course, any architecture that wants to move begs the question of direction. If the classic modernist building embraced the metaphor of the ship, sailing along its long axis, Gehry has managed to disperse this sense of movement, to make a more general condition of animation. And here the metaphor of the flower grows again. The idea is the opposite of Muybridge's and seeks not to observe by retardation but by acceleration, in the kinds of time-lapse photography that—by speeding up the succession of images— makes the opening of a flower or the construction of a building freshly accessible.

Although the blooming and the building might fairly be said to proceed to certain ends, what Gehry, in his most recent work, has captured is not the directed motion but the stationary dynamism of a flame. The evanescence of the reflective facades of the Weisman Museum and the Guggenheim achieve the feeling of motion, not by the conceit of stop-time, like the Kobe fish or Vitra, but via literal animation. This phantasmagoria of moving light is not projected on a simple screen—like minimalist mirrored facades that try to garner meaning from sun and clouds—but on a surface that is itself complex. Bilbao surely marks the mature phase of Gehry's cubist sensibility, in which he returns cubist two-dimensional depictions of three-dimensional space to the actual realm of volume. It is a masterpiece.

1999

Siza the Day

Until I went to Portugal a month ago, I had thought Alvaro Siza was simply an invention of Ken Frampton, the perfect, self-effacing modernist-regionalist. In spite of his 1992 Pritzker, and in spite of the reverential tones in which he is often spoken of, Siza's work had somehow escaped me. I just had not seen any, knew it only through photography. I expected sun-baked Aalto, desiccated curves, dried of their snap, white boxes in picturesque settings.

I had an object lesson in the perils of such distance viewing within half an hour of my arrival in Porto. There is a heroic column at the end of a long rising boulevard near the center of town that, seen from afar, looks like a gigantic, droopy palm tree. Closer inspection reveals, however, something else, something weird. What had appeared to be fronds turned out to be the limp wings of an enormous eagle. Sitting atop the prostrate bird (and apparently in the process of devouring it) was a smug-looking lion. The monument (Siza calls it the "copulation of the lion") celebrates a Portuguese victory over the Napoleonic armies during the Peninsular Wars.

Siza, viewed up close, also turned out to be a totally different story. His work, though compounded of a relatively austere material and formal palette, is very deep and very rich, luminous and controlled, full of allusions to other sun-dappled modernisms of the global periphery, from Luis Barragan to Richard Neutra. And it moves in a real variety of contexts, both international and local. Indeed, since the overthrow of the dictatorship in 1974, Portugal (which has a population of only ten million) has emerged as something of an architectural powerhouse. Among its leaders are Eduardo Souto de Moura, Carrilho da Graca, Concalo Byrne, and of course, Siza, the wellspring. Again, I hesitate to describe this community as simply regional, but it is, without a doubt, a community, filled with reciprocity and engaged with common issues of scale, culture, and climate. It is also a community that is clearly invested in elaborating the practices of a still vital modernity.

Siza is, of course, well aware of the fact that he is working in what is, in many ways, a marginal zone. In a small society, the lines of dispersion and influence are often very clear, and Siza described to me not only the CIAM-influenced teaching he experienced at Porto University in the 1940s but earlier, formative influences on Portuguese architecture from Austria, Germany, and Holland. These arrived both through publications of the twenties, thirties, and forties, and through the influence of two local architects who practiced between the wars, one of whom married a Dutch woman and the other a German. Their frequent trips to see their in-laws, he suggests, were key to the import of modern architecture.

Siza's affinity for an Aalto-protean prototype for a modernism of place is evident both in his work and his writing, and offers a clue to his "regionalism." In a fine 1983 text on Aalto written for the *Jornal de Letras, Artes e Ideias,* he quotes the following, which applies directly to his own practice and sensibility: "I don't think I have any propensity for folklore. The traditions which impress us are relegated mainly to the climate, to the material conditions, to the nature of the tragedies and comedies which touch us. I do not produce an ostensibly Finnish architecture, and I see no opposition between Finnish and international." Aalto's influence on Siza, though, is not simply in an understanding of a relationship of the local and the global, but more deeply, in an affinity for the tactile, physiognomic character of building. Like Aalto's architecture—and unlike Mies's mechanization and Corb's subjective universalization—Siza's work feels remarkably specific and sensual. Part of this surely lies in the presence of a sense of making, resulting from what Siza sees as a poignant local moment of transition from essentially handicraft building to the tactics of industrialization.

The building I went to Porto to see was Siza's new Museu Serralves, the first large-scale contemporary art museum in Portugal. Founded in 1989 as a public-private initiative, the Serralves Foundation has rapidly built up an extensive collection of post-sixties art, for which the 140,000-square-foot building is intended. Inescapably, the enterprise recalls Bilbao's, not too far away. Similarly scaled and with similar artistic content, the two museums take fundamentally different approaches to context. Unlike Bilbao, which dominates the cityscape, Siza's museum is hidden behind the high stone walls of the Serralves Park near the edge of town. The gardens, designed in a kind of Hollywood French style by Jacques Greber (landscape architect for a number of L.A. homes-of-the-stars in the thirties), originally belonged to a Portuguese textile baron. The big pink deco house on the grounds, completed in 1940 by the architect Marques da Silva, in a late-in-life stylistic conversion, has served as temporary museum for several years.

It is not exactly that Siza's large building is reticent (it is a very long white object), but rather that it wants to be understood in a gradual, unfolding, ambulatory way. Gehry's view of circulation is more modernist—more assembled, less rigorously sequential. For Siza, on the other hand, the management of circulation is central. He loves lengthy sequences of approach and entry, chains of goings in and out. At the museum, for example, one enters through a breach in the original stone wall, confronts a small entry pavilion, then passes down an elegantly long covered walkway, skirting a garden and finally arriving at the main entrance to the building itself. The motile sensibility is there from the first. The Ocean Swimming Pool of 1961–66—a beachside pool and changing pavilion—shows the same ambulatory verve with its dramatic sequence of ramps and turnings, descending to the beach.

The museum's organization is vaguely H-shaped—in essence, a double bank of galleries, with periodic lateral links. Instead of allowing these spaces to read as autonomous, however, Siza blurs the line between corridor and room, creating a sense of ambiguity, virtuality, thresholds. This ambiguity has created some problems for him. Siza's is an architecture of modulation—of light, of space, of use, of meaning—and his intention for the museum was to set up a rhythm between areas of circulation and areas of display, reflected in both the spaces' character and their function. As construction advanced, though, the curatorial powers realized that these nominal spaces of circulation also offered opportunities for displaying art. Although nothing had been hung at the time of my visit, Siza expressed some anxiety that the relief provided by the intermediate ambulatory spaces would be vitiated by a ubiquity of artwork.

In a short piece written in 1988, Siza offers a succinct credo about the architecture of museums: "In museums, the light becomes soft, careful, preferably impassive and immutable. It is necessary not to harm the delicacies of Vermeer, it must not compete with the violent light of Goya, or the semi-darkness, nor must we destroy the hot atmosphere of Titian on the point of dying out, or the universal light of Velázquez or the dissected light of Picasso, all this escapes time and place in Samothraces's flight of Victory.

"The architecture of the Museum probably cannot be other than classical, distant, or careful in relation to Geography and History; even [Frank] Lloyd Wright's ramp is suddenly stilled. . . . This is the Architecture of Museums, ideally without walls or doors or windows, or any of those defenses which are too obvious, too thought out or repeated. Museums which gather together objects that were in palaces or churches or cottages or attics, covered with glory or with dust, folded on the mattress of a pallet bed, and which now suddenly observe me, under a light which is indifferent to what moves too much."

You know how I love Paul Rudolph, an architect for whom light assumed a rare palpability. Siza is a brother creator, acutely sensible that a wall is both an object and the medium of void and luminosity. The tactic for the capture of light depends on its availability (think of how Rudolph's walls thickened after he moved north). My Portuguese visit took place under cobalt skies, in unabated sunshine. Clearly, this quality of place has been the study of a lifetime for Siza, and the Serralves Museum, which continues a focused research developed in his earlier museum in Santiago de Compostela in Spain, is a masterpiece of illumination. In that project, completed in 1994, Siza introduces a striking device for interior lighting, which reappears in about half the galleries in Porto. In these, suspended from the ceiling is what appears to be a very large, very thick, inverted Parsons table—legs cut down to cocktail length—creating the impression of a slightly scary monolith hovering overhead. This object, surmounted by an unseen skylight, also conceals air-conditioning equipment and artificial lighting.

The effect is magical—like one of those numinous perspectival Lauretta Vinciarelli paintings. Natural light pours over the table sides to wash the surrounding walls, topped up by artificial lighting as necessary. Originally, Siza wanted to treat each of the daylit galleries this way, but official skepticism forced him to use more conventional skylighting in half of the spaces. In fact, this variation contributes richness, as do differences in the rooms themselves. Generous and impeccably—if traditionally— proportioned, the rectilinear galleries often are on two or more levels, with balconies, view points, or internal ramps absorbing modest changes in elevation from surrounding spaces.

I saw the museum a couple of months before its opening, and although its main lines and character were clear, much of the detail was missing, and this provided the opportunity to observe something of Siza's working method. In one of the galleries, a metal railing had been partially mocked up, typical of the way he works with extensive calibration and modification on site. "Siza starts working where others would stop," I was told by the architect from his office who was touring with me, and I was then shown a fairly striking example. Disquieted by a double pillar in the foyer of the building's auditorium, Siza had one removed, necessitating the reinforcement of an adjacent stair to take the load but yielding a more satisfactory space. This is the extravagance of an architect.

How could I have missed all this? The new museum is superb without heroics, and rich without flamboyance, impressing with a supple curve to the auditorium roof, a projecting shadow-casting fin, a window strip inserted just so, a perfect rail, stone and tile finishes impeccably applied. It is the work of a master: Siza is a worthy heir to the legacy of that earlier Alvar, Aalto.

1999

The Borders of Islamic Architecture

The winners of the Aga Kahn Award for architecture were announced the other day, and it is an interesting list. This is the eighth cycle of the award—begun in 1977 and given every three years—and the winners reflect both the strengths and the idiosyncrasies of the program.

Idiosyncrasy is especially important. For a prize that has as one of its objectives the celebration of the idea of architectural plurality, the ability to acknowledge a set of cultural differences that can be extremely local is crucial. Idiosyncrasy is also the great hedge against the kind of spurious universality that has long dominated architectural thinking and that is a bedrock of religion. Greatness, though, always sets a standard of deviation from the norm: this is how it advances perception and thinking.

Idiosyncrasy is likewise crucial to the self-definition of an award, to the idea that giving a prize itself constitutes a form of work, that *awarding* has a purpose beyond publicity. Indeed, if anything distinguishes this award from, say, the better known Pritzker Prize, it is exactly the expectation that the results, in any given cycle, will exceed the expected, will reveal something new about what can be architecture. The Pritzker never defies expectations except perhaps in the order in which the prize is doled out to the usual suspects.

The formal mission of the Aga Khan award is to recognize both architecture in the "Muslim world" and architecture elsewhere that speaks to Muslim aspirations. The ongoing project and character of the award are inextricably bound up with that of its progenitor. Hereditary head of the Ismaili branch of Islam (a subset of Shi'a), the Aga Khan is probably as well known for his material as his spiritual interests, a thoroughly modern and somewhat paradoxical religious leader whose extravagant lifestyle and flamboyant entrepreneurship make him part spirit guide, part socialite, and part head of state.

Indeed, the problematic of the Aga Khan's person parallels that of the award: how to combine traditional values with modernity in the full Western sense and how to both socialize and aestheticize spirituality in a manner that will strip it of its sting and foreground the ideas of art and of service. These questions are thrown into greater relief by the remorselessly hostile and stereotyping coverage of Islam in the Western media. From the Aga Khan's standpoint, the award is surely useful both in increasing his own prestige and establishing a progressive cultural vector for Islam in general as well as in celebrating its architecture. This multiple agenda legitimates—even necessitates—a careful political reading of the results since there are such clear political imperatives behind the award and because any comprehensive statement about Islam is bound to be controversial to someone. Make no mistake, however, this insistent politics is one of the strengths of the award, the source and substance of its mission. Behind the high-minded (and inevitable) rhetoric of "quality" lies a more refined agenda.

"Quality" is itself a highly vexed concept. As we have learned from our own cultural wars, the idea of quality can be used as a strategy of mystification, perpetrated by elites to devalue cultures not their own. If the award has made a lasting contribution to the discourse of quality in architecture, it lies precisely in its tenacious enlargement of architecture's scope, in its insistence on a conceptual parity between high cultural manifestations and their mainstream designers and extremely local expressions by architects outside the range of the media, including local organizers and craftspeople who certainly never think of themselves as "architects" in the familiar sense.

Producing this result is no accident. Under the able direction of the brilliant and astute Suha Ozkan, the awards committee receives nominations (which have grown dramatically in number as the award has established itself over the years) from a very large number of nominators around the world. After an initial vetting by the jury to reduce the nominations to a manageable number, the awards committee dispatches experts to each site to prepare a dossier about the work (this is a *project*-based award), which is then presented to the jury, the expert remaining to answer any questions about the project under his or her purview.

The jury is itself something of a seismograph of the development and expression of these concerns, anticipating the character of the award in its makeup. This year's jury comprised a fairly typical group, including Zaha Hadid, Arata Isozaki, regionally well-known architects from Pakistan, Saudi Arabia, India, Indonesia, and Turkey, Mohammed Arkoun, an Islamic intellectual historian from Paris and a perennial ideologue for the award, and Fred Jameson, the cultural theorist from Duke and a leading neo-Marxist thinker. The steering committee for the award (responsible for the appointment of the jury) includes both Peter Eisenman and Charles Jencks, among its better-known members.

As should be clear from this mix (which has typified the award from the get-go), a certain operation of cultural straddling is central to both the jury and the award. The award's catholic gaze is both predicated on and achieved via its own tolerance—indeed crafting—of diversity, and at its best achieves almost a World-War-Two-movie-bomber-crew selection of backgrounds and ethnicities: the Diasporan theorist, the Marxist, the woman, the superstar, the Jew. This skillful combination of pluralism with the nominal monolith of "Islam" assures the continued relevance and credibility of the award and the expansion of its possibilities.

We know, however, that images can tell many stories at once. For example, whatever the failures of his administration, Clinton has been presented by the ravening media—in a purely parenthetical way—as a white man with black friends and colleagues. This is a revelation: every time we see Bill tooling around the golf course with Vernon Jordan, tee clenched between his teeth, we see something beyond the v.o. about Monica. Like a president, a religious leader is obliged to exemplary—demonstrative—acts, to the visibility of content, whatever the back story. I say god bless a jury with a theologian, a Marxist, a woman, and a Jew for understanding the cultural underpinnings of architecture and seeking to represent *its* diversity through diversity at every level.

This spirit carries over into the very careful range of the projects awarded. Although it is not mandated, the jury invariably chooses to honor a wide variety of project types, a spread that—in its consistencies and shifts from year to year—can be read for its contribution to the larger, cumulative project of the award. The relatively large number of projects typically premiated—in past years as many as fifteen projects have been selected—allows the award to function as a measure both of architectural developments in the Muslim world and of the shifting of its own preoccupations and tastes.

Large numbers beg, if only statistically, the question of representation (in the old sense of the term). One begins by what is conspicuous by absence. As in the awarding of the Pritzker, women are invisible. Broadening the range of projects has not proven to be a formula for inclusion, at least not a broadening as the award has constituted it. On the other hand, there is a wide distribution by countries and a willingness to look in places—like Palestine, Iran, and Iraq—that are on the index of forbidden geography for much of the Western cultural media.

The most interesting and relevant distribution, though, is by project type. This is very broad, ranging from rural and urban self-help schemes accomplished for pennies, to planning and infrastructure projects, to landscaping and parks, to religious buildings, to houses, to civic structures of both austerity and magnificence. Harbored within this spread of projects—when coupled with the shifting dynamic of serial juries—is the possibility for considerable polemical nuance. This year's crop of winners is no exception.

To begin, there are only seven awards this year, giving rise to the interesting question of why a jury with half a million dollars to distribute would elect to give it to fewer people than are usually recognized. Clearly, it has nothing to do with the number of candidates—this year produced a record crop. Nor does it have to do with the particularly extraordinary quality of this year's selection (although it contains extraordinary projects). A more likely explanation is—according to my sources—the especially contentious jury deliberations this year and the attendant difficulty of trade-offs.

But let's get down to cases.

One winner in particular—an infrastructure project in the Indian city of Indore—struck me as brilliant and moving, a truly profound project. The scheme is the brainchild of Himanshu Parikh, an engineer, who recognized a relationship between several existing watercourses and the location of the greatest concentration of slums within the town, which, in turn, were using the Khan and Sarawati Rivers as sewers in lieu of an absent municipal system. By both recovering the natural character of the rivers and using their courses as an opportunity to lay in sewer lines, a squandered but indispensable resource has been ingeniously turned back to good use.

Part of the appeal of the project is the nature of the collaboration that produced it, a coalition including residents, government, NGOs, and industry. Sanitary improvements, including new sewers and treatment facilities as well as subsidized toilet hookups to the new lines, were combined with streetlighting, roadwork, and community halls to produce a dramatic improvement in the local environment and in the quality of life of slum dwellers. One of the by-products of these improvements in infrastructure has been a startling decrease in crime, previously centered on communal washhouses.

The Indore scheme was one of three projects in India given awards this year. This concentration—as well as the nature of the winners themselves—begs a number of questions. Certainly it raises the issue of the relationship of Islam and the nation-state, an obviously sensitive matter in light of the number of theocracies in the Islamic world and the continuing pressure for secular governments to Islamicize. By the time of the awards jury, the Indian government was in the hands of the BJP, the stridently Hindu nationalist party with its threatening stance vis-à-vis Islam.

It seems likely that the award meant to send a message of tolerance in premiating projects that—while in areas with substantial Muslim populations—are sure to be used by very mixed groups. More, I cannot imagine someone like Fred Jameson, the leading critic and expositor of postmodernity, bringing a strong advocacy for the relevance of the theocratic state as a way of siting a cultural prize.

The second Indian prize—for an elegantly simple Leper's Hospital sponsored by a Norwegian Evangelical Mission and designed by two Norwegian architectural students—is irreproachably worthy and the first such facility in a region desperate for them. Simply and sensitively built, the project provides a safe, self-sufficient, and reposeful environment for people accustomed to being treated as pariahs, offering them precious hope and real care.

The third project, Charles Correa's design for a new assembly building for the State of Madhya Pradesh in Bhopal, is the curiosity in the Indian selections. Like all of Correa's work, it is a beautiful job, at once formal and relaxed, very sensitive to site and climate, and replete with incorporations of and allusions to local architectural traditions. What is unusual is that the building's form is derived from a nine-part Hindu mandala, which Correa uses to organize the plan. Calling this building "Muslim" is surely a stretch, and Vidhan Bhavan's inclusion signals the elision of the prize's catchment area with the developing world in general. It also begs one of the perennial issues confronted by the award: the place of iconography.

If the award has more than a geographical understanding of Islamic architecture, the inscribed systems of meaning in the projects beg attention and clarification. There is an obvious dilemma here that springs from the award's mission to coalesce Islam—with its historic traditions of visual meaning—with modernity and its own historic preference for abstraction. In one way, religion—in expressing its own particulars—would seem to converge with the predilections of postmodernity and its readmission of iconography. The moment is an interesting one, as abstraction has ceased to be exactly politically correct in the worlds of art and architecture, which are now more open to other systems of meaning. The question is, must we now read all buildings symbolically, or—more relevantly—is it any longer possible *not* to foreground such readings, especially in a project in which they are so deliberately incorporated?

The awards this year have it both ways. Another fine winner (never mind the somewhat regressive social content), a deluxe country club in Saudi Arabia designed by Frei Otto and Omrania Architects, is celebrated for its relationship to the desert landscape, its inner garden, the Teflon tensile structures that are held to evoke the tents of the Bedouins, and the sinewy masonry walls, suggestive of fortresses. This fundamentally abstract work is legitimated by being embellished with iconic meanings. Context provides meaning here: certainly no one would describe the Munich Olympic Stadium as "Muslim"—iconography is not commutative. This is a little bit troubling as a rationale, allowing meaning to be detached (Bhopal) or attached (Riyadh) at will.

While this represents an obvious dilemma, it is one the award has historically tended to fudge via its inclusiveness, promoting Islam more as a cultural than a religious construct. The bifurcation of a cultural Islam with the apparatus of modernity naturally begs the question of colonialism. One of the representational ironies of all of this involves the persistent repatriation of at least one of the initiating images of modernism, the north African village, to its source. This suggests, in turn, the possibility for an interesting reverse colonialism in the reclamation of historic images from their abstraction in modernity.

The most obviously political award in the group was for the restoration of the historic center of Hebron, just such a cubistic ensemble. It looks like a good job was made of it: historically sensitive, fine standard of craft, training of townspeople in building skills, no displacement of neighborhood residents, revival of commerce and a sense of life, hygienic improvements, and so on. Of course, what distinguishes it is the site, ground zero for the territorial struggles of Palestinians and Israelis. Historic restoration has long been an instrument for Israeli assertions of their rights of inhabitation, for establishing the authenticity of their claims of ownership, and the Palestinians of Hebron now assert their own pride of nation by the reclamation of this inheritance. This in not the first time the award has indirectly chided the Israelis: the 1989 cycle premiated the restoration of a mosque in Sidon, Lebanon, that the Israelis had bombed during their invasion.

The remaining two awards are less impressive. An arts complex in Lahore by Nayyar Ali Dada exemplifies another dilemma. A decent if rather stiff piece of architecture that has apparently greatly enriched the cultural life of Lahore, the building itself—despite its scale—seems slightly beside the point. As, in a way, does a house by Jimmy Lim in Malaysia, a fine but unextraordinary work that continues a long-standing tradition of the award to recognize vaguely folkloric houses for the better classes. One of my sources on the inside tells me that Zaha, who apparently saw shades of a Proun in the plan juxtaposition of two triangles, was a strong advocate for this project.

1998

Filming Wright

Ken Burns's new documentary on Frank Lloyd Wright is an interesting and enjoyable film, very much in his familiar stately, plump, and elegant style. The viewer is immediately (and extensively) immersed in Wright and his work: as in *The Civil War* and *Baseball,* Burns wants to tell the whole story from beginning to end in languid chronology. The film is great to look at, although—until its climax at the Guggenheim—it keeps its buildings empty in fine ESTO style, fires crackling in summer, flowers just so, drawings rolled out with period drafting equipment lying ready to use. The buildings that Burns focuses on—Taliesin, Johnson's Wax, Unity Temple, the Guggenheim, Fallingwater—are wonderfully photographed, unfolding at a walker's pace in front of a camera that clearly knows what it likes.

The film, with its characteristic blend of period photography (the sound of hammering over every shot of construction drove me nuts), learned talking heads, voice-over narration (Edward Hermann, the designated voice of the History Channel) and spoken footnotes (Japanese accent for the reader of a letter from Japan), and historic clips, keeps a firm grip on the viewer's attention. I had, however, a frequent feeling that I was watching two different films at once, one about the architecture and another about the man. Burns sets up this difference from the get-go, makes it the spine of his film, which begins with an organizing epigram from Yeats: "The intellect of man is forced to choose, / Perfection of the life, or of the work, / And if it take the second must refuse, / A heavenly mansion, raging in the dark."

This heroic chiaroscuro proves irresistible to Burns. The architectural half of the film, if beautiful, is pure hero worship. The only opinion—the only real analysis—the film delivers about Wright's architecture is that it is the work of genius. This approach is a little short in the nuance department: every time the film focuses on Wright's architecture, it shifts like a smooth automatic transmission into high hagiographic mode. The music is all Beethoven, the *Emperor* Concerto or the "Ode to Joy" swelling from the soundtrack to corroborate the affinity between the great artist of music frozen and the World's Most Famous Composer (with whom Wright identified strongly). The talking heads jabber on in Shelby Footesque reverie about the way in which Wright's architecture is a bridge to the ineffable, about the way in which it touches the soul, about the sheer indescribability of the work in other than these dime-store metaphysical terms.

The second film—the one about Wright "the man"—is dramatically far tastier, and this narrative get-up-and-go makes a considerably more interesting film. Here we meet the terrible, crippling dad, the philanderer, the sybarite, the autocrat, the narcissist. Wright's life, after all, was sensational in the best *National Enquirer* sense of the word. And the talking heads who evoke Wright the man—including biographers Meryle Secrest and Brendan Gill, several Wright family members, and former Taliesin fellows—have a far more interesting story to tell. The best parts of the film, though, are interview footage with Wright himself, including snippets of a priceless journey down Fifth Avenue in an open carriage and bits of a TV interview with a chain-smoking Mike Wallace.

The idea of an unbridgeable divide between art and life that undergirds the film entails the admission (fatal for a reporter) that the difference simply exceeds understanding. Believing this, the film shortchanges the territory of explanation. Burns lacks a taste for the comparative, for context, much as he paints his portraits as if the unconscious had yet to be discovered. For Burns, the idea of influence is trivial, to be attended to in shorthand with a mention of Wright's mother and those famous building blocks. This idea that Wright's architecture could not possibly have been otherwise because of the inimitable genius of its creator kills the idea of culture and milieu. It is not so much that Wright's persona is mystified by the film (after all, this has a long and honorable history ranging from Ayn Rand—curiously unmentioned in the film—to the Wright industry still headquartered in Taliesin), but that Burns's view of art—in its legion of cultural and psychical contexts—is so restricted and old-fashioned.

Part of the problem is surely the talking heads, who cast disappointingly little light on the subject of the architecture. Vincent Scully, Bob Stern, and Philip Johnson—three men whose professional positions in architecture are totally anathema to Wright's own values—are trotted out to certify genius. Indeed, the Yalie/Scullyphile axis is the predominant critical voice in the film. There is more than a whiff of hypocrisy coming from a cadre that cut its critical teeth supporting the wave of historicism that grew out of the postmodern assault on modernity, for which Stern, Scully, Johnson, and Paul Goldberger (all of whom are charming in the film) were primary advocates.

Wright has long been buffeted by the fickle winds of taste. The film   **117** does dwell to some extent on the interregnum between Wright's early and late careers, and on his dramatic reemergence in the thirties, forties, and fifties. Unmentioned (and here the Scullyoid Yalie vector passes through) is the equally precipitous decline in Wright's reputation in the years following his death. Wright took it from both sides. The high modernist types in the saddle at the time of his death hated him for being too fecund and juicy, too much of an individual, a man uninterested in and threatening to the lockstep minimalism of the day. As time went on, the fashion for functionalism waned, but Wright was again the object of derision from the historicist belch of a postmodernity he would surely have reviled.

When I was a student at the Harvard architecture school (then in the depths of mediocrity) in the early seventies, Corb (and Gropius to a lesser degree) was the hero, and the name of Wright was never spoken. It was astonishing that the nation's greatest artistic genius should have been so scrupulously forgotten, but his overwhelming talent coupled with his remarkably artistic evolution were simply too much. In particular, Wright's late work—curvy, ornamental, histrionic, and borderline kitsch—was—and remains—something the architectural historical establishment cannot get its mind around—as if Wright had simply stopped at Fallingwater.

Part of the problem here has to do with the nature of his legacy. While the architectural main line had its problems with the old man, his legion of direct disciples did not. This was not a happy situation. While Wright certainly did his bit to help create his incredibly American image of sainthood and celebrity, the fawning treatment lavished on him by his successors is too much. Here, we come to the real conundrum of genius. Like Gaudi or Aalto, Wright is genuinely inimitable. Although he may have deluged the world with statements of his architectural principles, his greatness inhered in his forms, in nongeneric "organic" solutions. While principles may be defended, however, forms must be interpreted. The mistake is in thinking that imitating the form serves the principle. There is no Wrightian architecture outside of Wright, and the pale imitations of his disciples inevitably look both tacky and derivative.

Interestingly, the most vibrant line of succession to Wright runs through those architects who managed to break away. Bruce Goff, Herb Greene, John Lautner, and Bart Prince clearly flow in a taxonomic stream with Wright at its headwaters. The film, unfortunately, is completely silent on the question of influence. For an artist as protean as Wright, one would expect not simply a string of monuments but some larger effects on the landscape and consciousness. Burns does not deal with this, because he cannot. If the great genius is as hermetic and Olympian as the film insists, no progeny but acolytes can be produced, and no explanation can ever hope to account.

I enjoy Ken Burns's films a lot. Part of the reason for their success is the feeling that they have been made not simply by an artist but by an enthusiast, by someone truly interested in his subject matter. And this is also part of a problem: the enthusiasm (based on insistent reading of genius that can only be approached by examining all that is not genius) mystifies. There is a sense in these films that Burns is too interested in the subject matter, always presented as primal—and fabulous. Watching *The Civil War*, I was riveted by the tales and images but was never without the feeling that this was a film about the best of all possible civil wars. The same was true of *Baseball*, another film about a masculine cultural monument, about the best of all possible ball games. And the same is true about Wright, presented as the best of all possible architects.

A less obvious legatee of Wright—one for whom Wright was alpha but not omega—is the artist Tony Smith, currently the subject of a fine retrospective at the Museum of Modern Art. Smith started his career as an architect—working for Wright during his Usonian period after the war— and firmly cathected on the forms of Wright's hexagonal mode. For Smith, this geometry of assembly, the issue of creating irregularity and complexity from a regular figure, proved the wellspring for an obsession of a lifetime. But, like Goff or Lautner, he took this preoccupation and moved on with it.

Smith was a distiller who sought to purify his obsessions into eloquent form. For him, the architectural ideas of assembly, geometry, and the repetition of the module formed a point of departure for both his painting and later his sculpture. There is a kind of double cycle in his work, the architectural drawings leading to architectural construction, and the paintings leading to sculpture. The issue, though, is always to achieve the maximum in expression, variety, and nuance, with minimal means. The paintings use a limited palette of both color and shape to run a long set of compositional variations. The big geometrical sculptures for which Smith is best known are likewise preoccupied with the use of forms of consistent section that—through a variety of rotations at the joints—produce an array of forms. In a great work like *Moondog*, such simple sections and joints subjected to variation produce a work of deep complexity, never revealing itself to the viewer the same way twice.

This is very different from the triumphant minimalism of Donald **119**

Judd or Sol LeWitt (which in its dumb dogma shoved Smith somewhat aside), which used ever more reduced geometry (any angle as long as it is 90 degrees) to achieve ever more reduced effects. Admirers of this art also revere its purifying ice, the asymptotic style of the vanishing signifier. Ultimately the box, the square, and the line become art's highest expression because there is simply nothing less to be done. Smith looked for both a grave stability and for surprise. Particularly beautiful is the installation of Smith's big yellow *Light Up* in front of the Seagram Building. Not only is the geometrical counterpoint brilliant, the interaction of the strong yellow with the building's bronze is wonderful.

1998

Inside the Biosphere

At Davis Monthan Air Force Base near Tucson, standing wingtip to wingtip as far as the eye can see, four thousand decommissioned military aircraft stand baking in the Arizona sun. Made surplus by the end of the cold war or simply too old to fly, they await cannibalization, the scrap heap, or a crisis.

Most evocative are the B-52s, hundreds of them in various states of decay, huge wings drooping to the ground. Eerily herded, crewed by rattlesnakes and memories, they stand as an intense moment of the American sublime. Three times a day, a Russian satellite passes over the base to count them. Soon they will be broken up in a final potlatch of mutually assured destruction.

Davis Monthan is a magnificent monument to bad intentions. The government paid over twelve and a half billion dollars to buy those planes and helicopters, and countless billions more to keep them. Producing this stuff—thinking of it—distorted all of our lives. The tragedy is beyond waste: lethality co-opted the edge, became the national experiment. Star Wars and Stealth were official America's visionary mode.

Not far from Davis Monthan sits Biosphere II, a more constructive experiment mating technology and vision. The press has not been kind to Biosphere, treated it as a kind of sporting event. Have they been cheating (that oxygen added to remedy mysterious depletion and to save the gasping inhabitants)? Is the project "scientific"? Does Ed Bass, the man who is footing the $150-million bill, belong to a cult? But these are cavils, barely germane, queries of the wrong category. The real question is simply, what is it?

Physically, of course, it is an enormous, dramatic, space-framed greenhouse, 3.15 acres of the most intensely cultivated territory on the planet. Surrounding it is an extensive apparatus of support: the domed lungs that allow for the expansion and contraction of the air, the power plant and cooling towers that keep the thing at a livable temperature, the administrative and lab buildings, the little tourist village, the Inn at the Biosphere, the Café at the Biosphere. The visual ethos is strictly New Age: glue-lam and domes, whale murals and whimsical sculpture fashioned from detritus salvaged from the bomb lab at Los Alamos. If there were a sound track, it would be Kenny G. or songs of the humpback.

Biosphere is a deeply American place, a bit disingenuous but full of optimism. Predictably, there is that Disneyesque overtone. Billboards on the highway hawk the tour. The logo is as pervasive as Mickey. Instead of Fantasyland, Frontierland, and Tomorrowland, there are the Savannah Biome, the Rain Forest Biome, and the Ocean Biome. The vision is simultaneously loopy and serious, reductive and somehow grand. Like Disneyland or Epcot, Biosphere tries to encapsulate the world. It is a vision of paradise from a long line of visions of paradise, purposive and very particular.

The idea that every place can be anyplace is a historic one. For all the visionary hype, there is something deeply nostalgic about the Biosphere and its project to reproduce and regulate nature. Nature is an outgrowth of modernity, anthropocentric: nature needed to be invented before it could be manipulated. By the eighteenth century, nature had been both aestheticized and scientized, and its "wildness" emerged for the first time. Landscape gardening dilated on the rough or regulated nature of the natural, while philosophy argued about whether it was monstrous or benign.

Architecture joined this and addressed itself both to its own natural origins and to a new project for housing nature, another instance of something born at the instant of necessity: advances in the manufacture of glass and metal allowed the creation of the greenhouse. Capturable, nature became political. With the concurrent exploration and colonization by Europe of much of the rest of the world, nature fell under the acquisitive gaze of the modern imperium. What better place to keep it than a greenhouse.

Exotic winter gardens proliferated in Europe, each a little Eden. Here is a description of a visit to the winter garden of Ludwig II: "With a smile the king drew aside the curtain. I was speechless, for I saw an enormous garden, laid out in the Venetian manner, with palms, a lake, bridges, pavilions, and buildings like castles. 'Come,' said the king, and I followed him fascinated as Dante following Virgil into Paradise." Nature became a simulation of itself. And here is the text from one of the self-guided tour signs that ring Biosphere: "The swaying palms reveal the presence of the balmy trade wind, created by the air-handling units behind the holes in the cliff face."

The linking of the creation of such artificial Edens to a utopian social program was only natural. In the crowded cities of the industrial revolution, these greenhouses were a holiday. In America, however, the utopian garden had a far more visionary dimension. Dolores Hayden quotes a letter written by Ralph Waldo Emerson to Thomas Carlyle in 1840: "We are all a little wild here with numberless projects of social reform. Not a reading man but has a draft of a new community in his waistcoat pocket." Hundreds—thousands—of intentional communities were founded by social and religious reformers across the country.

American communitarians—from the Owenites to the Fourierites to the Perfectionists to the Harmonists—believed their communities and their land were gifts to be perfected, that their irregulated and harmonious relationship with each other was to enjoy a parallel in both their relationship to nature and in the relations within nature that were established under their stewardship. These "peaceable kingdoms" were deliberate microcosms of a larger order, manifestations of a theory about perfection: community was continuous with cosmology. The specific ideas that animated these places sprang variously from science, religion, and their mongrels, much as today.

The Biosphere, then, is long of pedigree. The aura of sympathetic, aestheticized regulation pervades. At the gift shops in the village, the best souvenirs are small glass biospheres, sealed marine environments containing tiny aquatic plants, snails, and shrimp that thrive for years in their sealed enclosures, requiring no more than a bit of light. Biosphere constantly begs the question of how much—how many plants make a savannah, how much water an ocean, how many biomes a world. The fantasy of the Biosphere is no more than this: a closed system, homeostatic and self-sustaining, the project of total autonomy, an American idea out there in everything from Shaker settlements to isolationist foreign policy to the dream of the suburban house to the madness at Waco.

Biosphere is a postmodern utopia under glass. Its mythos is ecology. Its innovation (and its fascination) is not the hoary project of the self-regulating garden—however fascinating—but the relationship of its eight inhabitants to the world beyond the glass. That relationship is vigorous and ubiquitous. Although no one goes in or out, the Biosphere is highly permeable electronically, informationally. This is its most striking transparency. During my visit, I had the sense of the greenhouse's inhabitants being constantly on the phone—wherever we went, somebody was talking to someone on the inside. Indeed, when it came time to interview Mark Nelson, a likable and articulate Biospherean, we spoke via closed-circuit TV.

It was hard to know who was in the fishbowl. We had spent an afternoon doing what tourists do at the Biosphere, prowling the perimeter looking zooishly for human life. When we finally found some—the next morning—it was anticlimactic: just a guy in old clothes puttering in the garden. But it was we who felt on display during the interview, sitting in the TV studio in the administration building, surrounded by technicians and a genial flack, chatting with an adept at such real-time televisual relations.

Nelson's initial answers ran long, tending to familiar-sounding riffs. Progressively, though, things became more relaxed, and a picture of a little culture emerged. Clearly, Biosphere embodies both the pleasures (common beliefs, unity of purpose, special intimacy) and problematics (the artificial uniformity of a world inhabited by eight white folks, hermetic delirium, loneliness) of utopian subjectivity. But what was most striking to me was the normalcy of it all, the way in which life in the Biosphere offered a series of intensifications of more familiar patterns of daily life. The kinds of cultural decisions Nelson spoke about with the greatest animation tended to be those by which the Biosphereans recaptured aspects of the world left behind, three-day weekends and working hours in sync with those of their colleagues on the outside.

I got the impression that the Biosphereans watch a lot of TV. What can you say about a utopia with access to Blockbuster? Certainly, that it is a lot like home. Enclaved against the curious or the malevolent behind tempered glass, fixated on their diets (dramatic drops in weight and cholesterol, two of the central anxieties of postmodernity, should guarantee the commercial viability of a thousand biospheres!), isolated from chemical toxins, and suspended in the electronic nexus, the Biosphere models utopian social and ecological relations on the inside while representing contemporary paranoia in its relationship with the world outside. If Biosphere is resonant architecturally, it is not simply for its many conventional—though very genuine—beauties but because it represents our already daily life in extremis.

Much has been written about the cultish aspects of the leadership cadre at Biosphere, and as far as I know, they may all be artful zombies waiting to be beamed off-planet. The visionary mode needs nuttiness to thrive, both to stir a sense of its own relevance (why live for two years sealed in a glass house, after all) and to protect itself from the skepticism of nonbelievers. But criticism of the cult is a red herring. What makes science science is never the scientist (the "I" is rigorously excluded) but the repeatability of the experiment. Biosphere is not simply repeatable, it is itself a repetition.

The Arizona landscape is especially rich in the compulsion. I had been previously to the cloister at Wright's Taliesin, and so concluded this trip with a visit to Paolo Soleri's Arcosanti, another community long tarred by the distorting charisma of its founder. Again I was skeptical, caught in the seemingly unreconcilable dissonance between those lovely little bronze bells and the megalomaniac megastructure schemes. I was unprepared for the charm of the place itself. Sited facing south on the lip of a little canyon, Arcosanti is at once intimate and elaborate, filled with craft, a cypress-lined hill town with eco-consciousness, and a brave rebuke to the remorseless ugliness and squandering sensibility of Phoenix or Tucson. One forgets, I suppose, that before he set out to save the world, Soleri was simply Italian.

Driving between Biosphere and Arcosanti, we descended into a spectacular, narrow river valley. On the opposite side, a fire was raging. Traffic was backed up, and the flames leapt uncontrolled through the brush. Suddenly, in the sky overhead, a huge airplane appeared. It slowly circled the fire and then raced toward it. The shadow of the big plane dived down ridge after ridge, growing larger and larger until it was over the fire. Suddenly, the plane released an enormous pink cloud of fire-suppressing chemical, flew in front of us and away.

The enormous plane was completely improbable in the place, both too big and too close: unnatural. The sight was easily one of the most amazing I have seen. Like the Biosphere, this was a weird but magnificent intersection of technology and nature, a kind of experiment, an attempt at regulation for some nominal good. The planes at Davis Monthan—an extreme attempt at a technical solution to the problem of "human nature"—are connected to all of this at some bitter, distorted edge. The vexation at Davis Monthan (especially for an aviation junkie like me) is with the sheer formal and technical magnificence of all those machines shoved up against the insanity that required them.

Which brings us back to the question of intentions. As a prototype for communities on Mars, Biosphere is interesting, if less than gripping. As a model of harmonious environmental and human relations on earth, it is quite beautiful. As a paradigm for theorizing the utility of technology, it is a work of exhilarating optimism. The point, after all, is not that we queue up to live in that particular ark, but that we reimagine our relationship to the one we have already got.

1993

Come and Getty

The fantasy was this: against the uniformly dreary assessments of the Getty Center, I would rise in defense of a project that could not possibly be that bad. After all, it has been branded in the press as everything from cultural imperialism to elitism to autoplagarism to gigantism. Burdened by its brush with the millennium, its giant budget, and extended gestation, the Getty has even been saddled, it seems, with a duty to account for the very existence of Los Angeles.

Some of these criticisms would have been advanced for any project on the site that represented such a huge concentration of resources, and the relevance of such old-fashioned styles of bigness and isolation to a city of sprawl where needs and neighborhoods are so evidently dispersed has been legitimately questioned. I, however, have never had any problem with the idea of a big complex on that Brentwood hill. The site, after all, is superb and commanding and clearly not a place for false architectural modesty. And I am down with the idea of an Acropolitan solution, pristine temples glinting in the sun.

Nor does the institutional magnitude of the Getty trouble me. Much of the criticism of the project, understandably, has seen the Getty collection—the museum component—as synonymous with the institution. The collection is not fabulous (although it contains quite a few top-dollar items), but its strengths are more those of an academic collection than a concentration of masterpieces. It is the ancillaries, though, that make this an amazing place: the superb research labs, the luxurious scholars' center with its excellent library, the programs of public education, the grants and conservation subsidies. We do not make institutions like these often anymore, and the creation of the center is more like the founding of a university than the opening of museum. This is one of the strongest arguments for the consolidation, the idea that components will work synergistically in the peripatetic, cross-fertilizing interchanges that only come with concentration.

But, of course, the museum *is* the focus for most visitors, and it is unfortunately the weakest component of the complex architecturally. Disposed in a clumsy set of connected pavilions, the building's logic is to concentrate painting on the upper level and to suggest intimacy by breaking down scale via the pavilionization. The result, though, is a cumbersome and confusing pattern of circulation that—given the proportions of the buildings—gives excess weight to the vertical. I had too many trips up and down stairs, confronted too many elevators, caught in a circulation yo-yo.

The interior spaces are also largely unsatisfying. Much has been made by a variety of writers (including Richard Meier himself, who issued an unprecedented book-length apologia for the project) over the imposition of a decorator—Thierry Despont—with the responsibility for doing up the period rooms in period style. I am strictly with Meier on this one. While I have no problem with museums installing period rooms *from the period,* the generic ersatz is tacky. Even the relatively undecorated rooms are done in lugubrious colors and unimpressive detail. It all feels wrong.

But the real problem is size. Although the upper rooms are based on John Soane's beloved Dulwich museum (Meier himself allowing the historicist camel to poke its nose through the flap), with its high pyramidal ceilings surmounted by skylights, they mainly seem too small. The strategy for intimacy is both out of scale with the grandeur of the enterprise and cramped in absolute terms. And on a Sunday, with thousands of visitors, it is a jungle. To be sure, the natural lighting is pretty pellucid, but the cost in scale and proportion is too high.

Hardly an original insight, still the Getty is in Brentwood, land of O.J. and Monica Lewinsky. The reigning sensibility here is the decorator's, and the Getty certainly begs the alpha question of Angelene decor: what goes? Brentwood answers with a radical eclecticism in which anything goes with anything as long as the decorator agrees. This is more or less the strategy at the Getty (and at most old-line museums of encyclopedic grasp), which collects all over the map: Louis XIV furniture to Old Master paintings to the shards of classical antiquity. The architect and the decorator struggle in a turf war that parallels that of the museum departments in the inevitable battle for space and funds.

The decorator insertions inevitably raise a question that the institution's overwhelming aura of respectability is designed to forestall. The question is kitsch. Meier's mainline modernity is critical in letting the museum rise above its roots, including the legendary kitsch of its predecessor, the reconstructed (with underground parking) Roman villa overlooking the beach at Malibu. That museum is itself being reconstructed by architects of classical inclinations who are treating the phony villa as if it were itself an archaeological site, a *truly* kitschy conceit. **127**

There is another much-spoken-of imposition on the Meier project that also begs this question. At some point in the development of the buildings, the museum, worried, it seems, about Meier's Olympian stiffness, decided to invite the artist Robert Irwin to work on a large formal garden in a cleft between the museum and the scholars' center. This was a portion of the project that Meier himself had already designed, and he was reportedly furious to have yet another collaborator foisted on him. The two were apparently so overcome with mutual loathing that they were unable to connect their two projects. Indeed, the most symbolically fraught moment in the whole complex is a dirt DMZ (as everyone refers to it up on Parnassus) that stretches between Meier's plaza and Irwin's garden. On a rainy day, one slogs through the mud as a result.

Irwin certainly does his bit to advance the kitschiness. Again, there is that sense of disproportion and excess. Tiny mounds of earth are retained behind inch-thick Cor-Ten steel walls, of which there seems to be enough to build a battleship. Hundreds of plant species have been assembled and laid on—reproducing the taste of the institution itself—a floral smorgasbord evoking the sentimentality of surfeit. And the garden has a graceless geometrical order. Although the impulse might seem to tithe Meier—the master geometer—the garden scheme is klutzy and overwrought, filled with circles and switchbacks and undercooked detail, the antithesis of Meier's cool grids and curves.

Even Meier, though, falls into the trap. Modernism is the timeless and self-declared enemy of kitsch. Unfortunately, as the forms age, modernism becomes increasingly engaged in self-recollection, adducing its relevancies via nostalgia and aroma. Nostalgia plus excess equal kitsch, and the Getty is nothing if not excessive. Kitsch compares means and ends, looking for signs of *too much*. Unlike, say, the Baroque, which produced excess by a decorative piling on and elaboration, modernism's special style of excess is founded in repetition.

Meier's kitsch involves both the numerousness of the building elements in the complex and the extreme deployment of his regular kit of parts, the orthogonal grid, the piano curve, the pipe railing. There is a relationship between delicacy and scale, and the sheer repetition of detail—however artful—dulls any sense of the particular. Of course, in Hollywood, the studio standard of quality is tied up in quantity (e.g., *Titanic*), and this is generally a winning formula for kitsch. What seemed precise in the Atlanta Museum or the New Harmony Center becomes—when multiplied to enormous proportions—a blur. Yes, the travertine is a beautiful, sensuous material, but the acres of it at the Getty, used simply as surface, are vulgar.

The neighbors also did their share. Meier, whose whole career has been devoted to making white buildings, was obliged to promise that he would not do so here. Bad move. White is the most volumetric color, and it is Meier's signature. The road to perdition began with the locals' demand that the buildings be beige. And so the complex has been dulled once more by the decorator deal. Most of the metal-cladding panels are indeed of an ambivalent tan, suggesting shade where there is none, dulling the crispness of edge, and adding a needless complication to an architecture that has always sought to pare.

Sentimentality is at the core of kitsch. The Getty shows its sentiment in its studied evocation of the icons of the past. The Acropolis to be sure, the whiff of Tuscany, Hadrian's Villa, Soane, and most especially the now almost parodistic reaching back to the forms of the Corbusian villas, which have long been an inspiration to Meier. Indeed, that referent has long ago ceased to be Corb and has become Meier himself. And this effect is heightened by the fact that there are many Meier buildings on the hillside, facing each other in various juxtapositions. Lacking in irony, Meier's compulsive repetition produces Meierland.

Searching for a reading of multiple buildings, we rely on certain conventions. The acropolis, the campus, the corporate office park, the theme park. The Getty elides all of these. With its mechanical sequences from car to garage to robot train to plaza to café to attraction, it offers more than a suggestion of the Disnoid, a reading reinforced by the touchy-feely ad banners hung on thousands of L.A. lampposts, picturing a young black boy and offering the invitation to visit "your Getty."

In 1967, I spent some months living and working on a kibbutz. Shortly after the Six-Day War, I went to Jerusalem to check things out and offer my services. The task I was assigned was helping to clean up the old Hebrew University campus on Mount Scopus, abandoned to the Jordanians in 1948. Like the Getty, the complex enjoyed a certain Acropolitan splendor, crowning the little mount. The buildings were also the product of one hand, that of Erich Mendelsohn in his Holy Land phase. And Scopus was earth-toned, clad in the luminously gold local stone. Although, at the time, I was unenthusiastic about the rough dressing of the stone (I was into a more Meieresque machined look in my impressionable youth), I came to appreciate the building complex for the way in which it appeared to be not on the hill but of it.

The Getty has many pleasures. The views over the city are incredible, **129** and the landscaping luxuriant. The complex organizes many wonderful internal vistas: the view back from the delightful cactus garden through the museum court to the drum of the rotunda is one of the best and my favorite. The scholars' building is a very good piece of Meier (which means a very good building) and easily the best working environment in the complex. But these are obscured by nuance-dulling extent, by the fact that every detail is too similarly produced, by the fact that the complex does not grow from the site but overwhelms it.

1998

Habitat and After

Habitat gave clarity to one of modernism's main befuddlements: the styles of equality. We know that modernity has both technical and political vectors, that it was enabled by ideas of both science and rights. This conjunction produced a predictable consequence: the attempt to measure the dimensions of right. For architecture, there were a number of implications. Perhaps foremost, housing became the privileged site of architectural modernism. Only logical. Shelter is *the* fundamental right in architectural terms. And mass housing maps a relationship of social breadth, encapsulating a theory of equality: it specifies.

If Marx's great contribution was to clarify the economic engine of history, to show the informative underpinning of economy in virtually every cultural expression, housing provided the spatial analog for the polemic of economic equality. As modernity produced its "new man," his domain was surely to express his rights vis-à-vis property. Housing was to be a principal organ in shaping his attitudes and character. Rationalism and economism, however, were not the only pillars of modernity; a teleological psychologism was also a staple of the age, another scientific notion of "man-environment" relations that further flavored architecture with a spirit of determinism.

The atmosphere of scientific precision that is so characteristic of the age entered the housing question via several axes. One was dimensional, the ongoing debate about the *Existenzminimum,* a kind of quantum of shelter, a suitably hygienic, dignified, and functional unit of housing that would guarantee and describe this basic right. To this day, this discussion has devolved on insanely asymptotic dimensioning, on a measuring of rights by inches. Of course, in a conservative climate in which housing is considered a privilege and not a right, this same obsession with measure is inverted, deformed into a question of excess rather than entitlement.

The therapeutic aspects of the crusade for housing grew, however, not simply from the dimensional or volumetric aspects of equality but also from the character of the space itself. High-modernist housing tended to retain the Calvinist parsimony of character that offered both a kind of chaste, disciplinary atmosphere and the putative rationality of visibility of construction and arrangement that guaranteed a clarity of replicability, the sure knowledge that the characteristics of one's own dwelling would be repeated in those of one's neighbors.

The medium for the creation of these interacting sets of relations was geometry. The association of the grid with the supreme philosopher of rationality, Descartes, reinforced the apparent logic of orthogonality. High modernism is certainly characterized by its zeal for the right angle, for the clarifying therapy of social relations made geometrical. Perhaps no more succinct statement of the impulse is to be found than Ildelfonso Cerda's explanation of his plans for the enlargement of Barcelona: "the squared block is the clear and genuine expression of mathematical equality which is the equality of rights and interests, of justice itself." Squared forms in repetition assumed not simply the aura but the substance of democracy.

This conjunction has been pursued insanely, the putative democratic content of the grid serving as a kind of cover for the sciences of discipline. What are we really to make of the schemes of Hilbesheimer, Gropius, Le Corbusier, of the thralled housing authorities of New York or Chicago and their exaltation of what, retrospectively, can only be seen as landscapes of alienation and incarceration? Then, again, this fantasy of infinite parity is the Janus of the age. What do a billion Chinese in Mao suits tell us, tell them? That all men are equal? That all men are miserable? That no one is in chains? That everyone is in chains?

Modern architecture tends to be read at one extreme or another, either as the good-faith experiment of generations gripped with the desire to put the world right or the delusional communism of dupes and fellow travelers. The real situation, naturally, is more complicated. We are past the point where such uniform readings are the only ones available, and can now look back at an architecture that has long embraced both nuance and productive contradictions. Corb's are emblematic. As theorist, his contribution is all mechanism and megalomania, universal principles and an architecture of mesmerizing replicability. As practitioner, his production speaks of values that spring from sources quite different, of sculptural modulation and the inflections of eccentricity.

All that crisp white architecture produced by the modern movement is, however, not just a fantasy of purity and reflectivity but of a very particular place in the sun. One of European modernism's deepest roots is Mediterranean: the prismatic, sun-dappled modularity of the hill towns of Italy and the villages of North Africa. The accidental "natural" cubism of these places inspired the movement both for its dramatic sculpturality and high-key chiaroscuro, for its primary simplicity, and for its accretive genesis, for the way in which a set of simple volumes acquires, in growth, a labyrinthine complexity. The isolation of modernism from this primary source is one its sad ironies.

Perhaps one of the reasons for this is modernism's much remarked elevation of space over mass and its preference for the legibility of the object over that of the ensemble. Scientific modernism was, in this sense, antiorganic, seeking constant objects in constant relations, an interstice as "squared" and predictable as the objects that hemmed its edges. This universal lack of tension, this insistence of an absolutely continuous and noncontradictory reading is at the heart of modern architecture's failure to produce a habitable urbanism. Its devotion to perfection left no room for the structures of apparent anomaly that the natural world is so brilliant at producing, structures that, indeed, form one of the fundamental consistencies of nature.

Which brings me back to Habitat, to Moshe Safdie's repatriation of modernism to this neglected point of origin. Biography, of course, is an unreliable guide but a convenient source of metaphor, and Safdie's is perhaps too apt. Mediterranean-born and relocated to icy rationalist climes, his architecture—at its own origin—is one of reconciliation. There is something unusually North American about the synthesis. From the start, Safdie has been conscious of his comminglings, happy both in the patterns of village life and in the gleamy technicality of construction. Indeed, it is the frank imagibilty of the ensemble that sets Habitat apart: the image of the village is the medium by which the product of the factory is individuated.

Safdie has invoked the analogy of the automobile industry in describing the project. His use of this comparison, though, seems to be more about mechanization than individuation, about the efficiencies of indoor assembly-line construction rather than the possibilities for a mechanistic entry into the territories of variety. But the life cycle of the American car also suggests a formal mode, the styling of a taste- and function-sensitive envelope offering possibilities for the accumulation of an aesthetic of excess in the susceptibility of the car to customization, addition, and individual whim. One of the joys of Habitat is precisely this: it has accreted all the physical extensions—the awnings, draperies, potted plants, and deck furnishings—of individual occupancy.

Habitat impresses precisely for its openness to such alterations. The relatively mute and prismatic forms of the stacked boxes are especially fine for their failures of coercion, their subtle underexpression. Simple **133** openings, plane surfaces, and copious terraces are exactly the territories of self-expression so well advanced in the North American suburbs. If the Habitat *parti* were to become more general, one would expect the individuation of its elements to become still more particular. Habitat's tragedy, of course, is that it has remained so singular, iconic. The result is a theft of latitude: one does not mess with a work of art. A *community* of Habitats would, one expects, be daubed in competing colors, encrusted with vines, hung with shutters, reglazed with sash, wildly morphed into the flamboyance of form and image of a bourgeois favela (the great sixties addition to the lexicon of democratic architecture's sources). If only. . . .

This paradigm of unspecified extension (as opposed to various overbearing "kit of parts" fantasies that were more or less contemporaneous with it) is Habitat's most important conceptual contribution. It is also here that Habitat's most resonant analogy with the city lies. Safdie was explicit in the urbanistic rationale for Habitat, the idea of combining urban scale and density with the family-object of the suburban pattern. The appeal of the suburbs is a compound of safe homogeneity, open space and fresh air, and—perhaps paramount—a sense of territoriality that extends beyond the walls, the bufferings of a proprietary spatial envelope. Safdie's canniness is in the calibration of the dimensions of this hemming space, in providing an envelopment (not just of the terrace but of the airspace that surrounds the suspended pods on all sides) that is usefully assertive in making a place that each dweller can call his or her own.

It would thus be a mistake to associate Habitat too closely with the culture of pods that grew concurrently with it. Habitat's capsules were always a means rather than an end. One cannot emphasize how pervasive (and pervasively ambiguous) the fantasy of the module was in those days. Habitat is a line strider, disposed between the close-packed nightmare of endless monads, the high-stacked, universally equipped, crouch-height pods of Japanese love hotels and of various delirious filing cabinet fantasies of the hive on the one hand and, on the other, the benign seriality of the idea of a house for everyone, delivered by a technology harnessed for good.

Of course, Habitat was also a victim of a loss of faith. Opened at the apogee of the technological slaughter of Vietnam, it fell afoul both of a society that was favoring guns over butter for its capital investments as well as a more generally rising conviction that large-scale "heavy" technology was the answer to nothing benign. An irony, this, as Habitat was one of the first of the "mass-produced" projects to engage a problematic beyond cost, to incorporate a meaningful theory of contemporary collectivity. *For Everyone a Garden* is the title of one of Safdie's books, and the argument that it (and Habitat) embraces is transformative: architecture should take as its ambition the provision of a fragment of paradise for everyone, not the just the regressive calculus of the minimum turf of daily existence.

The series of unrealized projects that followed Habitat, including a variety of sisters and brothers initiated in the flush of enthusiasm for the new system and then abandoned by failures of commitment to the necessary scale of its industrial aspect, are sad witness to a general decline of the sciences of optimism and their displacement by the decade and a half of suspicion and venality that followed the collapse of the sixties. Of particular poignancy is the unbuilt project for a student union at San Francisco State University, scene of some of the most vigorous student activism of the time (presided over by the ridiculous repressions of its president S. I. Hayakawa). The union project pointed the way to Habitat's logical advance, refining the module, embodying a much more activated notion of user input, and—most dramatically—realizing Habitat's destiny as artificial topography, inhabited mountain, its outer surface almost completely negotiable. A beautiful direction.

It is another of Habitat's historical ironies that the first instance of the construction of a seminal idea was also the end of the road. This is a characteristic Habitat shares with a nearly contemporaneous project, which both crystallized and finalized another set of ideas dear to architectural modernity. The Plateau Beaubourg also stood for a juncture between technology and freedom but reconciled them in terms of potential rather than individuation. This was another of the beaux ideals of modernity, the anticipating void, the idea of "equipotentiality," the location of the idea of malleability in the absence of intervention, the space of all possibilities awaiting freedom's own (unspecified) creativity, space that could in its nonparticularity be (potentially) all things to all people.

The well-serviced shed attempted to do much of the same conceptual work as the metastasizing pod. At Beaubourg, football-field-sized spaces, open and untrammeled, were supported by the migration of all structure and services to the building perimeter or to deep "servant" (technology also takes care of the class system) interstices between floors. These voids were to await the defining particularities of an endlessly shifting flow of use. This is a fantasy that clearly has its limits, too coy about its own modulations and necessarily deeply invested in the specific tectonics of its long-spanning strategies. The pressure is for the greatest possible leap **135** as that which liberates the greatest possible set of potentials. Size is crucially bound to possibility in this expressive economy.

Habitat suggests a more nuanced strategy for the collaboration of structure and complex possibility. In Safdie's initial design, Habitat isolated its dwelling pods from the structure that supported them, a "plug-in" in the lingo of the time. In this incarnation, the form of the dwelling cliff faces was very much subordinated to the heroic tectonics of the apparatus of support, taking on a megascaled rhythm and regularity. In the reduced scheme eventually built, however, the means of support has been incorporated into the pods themselves, yielding a far richer and more eccentric statical condition. To me, this is one of the beauties of Habitat: the complexities of its loading and the fiendish negotiated transfer of the forces that stabilize the structure. Here is a fine metaphor for the culture of cooperation that informs the city of real choice, each element playing its singular part in a structure that is sustained by a complex negotiation among it citizens/components.

We are once again at a moment in architecture in which the sources of form have become a troubled subject, in which the bases of architecture's authority are in dispute. Habitat provides what remains a remarkably coherent set of arguments about the origins of form, invoking both rationalism's orders of objectivity in construction and purpose but leavening their mathematical reduction with a vision of life. For Safdie, abstraction is a medium for solving the problems of housing a vibrant daily existence, not an end-all means for *representing* the character of modern living. Logical, too, that Safdie's best post-Habitat work signals a more literal return of modernism's Mediterranean repressed, inspired by the glowing simple modularities and complex ensemble of Jerusalem.

1998

MOR Is Less

In an embarrassment (of this more later) of riches, the Museum of Modern Art in New York currently boasts *three* architecture shows, surely a record. There are "Fabrications," a set of installations in the garden that is part of a joint project with the Wexner Center at Ohio State and the San Francisco Museum of Modern Art; a retrospective of the work of Alvar Aalto on the main floor; and in the design galleries, an exhibition of the submissions of the three finalists for the recent competition for the museum's own expansion.

The first architectural piece I wrote for the *Village Voice* covered a retrospective exhibition of Aalto's work at MoMA, which would seem to put him on about a twenty-year cycle. I was and am an Aalto enthusiast, but—in spite of close attention paid—he has always been a somewhat elusive figure. It is not simply the usual inaccessibilities of hard-drinking genius, it is that Aalto falls afoul of the main historiographical lines of interpretation of modern architecture. On the one hand, he lies outside the Miesian-Corporatist strain of late functionalism. On the other, his work—with its delicacy, curvilinearity, and warm materiality—cannot really be compared to the thick plasticity of the Corbusian line, despite kindred organicisms.

What Aalto lacks—to his credit—is an old-fashioned sense of the heroic: his was a nonhistrionic style of genius. This is true of his sparse polemical writings and especially of his architecture, all about comfort and the wash of architecture into its environment. What steel was to Mies, concrete to Corb, and brick to Kahn, wood is to Aalto, the sensualist. Mies, Corb, and Kahn were—in many ways—architects of the nineteenth century, representing the spatial destinies of industrialization and integrating their new possibilities with a known history, stretching back to Schinkel, Boullée, even the Romans, a tradition that found its highest expression in monumentality.

Aalto represents a rupture. In his elegant domesticity, his transcendence of austerity, and his remarkable and rich materiality—deep blue ceramic tiles, birch paneling, columns wrapped in leather—Aalto preferred his pleasure more directly, straight from the bottle, as it were. His episodic buildings resist the reductive whole, preferring an unfolding accumulation of quirky delights. For Aalto, the idea of the integration of building and landscape holds the status of principle, and this pervasive sense of flow is not simply a by-product of a scrupulous *Raumplan,* it is parcel of Aalto's conviction that the membrane separating in and out should be as invisible as possible, that sitting in the living room, one also sits in the woods.

Curves—like the shape of a musical line—have great particularity, Aalto's curves are the best architecture has produced. This is partially a matter of taste and partially a reflection of the way in which those curves were found. For Aalto, the sources were embedded in whatever corner of the unconscious produces an affinity for shape but also in nature. That is not to say that Aalto lifted his shapes directly from natural forms, but that many of his curves are the result of a collaboration between the will to curve and the character of the environment through which the curve was to pass.

At Baker House, Aalto's superb dorm at MIT, the sinewy bend of the building is wiggled by Aalto's desire to give the riverfront rooms views *along* the Charles and not simply across it. In the apartment house at Bremen—a rare Aalto high-rise—the curve in the facade is the result of a graceful reconciliation of apartment layouts, the freedom of the wrist, and the desire to orient each opening to maximize solar exposure over the course of the day and the seasons. In the spectacular auditorium at Otaniemi, near Helsinki, the regular curve of the plan is derived from the play of sunlighting, acoustics, and the drama of its own geometry.

One always hears the same complaint directed at architecture shows, based on the simple fact that what is on display is not, after all, the building. Gripes I have read about the Aalto show take essentially the same line, focusing on a lack of prima facie evidence—models, drawings, photos, and videos being somehow not enough. Of course, an architecture show can *only* be about artifacts prior or anterior to the building, and this can be quite OK—indeed, it forms the challenge in mounting such a show. The advantage of the museum is in its careful exposure and arrangement of originating documents, not as a space of spatiotemporal economy, the institution that saves a trip to the site. The best architecture shows teach us something about the way in which an architect *imagines,* and the Aalto show offers a stunning dose of sketches and working drawings, of models from the office, not to mention of the amazing glass and furniture pieces at which Aalto was peerless. I was blown away by the directness of his technique and the succinctness of his imagination. I keep thinking, in particular, of a sectional model of the Maison Carrée near Paris in which all that is shown is the shape and thickness of the rooflike upper story and the line of the ground plane. It is one of the pithiest models ever made.

"Fabrications"—the show in the garden—is, on the other hand, an exhibition in which privilege is given to the work "itself," not its representation. The catalog is explicit on this point, proposing that the installations are a kind of redress for the analogous content of most architecture shows. Twelve architects were invited by three museums to fabricate installations inspired by a set of vague thematics: "bodybuildings," "full scale," and (at MoMA) the "tectonic garden." I have seen both the SFMOMA and MoMA shows (although not the Wexner), and the results are fair to good. Although there is no doubt of the presentness of the work, the physical inhabitation of the literal and conceptual space of the museums does not—by and large—beg any particularly pregnant questions. And the familiar materiality—so much metal and glass—of the MoMA pieces contributes to the sense of ho-hum.

Indeed, of all three shows at MoMA, Aalto is about as outlaw as it gets. Even the youthful contributors to the "Fabrications" show (MoMA installment) seem tepid and old-fashioned, out of doors merely. The one exception is the work of a young collaboration called "Office dA." Very much of the moment formally—especially in its concern with the mock-Deleuzian fold—the pair has made a flamboyant, stairlike, folded metal screen that soars up and over the MoMA garden wall (while leaning on it for support). The combination of conceptual simplicity and formal extravagance of the piece is most winning. In San Francisco, I was taken with a big felt piece by Kuth/Ranieri that erodes a long gallery wall with a space that can actually be occupied.

Speaking of occupation, le tout New York has been gibbering for what seems like years over the Modern's proposal for another expansion. Given the city's almost total lack of commitment to avant-garde (or even good) architecture, this competition—with the certainty of a constructed outcome—attracted a certain level of hope. Not that there was any strong reason for this. MoMA's expansions over the years have had a decidedly MOR flavor, whether Philip Johnson's mock-Miesian end pieces or Cesar Pelli's mock-Miesian garden expansion and condo tower. This sort of refined but less than daring taste was reinforced as the local standard by the one synthesizing and polemical show of the current curatorial regime, the enjoyable "Light Constructions" of a couple of years ago.

That show exhibited a clear and consistent enthusiasm for a crisply **139** wrought late-modernist stylistics, compounded from an industrial palette (especially glass) and highly austere in its geometries. This was a neofunctionalist architecture, modernism for a post-technological scene. The resituation pointed up a crucial fact about the fate of modernism, illustrating that its forms and structural strategies could no longer advance any real claim to being in the technical vanguard. Indeed, what struck me most in "Light Constructions" was the emergence of a particular new building type—the "Media Center"—preoccupied with an attempt at reconciliation between modern architecture and the technologies of virtuality that seek to supplant it. On the one hand, these buildings (whether by Koolhaas, Herzog and de Meuron, Ito, or Meccanoo) are consistently cubic, as if that most platonic architectural form were the best hope for substantiating the vagaries of the ephemeral program. And on the other, all of these buildings seemed to be about the idea of a signaling skin, the conversion of the surfaces of the buildings into a space of projection or representation, on which fleeting electronic images would serve the function of architecture. Whether one sees this as an apotheosis of turn-of-the century fascinations with illumination and advert, vulgar Venturian semiotic revenge or simply another rendition of the metaphor of the cave, the dissipation of the power of physical construction (the power that "Fabrications" makes a stab at recovering) was surely one of the problematics usefully engaged by the show.

All three of the competition finalists are squarely (and unsurprisingly) in the Light Constructions camp. Herzog and de Meuron (who most handicappers thought would not win because they already have the project to do the expansion of the Tate in London, a presumptive MoMA rival) produced a competent scheme with a truly misbegotten stump of a tower as its main visual feature. The real strength of this firm, though, was unrevealed by its boards; the suave elegance of detail for which they are known would, presumably, have been elaborated in design development.

Bernard Tschumi—an earlier subject of a solo show at the Modern as well as one of the famous MoMA Decon cohort—produced the most impressively massed and expressed scheme of the final three. Formally speaking, Tschumi is also a modernist revivalist and very European in sensibility. He was certainly my pick and struck me—for professional, political, and architectural reasons—as a shoo-in, although his scheme did have circulation problems and a somewhat uncompelling ground-floor plan. The real causes of his failure to get the commission are doubtless mired in the politics of the moment. Indeed, commissions of this sort—especially given the undramatic (if real) nature of the differences among the finalists—are often decided on the basis of with whom the client feels the highest comfort level. Which is to say, the reason for the failure to win is most likely because someone (and there is plenty of speculation as to whom) did not like Bernard.

The winner of the competition, Yoshio Taniguchi, a Japanese architect relatively little known in the United States, all of whose (extensive) work to date has been in Japan, certainly delivered a well-organized project, carefully attuned to the Lite spirit. Its entry level is clearly the best of the three, and it solves the key question of the expansion—where to put the café—with gracious aplomb. In its way, the project also inverts (and renders static) the media center proposition. Behind facades of perfect blandness, there will lie the extraordinary collection of framed images in the museum collection—snapshots of modernity. This is very much in line with the idea of effacement that lay at the core of Light Constructions. Indeed, this is very much in line with the idea that has lain behind the successive expansions of MoMA, a conceptual preservationism in which virtue is assigned to strategies of literal and qualitative continuity with what is. The Taniguchi scheme offers a compelling caution against the devolutionary effects of taking cues from this particular context, the gridded glass curtain walls of its predecessors.

The show of the finalists was called "Rethinking the Modern." Unfortunately, the rethink *revises* nothing.

1998

Far, Far AwAIA

Here is the nightmare. Vincent Scully has been taken ill. I find myself at the lectern in the front of a darkened auditorium as pairs of slides flash on the screen. The pressure is on for a lecture both witty and deep. I do not recognize most of the buildings.

Crouched over a loupe, staring at pairs of slides of the winners of the 1997 AIA awards, I am having a similar feeling. The pressure is a little more attenuated, but it is still the job of an old-style CIA Kremlinologist, trying to come to sweeping generalizations from satellite photography. This is a risky business at best: after years of analyzing the May Day guest list atop Lenin's tomb, they still missed the collapse of Communism.

Certainly, one of the striking things about the *representation* of the awarded work is the classic depopulated quality of the photographs. Emptiness is one of the stable characteristics of architectural photography, the perennial assumption that the most essential image of a building is one in which the inanimate is foregrounded. This is not trivial, however familiar the lament. As architecture is increasingly mediated by the mechanics of publicity, such standard tropes of observation increasingly come to stand for architecture itself. The risk is that the values of the photograph more and more double back to inform the character of building, arguing against an episodic and changeable architecture and for more totalized and graspable forms.

A striking case in point among the winners is the very extensively published Neurosciences Institute by Tod Williams and Billie Tsien. Seeing the project presented in one or two photographs over and over, I could not form a picture of it until I finally saw a set of drawings. The sophistication of this building is firmly elusive to conventional photography, at least to the kind of conventional photography that seeks to capture the work in a single view. The camera—with its established routines of framing and its preference for the iconic—circumvents the *parti*, the real fundamentals of order. But this is a building that resists summary, and it is a testament to the suppleness of the design that it seems to evade adding up when reduced.

Still, there does seem to be some territory for generalization: looking at the pairs of photographs the AIA has supplied, I can only observe that the group of projects selected is very clean indeed. The buildings appear much like their photographs, crisp, well composed, no mess anywhere, nothing challenging to easy comprehension. Perhaps in the wake of the decorative excesses of postmodernity, the AIA is simply trying to lower the temperature. They have succeeded: the awarded work is consistent if very slightly hybrid in feeling—almost all of it comfortable under the unmodified rubric of "modern architecture." The historic creeps in either in the several fine renovations premiated or in structures—such as a guest house in Mississippi, a little housing project, and several buildings described as the legatees of "California modernity"—which directly riff familiar forms. It is all very fastidious, inflected rather than inspired.

Looking at this work, I was struck with the impression that all of it seemed to be from one place, somewhere kempt and peaceful and very upper middle class, a world of fine homes and guest houses (for, among others, Bill Gates), of prestige universities, of mammoth convention centers, of ad agencies, of expensive boutiques and glamorous hotels, of public libraries in good neighborhoods. Even the low-cost housing is suburban. To be sure, there is an indecipherable redo of a Pruitt-Igoe–style public project in Baltimore, but it is a token, another historic renovation—urban public housing being something from a bygone era. Taken all together—and despite claims to the contrary—this is a collection of buildings that share a sense of place, never mind it is everywhere. Perhaps this is inevitable in a global environment in which regionality is so malleable it seems like affectation.

The big-scale, from scratch, urbanism is much the same. The two schemes awarded are both in fairly exotic situations—Honolulu and Ho Chi Minh City—and are big, decent, if not particularly innovative projects. Not to overplay the CIA metaphor, but it does seem that if SOM is directing the urban future of Vietnam, creating a glamorous haven for multinationals in old Saigon, it may be that we won the war after all. What is most striking about the urbanity of the winners taken as a whole, though, is that most are projects for communities of modest, suburban scale. There is a kind of arcadia here, a place that seems far away from the real problems of cities, a place where things work, where density is low and cleanliness high, where things are easy and the weather is always warm—the "new" urbanism. And this gives me a little chill: one movement's suburban paradise is another's gated community.

Which brings me back to the question of the people missing from these images. Although humans never appear, plant life often does. The **143** subjectivity of plants—visible in the perfect arrangements of flowers (never food) on the dining room table, the elegant oak in the foreground, the garland of leaves surrounding the long shot—comes to stand in for human subjectivity in this sunny universe. Certainly, over the past decade or so, architects have come to be more and more sensitized to questions of the environment and of ecology. What these representations suggest to me is that the "environment" (something that continues to be represented as essentially outside human ecology) has become a surrogate for human occupation, which—unlike the well-disciplined plant—has the effect of messing up architecture.

Reading through this photography, most of the winners do seem to be fine buildings, some exciting. But—as an inveterate New Yorker—I am left with the feeling that these projects—taken all together—are celebrations of a place where I spend very little time, a place that may not even exist. Except, of course, in the magazines.

1997

Amazing Archigram

1964 was the year of the great British Invasion. Capped by the world historical appearance of the Beatles on the Ed Sullivan Show, a deluge of male rock groups, including not simply the Fab Four but the Rolling Stones, the Searchers, the Animals, Jerry and the Pacemakers, and Herman's Hermits, took control of the charts and held on for almost a decade.

The British Invasion was, among other things, the return of the repressed. In the post-Elvis years, American rock and roll had become anemic and stupid, filled with Fabians and Bobby Rydells, Elvis wanna-bes whose music was both saccharine and almost completely disconnected from the blues-based sources that formed the foundation for Elvis's own great leap. Independently, the Brits rediscovered Chuck Berry, Little Richard, and earlier blues titans like Howlin' Wolf and Big Bill Broonzy and reconstituted, electrified, and transformed a tradition that we had squandered. At the same time, they Europeanized rock by introducing their own sonorities and sensibilities and opened the door for globalized production.

But rock and roll was not the only restoration happening in Britain. In 1960, Archigram, a collaboration of Warren Chalk, Peter Cook, Dennis Crompton, Ron Herron, David Greene, and Mike Webb, coalesced and began an inventive run that in many ways paralleled that of the Beatles, including the ultimate, amicable split and the continuation of a number of solo careers. Like the Beatles, Archigram was not founded on clarion principles but came together almost casually, like-minded lads with a childhood in common and the desire to jam. And like the Beatles, Archigram reconnected with an abandoned tradition, reinvestigating sites mainstream architecture had written off—machines in the garden, the joys of consumption, the universal family of the object, the circus of new ideas.

That they were lads was not entirely irrelevant to what they became. The work of Archigram is filled with both a boy's love of technology and a certain testosterone confidence. The group was part of a historic British movement—visible in a line of engineered structures running through the Crystal Palace, the *Dreadnought,* the Firth Bridge, the Sopwith Camel, and the E-Jag—which by the end of the nineteenth century had roared past a main-line architectural tradition fallen into nostalgia. The progenitor of this school of British design was Isambard Kingdom Brunel, the great nineteenth-century engineer and builder of, among other things, much of the British railway system. Brunel was a systems thinker who joined a romance with the forms of technical construction to a global reach, apt to the high noon of Empire.

But what happens to megalomania when leavened by the Beatles and the Goons, by the simultaneous skepticism and optimism that mark the sixties? Early Archigram was not shy about Bucky-style scope, about the sort of technological utopianism that was soon to crash and burn in the "rage at the machine" that sought to overthrow the blind halcyon of an Americanized fifties. These projects were big-scale, focused on a variety of "plug-in," "walking," and other mechanized fantasies of the city of the future. But they also sought to harness the apparatus of global production and consumption to what seemed to be a more progressive, democratic vision of urban invention.

The political side of this work—part of a current of the times—was sited in the idea of malleability, the idea of consumer choice applied to the environment, a synthesis of optimized technology, nomadism, miniaturization, and the giddy styles of customization founded in Detroit. Of course, functionalism—the received architecture of the day—had advanced a similar agenda. But because of functionalism's philosophical roots in the utopian socialist tradition, the forms it preferred had a more narrowly industrial content, and the "lifestyle" it idealized tended to a dreary good-taste proletarianism, workers flats furnished from the MoMA gift shop.

One of the ironies of the modernist so-called machine aesthetic was that it was not all that machinelike. To be sure, it was austere and often highly "machined" both in its smoothness and in the use of materials of industrial origin. But the prismatic, white, orthogonal architecture of the International Style owed far more of its form and massing to the traditional building culture of the Mediterranean than to any riff on machinery. By Archigram's inception, a deep, cookie-cutter dreariness was predominant in British and world architectural culture. Gone were the brighter days of modernity when architecture bore the aura of progress and social amelioration. What was new was the New Brutalism, expressed either in an aggressive austerity or in a Corb-influenced heavy concrete. Although there was much intelligence in this work, there was little joy.

This was the kind of architecture that expressed the anger of angry young men (and women).

Archigram—never angry in either mood or form—was thinking about something else: Gropius could never have imagined the Cushicle, architecture reduced to a pneumatic suit. To be sure, much of their early work showed their thrall to the big constructions of the era, the skyscrapers and moon shots and refineries. But this was leavened by another set of images that included not only the Spitfires and Meccano sets of their common childhood but also the rogue architecture of the fun-fair with its roller coasters and parachute jumps, a highly elaborated and very refined construction technology devoted to the production not of goods but of pleasure.

And Archigram were *Brits,* frank exponents of a sweet petit-bourgeois sensibility that had little use for the class-based architectures of tradition (or, for that matter, the class-bashing architecture of modernity). Archigram started not simply from the refinements of metal joinery but from a love for the Britain of toby mugs and caged budgies, of flying aspidistras and Callard and Bowser's toffees. This may be the root of the group's strongest contribution, the loving domestication of technology and the clear consciousness that taste had a role to play in the mediation of means and uses. Perhaps more than any other architects, Archigram made a lunge at the throat of the parsimonious aesthetic of modernity, putting the fun back in functionalism.

In an essay about Archigram, Barry Curtis excavates a (then) famous fifties publication, the "Eagle," a weekly comic strip featuring both boldly and complexly imagined Captain America–style images of a heroic sci-fi future filled with moral, artistic, and technical hyperbole as well as intoxicating cutaways of current technology, sections through the Morris Mini, the Comet, and so on. This is certainly a nice source both for a certain conceptual enthusiasm and for the reborn aura of benign technology. Archigram borrows both from these images and from the way in which the "Eagle" collapses analysis and fantasy. There is a beautiful, innocent positivism about the way in which contemporary innovations seamlessly blend with a happy hypothesis about a future in which every subject would have superpowers, a sensibility now drowned in the maelstrom of dystopianism that characterizes sci-fi.

Even more consequential, though, is the deeply resonant drawing style of the magazine. For Archigram, as for the "Eagle," there is the combination of the technical (per Mike Webb's obsessive perspectives and fiendish compound curves, for example) with the cartoon. Indeed, the **147** cartoon—a vehicle for narrative—emerges as a primary instrument of meaning for Archigram. In the pre-computer, pre-video (but high tele-visual) age in which Archigram grew up, time (particularly the kind of big sweep projective time of the futurist) lived in narrative. The sixties were a time of rebirth and reappropriation for the depth of cartooning. In the United States, R. Crumb—the Daumier of the drop-out—produced what may be—along with a variety of psychedelic ephemera—the most enduring visual imagery of the era. Unconstrained by the hyperaestheti-cized standards of modernity and abstraction, or by the strictures of "good taste," Crumb collapsed raunch and charm to brilliant effect.

While Archigram cannot exactly be called raunchy, they certainly moved in the spirit of pop. And like the Beatles, Archigram went straight to the source. Strikingly, the Archigrammers are near contemporaries of Robert Venturi, who plays a learned Fabian (in both senses) to Archi-gram's mop tops. Both aimed at an architecture that tapped into a vivid cultural lode, at acquiring a set of images and procedures just entering the pale of art. Archigram's appropriation, though, was drafted into ser-vice at the source: this *was* their culture. Venturi took a more mediated, anthropological approach, journeying like Richard Burton to the Mecca of Vegas, producing wimpy building that foundered on its own compro-mise, on the idea that pop-cultural sources needed to be transformed to enter the state of Architecture, and on his own private absorption with the classical tradition (and, indeed, with tradition in general in the T. S. Eliot sense). Venturi wound up as an astute swordsman of the signifier in the best postmodern fashion. Archigram was never much interested in signification, but with objects. And with fantasies both gentle (not gen-teel) and exciting.

The gentle style of Archigram may have been its undoing. Over time, their trajectory became more and more arcadian, more and more hippie mode, less and less edgy. By the later sixties, Archigram's work had be-come increasingly preoccupied with its own invisibility, with a weight-less nomadology. The various manifestations of a "bugged ground," the Logplugs and Rockplugs and Quietly Technologized Folk Suburbias, the Hedgerow Village, the Crater City, the Prepared Landscape, all stood for a crisis in optimism that must surely have been informed by the mis-appropriated technology of the war in Vietnam, with its own prepared landscape of the electronic battlefield and its co-optation of the ro-mance and potential beneficence of the machine for murder. As we de-foliated Asia, the movement for a more rational sense of global ecology was born, and Archigram must have concluded that the only logical means of resisting was to fight to leave things pretty much alone. At least on the surface.

The end of Archigram began in a perverse moment of success and failure. In 1969, Archigram won a competition for an entertainment center in Monaco. The project they proposed was for a big domed, circular hall, buried underground in a park along the Mediterranean. All the essential late-Archigram ideas were here: the building disguised in the landscape, the double-tiered overlay of technology and arcadia, the population of helpful machines. Below the dome, the building was completely flexible: seats, toilets, lighting, and so on all autonomous wheeled creatures ready to be reassembled at a moment's notice to accommodate new uses and configurations. It was a wonderful realization of Archigram's master fantasy, the circus. The bestiary of parts, the rock-palace-big-top filled with its disco synesthesia of cathode and strobe, the throngs at play had all been made ready for the real.

Unfortunately, the project collapsed, and with it, it seemed, the energy went out of Archigram. It is a widely noted irony that Archigram's obvious masterpiece was eventually constructed by someone else, Renzo Piano and Richard Rogers's Beaubourg Center in Paris. Here, finally, was the built version of Archigram's heroic early program. Not simply was the Beaubourg a monument to their hyperserviced mechanical metallic shed, it was premised on that idea of flexibility that served as a politics for so much of the architecture of the time. If Beaubourg (built in France) is the founding monument of British hi-tech, Archigram (built in air) was the founding sensibility, the first to make the persuasive synthesis.

While Archigram may have been the last great architects of the twentieth century, there is no doubt that they are also among the first of the twenty-first. Environmentalists avant la lettre, Archigram deeply disturbed architecture's flow, chipping away at its sense of discontinuity, eliding it with fields of objects and dreams. For Archigram, there was no need for tension between consumption and self-determination, between malleability and stability, between expendability and conservation, between high culture and low, and between freaks and swells. The proof was in the drawing, and for a generation (mine), those drawings changed everything.

1998

Admitting the Fold

One of the problems of living in New York is the Visiting Fireman Question, the call from an out-of-town colleague who wants to know what interesting new buildings to see. This is tough. While plenty have been built in recent years, their interest has generally been more cautionary than aesthetic, examples of too big, too commercial, too bland, too bad. Major projects in the city have gone to business-as-usual corporate firms, while local talents languish at home with shop fronts, interiors, and competitions and build their careers out of town. By my estimate, the last really convincing building in Manhattan was the Ford Foundation, and that was thirty years ago.

The situation seems to be changing a bit. Two buildings in particular—one just finished, one just started, both smallish—offer hope. The most promising of these is Raimund Abraham's Austrian Cultural Institute on East Fifty-second Street, a tough but dramatic and beautifully disciplined little tower with a cascading, guillotine-like glass front, just emerging from the ground. The other is the newly completed twenty-three-story LVMH (the French luxury goods conglomerate) tower on East Fifty-seventh by Christian de Portzamparc, a fifty-five-year-old Frenchman who, improbably young, won the Pritzker Prize a few years back.

Both buildings are clear responses to local zoning constraints, our municipal prosody. Because of New York's complex system of air-rights transfers, density maxima, and sky-exposure setbacks, the law has produced a characteristic building type: the "sliver," skinny buildings rising to twenty or thirty stories midblock, as if a row house had simply shot up. While there are good arguments to be made about the negative effects of this densification—on urban character, crowding, and shadowing—sliver buildings have happily restored some sense of vertical proportion to a building type—the skyscraper—grown too fat. And they have opened up a fine field for formal research, if few, so far, have risen to the challenge.

East Fifty-seventh between Fifth and Madison Avenue in Manhattan—site of the LVMH tower—is a block very much about things in a row, lined with deluxe boutiques, Escada, Burberry, Hermes, Chanel (not to mention—culture, location, and rents being what they are—Swatch, Levi's, and Niketown). In fact, Chanel itself occupies a new sliver tower right next door to LVMH, all dignified granite and regular setbacks, a classic wedding-cake profile Marcel Marceauing up the sky-exposure plane. It is typical of the type: good scale, careful detail, dull.

LVMH is a more lively. While housing the same uses as its neighbor, LVMH manages the legal requirement to move mass away from the street by both stepping back in the traditional way and by folding its facade inward. The organizing compositional move is a slightly curving diagonal running from lower left to upper right, the right side of the building pushed forward, and the left folded back. This angling seam is reinforced by a difference in materiality: greenish to the left and sandblasted panes— wonderfully white—to the right. At night, neon tubes along the seam wash light effects over the building.

Without question, this facade is a leap forward by local standards, a complex object with its push-pull, creases, and bulges. The building's angularity and glassiness enliven the street, provide unexpected views, and relieve midtown's relentless orthogonality. And because of the tiny site, the building's floors are usefully small (if largely lightless save for the front offices, enforcing the usual hierarchies). The architectural pièce de résistance, however, is an exhilarating, thirty-foot-high, glassed-in party space at the top, with a curving stair designed for fabulous entrances, an aerie surely destined to become one of the city's most sought-after party rooms. May the supermodels and CEOs enjoy it!

A recent publication of Portzamparc's work includes a set of studies for LVMH, which—they reveal—started life as a cubist composition—a still life with highly autonomous, pretty Euclidean parts—and moved by stages to its present form. Although the final version struggles to be a rose unfolding (even the flacks are retailing the floral metaphor), grasping at the conceit of kinesis, it recalls its origins as a pile of shapes. The elegant new skin feels like it is drawn over the old body, a form caught somewhere in the middle of its own evolution.

Part of the problem here is admittedly my own taste. I am a devoted and emotional connoisseur of curves, and I have always found Portzamparc's clumsy. And the work simply seems undercooked to me, without persuasive detail, not an opinion—judging by the hype—universally shared. On Fifty-seventh Street, it is not just that the curves lack the lovely line of an Alvar Aalto or a Jorn Utzon, the facade feels confined. Hemmed in by thick horizontals that mark the top of the building and the second floor like pieces of some remnant entablature, and bookended on both sides by neighboring structures, the building looks like it is in a box, resting on the glass of the Vuitton shop front.

In a recent piece, in which he compared LVMH's style to art deco, Herbert Muschamp, architecture critic of the *New York Times,* cheered Portzamparc for standing outside the camp of "theory," therefore, presumably, lending him, in the innocence of his artistry, extra conceptual heft. Although Muschamp's view of Portzamparc as nature boy may or may not be on the money, he misses a point about the origins of LVMH's style. Those forms are not accidental but very much the product of "theoretical" research—particularly the "folded" facade Muschamp so admires.

For some time, many architects—anxious at the loss of architectural meaning through commercialization, bureaucratization, Disneyfication, simulation, and the other assaults of modernity and post—have been enthralled with philosophy, especially (like everyone else) recent French theory. One of the ideas that has made the rounds has been a version of the concept of the "fold" elaborated by Gilles Deleuze. This idea is extremely difficult—descending from Leibniz—and requires some knowledge of mathematical theory (though Deleuze himself "organicizes" the notion). *This* idea of the fold has almost nothing to do with the mechanical and spatial logic of folding paper or fabric (or buildings). Architecture theorists, however, have pounced on the concept and destroyed it by reducing it to a metaphor.

It has, however, proved an extremely *useful* metaphor—folds have been tearing up the schools and magazines for years. A final review at Columbia or the AA is likely to include at least one project done in amazing computer-generated folds. Most recently, Peter Eisenman, guru of such theory-as-metaphor-driven practice has done a number of projects for buildings that are more or less creased, including a new proposal for Manhattan's West Side rail yards, a huge lateral version of the LVMH facade. While it may be refreshing to encounter an architect, like Portzamparc, with no need to pre-certify the intellectual content of his work, both the metaphor and the forms do have a history.

Portzamparc's work is simply *derivative:* his projects always look vaguely familiar. This is no crime. But is there actually a difference between origin and spin-off? Architecture is flailing for paradigms these days, and the angularity and dynamism of a large group of "deconstructivist" architects (including Eisenman)—whose theoretical ad hocism has led them from Derrida to Deleuze with many detours on the way—

form one of the strongest available. This bank of images clearly appeals to Portzamparc, who uses similar-looking moves at LVMH. But he uses them simply to cover an object, not to invent or structure one.

Why deride the derivative? It is mainly the magpie question, the architect who takes hold of an idea that is developing, does his best with it, but does not really advance the research, does not invent any new detail, does not get under the skin. LVMH is all surface, it lacks a genuinely *tectonic* character, fails satisfyingly to integrate form and structure. This is what those studies really show: as Portzamparc moves from the prismatic assemblages of the early models to the folded final version, nothing changes but the look. A "folded" skin is drawn over a massing arrived at on the basis of the previous tectonic conceit, the image of the pile.

Architecture's fascination with Theory is, among other things, a search for a successor to functionalism, the logic that has always been modern architecture's ultimate claim for itself, the succinct mating of form and use. A tectonic idea of architecture is more purely physical, describing the union of form and means. A satisfying tectonic of folds must involve their fundamental physical properties, the inherently structural character of the fold (think of the way a folded piece of paper gains strength or of the fold-producing interaction of tectonic plates). Portzamparc's work is derivative—not a part of the research—because the tectonic is eliminated, reduced to decoration, just angles.

Portzamparc is a modernist eclecticist, a bit of a Philip Johnson. Plural sourcing can produce winning complexity and challenging juxtapositions, or it can produce kitsch. Portzamparc is on the edge, his work well received, I think, because it is unfamiliar and because he is a real architect and not just the face of a corporation. Competent but sparkless, this architecture has become the mass-market, trickle-down version of something, and, I suspect, for the graybeards and rinses on the Pritzker Jury, that something is "youth." With its narrow formula of respectability, the Pritzker has shown little interest to date in challenging architecture (something youth has often insisted upon), and so Portzamparc takes the prize that might have gone to Zaha Hadid or Coop Himmelblau or Morphosis.

Still, LVMH is, at least, a try (and certainly something to put on the list for the next fireman's call).

A skyscraper—even a sliver—is a density engine, a machine for increasing the concentration of human resources on a site. The greater the density, the greater the demands on the means of movement that serve it: skyscrapers are part of a larger system that can only function if it is sufficiently   **153** infused with people and goods. A skyscraper is not simply an object, it has effects, and traffic is one of them.

Just down the street from LVMH at the Museum of Modern Art, there is a show called "Different Roads," which displays nine new automobiles—prototypes, production models, and "concept" cars, ranging from the adorable little Swatch Smart Car to the more traditionally penile GM EV 1 electric, the most aerodynamically slippery item on the road. A PC whiff hangs over this show of small, efficient cars, manufacturer self-congratulation at being coerced by the government into producing a statistically trivial number of better cars. If the show truly reveals anything, it is the amazing lack of progress in transforming the car into something more logical and sustainable, although one or two cute items lurk in the garden among the Brancusi's and the Moore's, an adman's dream image.

I remember sitting at an awards dinner several years ago at a table with, among others, a senior designer from Chrysler and a traffic planner from L.A. with a fairly jaundiced view of automotive technology as an ideal movement system. As the evening wore on, and our glasses of chardonnay were repeatedly topped up, the man from Chrysler—a Brit and an enthusiast for cars from boyhood on—began to dilate about the "concept cars" he had been involved with, kvelling about their zootiness. As he waxed on about the beauties of his favorites, my friend the planner leaned toward him and said, "But tell me, Trevor, what's the concept?"

Indeed. The history of concept cars is a history of no concept save styling, a projection of a formal future of speed and fins (the *appearance* of speed) that always begged a classic schoolboy question that automatically deconstructs the industry: if they can make cars so great, why don't they simply build them like that in the first place! At MoMA, the concept is slightly more substantial than the testosterone/growth hormone basis of mainstream automotive design. The real interest of these cars is in the degree to which they have implications not simply for the object but for the system. In particular, one reads between the lines of this deeply uncritical show a glimpse of attention to a new attitude toward the *urban* car emerging in Europe and Japan, a type hitherto traditionally treated by American manufacturers (the Lincoln Town Car, the Chrysler New Yorker, etc.) as still another excuse for boat building, witness the fleets of aging yuppies and drug dealers trying to cement their status and occlude their insecurities with lethal, air-fouling, semimilitary SUVs.

Refreshingly, the MoMA cars employ different strategies: smaller, lighter vehicles and cleaner, more efficient engines. While these may be less than revolutionary changes, the greenish vibe that attends these new cars harbingers a more rational future. However, while small and clean are certainly a start, little thought has been given to the integration of this new class of automotive gadgets into the larger traffic system. Cars are still imagined as *cars,* autonomous pods for every individual, with the same absolute rights to the same streets and roads as previous vehicles, their aggrandizement not relaxed but potentially extended. The larger philosophy of movement remains that of the traffic engineer, fixated on maximizing vehicular flow. For this mentality, a smaller car simply represents the possibility of putting more vehicles on the street. After all, a half-size car not only doubles the available number of parking spaces, it increases the carrying capacity of roadways, which—as years of experience have invariably shown—simply increases the amount of traffic.

At the art museum, as fascinated with hardware as Detroit, the system continues its distracting preoccupation with style. But why not look a bit beyond it. One possible outcome of a reduction in the size of cars is, for example, the reduction of the automotive space of the street, the greatest area of public space in the city, now given over to the private storage of vehicles. Imagine that in New York City one lane on each thoroughfare has been removed from the automotive system, transformed into a space of real community use, into green space, seating areas, bike storage, and a system of managing the mounds of waste otherwise piled in plastic bags on the curb. And what about the suggestion of other strategies for sharing urban cars to reduce their number and increase their efficiency? And what about the integration of the car with other modes of movement more suited to the urban environment? And what about a real consideration of the necessary speed of cars in the city?

These seem, alas, to be beyond the purview of art.

1999

Forms of Attachment

Is anything more confusing than adjacency nowadays? Adjudications of the juxtaposable, of what goes with what, comprise the main artistic activity of postmodernity. The era prefers legislation to invention, disputations at the margin to the more lusty speculations at the center of things. When it is not simply about money, so much of our art seems to be merely about art, all Jeff Koons, Jesse Helms, and Jenny Holzer. Real politics and its aesthetics, though, both lie at the seam.

To be sure, it is tough to make sense of what goes with what in the age of television. TV is about anything goes, about a gyre of pure iteration, doing continual violence to a stable politics of propinquity. Images of bodies laid out in Vukovar follow the commercial for new Ban Roll-On. Starvation in the Sudan yields to Beasty-Feast Gourmet Cat Food. This total, hallucinatory, recombinant delirium is a great machine for simultaneous invention and devaluation, somehow akin to Groucho's ravioli stuffed with bicarb that simultaneously caused and cured indigestion.

It is no surprise that these questions of possibility are most architecturally acute in conditions of literally stitching on. While any renovation of the city begs the issue generically, the most emblematic architectural production of the moment, the most taken up in architecture's public discourse, is the issue of adding to cultural monuments, especially museums. In an age of avarice, the main scenes of artistic accumulation are clearly most favored for attention, although, in the United States, the current collapse seems likely to signal the end of this era of breathless expansion.

Any addition challenges the predecessor aura. At a time in which no historic construction ever appears subject to invalidation, in which "preservation" is the only architectural value anyone is able to agree upon, the issue (not to mention the building) is almost always joined from the same perspective: the official rhetoric is respectful and expansive, the addition an augmentation, never a compromise. Surely, this is the central fiction of postmodernity, the Shiva-like ability to assume any form at any moment, the TV version of modernism's own hubris of universality.

The irony here is that postmodernity is so often applied as proximodernity: most of the truly controversial American additions of recent years are expansions of celebrated modernist buildings. We have now come full circle from the predecessor crisis. When modernism claimed exclusive authenticity, offering itself as the only mode of extension, the crisis of virtue was over the modern addition to the neoclassical museum or Richardsonian library. The irony (and postmodernity always entails a little irony) is that modernism can now be relegated to the same chameleon portmanteau as everything else, just another available historical style. But let us get down to cases.

The most over-the-toppishly schematic proposal of the decade was certainly Romaldo Giurgola's short-lived plan to expand Louis Kahn's Kimbell Museum in Forth Worth, Texas. Here was that irony from the get-go. To begin, the project that first put Kahn himself on the map was a bang-on modernist addition to a neo-Gothic gallery at Yale. Giurgola's strategy, however, was more contemporary, more hormonal, a literal stretching of the building by the xerographic extension of Kahn's vaults to make a longer version of the original, the way airplane and limousine manufacturers create "stretch" versions by interpolating additional elements of the original section.

The project was quickly hooted down because the Kimbell was widely agreed to be an absolute masterpiece. The architectural community readily accepted a notion that any intrusion on its aura would cause it to become a building other than that which it was. The Kimbell's quality was so esteemed that there was easy agreement about its untouchability—people simply loved it too much to see it changed. More, the replicant character of the addition made it clear that it was counterfeit, that Giurgola proposed to trade in what appeared to be Kahn's literal currency, obviously touchy ground for an art museum. By seaming it directly to the original, Giurgola clearly crossed the line between flattery and mendacity.

The proposal could not more vividly evoke the crisis of proxi-modernity. Giurgola defended his scheme by means of several characteristic fallacies, almost invariably cited in such cases of troubled adjunction. To begin, he offered that most troubled fallacy of all, an argument from Kahn's original intention, suggesting that Kahn had, at some point in the development of the scheme, himself contemplated a longer building. As a cultural artifact, the return of the notion of intentionality, of the idea that a work is to be read and judged on the basis of its success in representing some specified set of authorial intentions, is clearly a reversion to a standard one had thought long gone. Still, the first defense of the counterfeiter is always to claim that the bill is genuine.

This discourse does carry the flavor of the time. This reversion to the **157** standard of intent typifies this period of historical fundamentalism and political counterfeit. Reactionary jurists develop their theories of constitutionality on the basis of "strict constructionism," Bible-thumping preachers call down their imprecations with like-minded literalism, demanding a single authentic reading, and politicians call for a thousand reversions to the will of the founding fathers. In the architectural arena, the evocation of these instances of intention are generally used as a strategy to de-authenticate the voice of the work itself, to substitute an authority allegedly strong enough to supersede it. If you can't tell I'm lip-synching, how do you really know I'm not James Brown?

Similar arguments were heard when Charles Gwathmey presented his (now nearly completed) scheme for expanding Frank Lloyd Wright's Guggenheim Museum in New York. As with the Kimbell, the question was how to develop a strictly architectural argument (as opposed to a curatorial or economic one) for the expansion and alteration of a building that most considered to be superb and in no need of modification. Like Giurgola riffing Kahn, Gwathmey argued that Wright had, in the course of designing the building, himself made drawings of an another element that was, at least, similar to the proposed addition.

A somewhat different version of this argument from original intent was also suggested during the debate about the Guggenheim, a claim that invokes what might be called the Stanislavskian or Method fallacy. The architects of the addition argued, by means of a series of geometric, art-historical analyses of the proportions of the Guggenheim, not simply that they were recuperating a literal, unfulfilled intention of Wright's (Giurgola's claim for Kahn), but that the new elements they themselves were designing were in concert with some Wrightian quintessence. Here was the true moment of the postmodernist elision, the fuzzing of the seam, the conceptual eradication of difference, the appropriation of both object and aura.

As suggested, this co-optation of aura is continuous with the long history of "correct" forms. Its end product, of course, is Disneyland, the architecture and culture that are "just like the real thing." The most perverse moment in this system comes at the point where the invisibility of the seam is most complete—the system's ultimate aspiration is the seam's total superannuation, the final inaccessibility of any memory of the initiating reality. By this standard, Giurgola's proposition (never mind how "well-intentioned") was as weird and canny as any of today's hyper-hip, ironicizing art product. It is the postmodern counterfeiter's first line of defense—call it art.

The Giurgola extension, predicated on the modular, incremental character of the original, was actually about producing more of the same, an addition to the building that would have used precisely replicated elements of the original to obliterate it. The study—the connoisseurship—in all of this would have been to actually detect the seam, the tiny differences in the concrete mix or the weathering of the stone that betrayed the counterfeit, that might distinguish the appropriation from the appropriated. It would have been a succinct moment of postmodernity, a moment of judging, of asking the question of "how real." Naturally, we were all outraged at the prospective violation, but what an amazing moment it was to see the dependable and elegant architect Giurgola aspire to a realm hitherto reserved for the likes of Sherrie Levine or Milli Vanilli.

The intentional or Stanislavskian fallacies employ a particular strategy of camouflage, a notion that one can snuggle under an aura like a blanket. The question begged by schemes like those by Gwathmey or Giurgola is precisely the radius of aura, of whether or not an aura can be snatched. If the pressures to address genius are intense when an addition literally impinges, do they relax with distance? Where is the line over which rip-off, idolatry, or slavishness becomes homage or merely influence? One does not disqualify every vaguely Kahnian construction on the planet, but asks how close to the original can a similarly charged derivation come (both literally and figuratively) before the forces of repulsion go to work?

Controversy currently surrounds a proposal by the architects Anshen and Allen to add to another of Louis Kahn's greatest works, the Salk Institute. Here, the addition does not literally touch the original but occupies a site clearly calculated to deform its aura. This is a fine instance of aura-snatch from a (small) distance and in the face, for what it is worth, of clear contrary authorial intent. Kahn, after all, had developed (and drawn up) a site plan for the expansion of the institute that deployed its elements according to a certain hierarchy of deference to the main building. In this case, it seems reasonable to include the specifics of the approach and view it as part of the original.

The new facility sits in the filtering grove of trees directly athwart Salk's ineffable central axis, that magic water line pointing to the setting sun. It is a bad piece of work, clumsily sited and deeply un-Kahnian in its spatiality. Still, the arguments pro are all via the authenticating aura graft. The addition's simple geometry is alleged to be "like" Kahn's. Indeed, the lead architect on the job is advertised as a previous collaborator of the master's, as if such association (like Gwathmey's "authentic" geometric analysis) were somehow the guarantor of the quality of the results.   **159**

But the building is *too close,* especially when obvious and superior sitings are available. As with the Kimbell and the Guggenheim, an Oedipal drama is being enacted, patricide and blindness rolled out on a rhetoric of responsibility.

The most emboldened recent American experiment in camouflaging postmodernist proxi-modernity, however, is Michael Graves's ongoing attempt at the expansion of the Whitney Museum in New York City. Here the problem has gained a somewhat more succinct expression, inverted, returned to the source of its crisis. Unlike those architects too much protesting their reverence for Kahn and Wright, Graves, it was clear from the outset, abhorred Breuer. Graves's strategy was to try to overwhelm the original building, to turn it into a subsidiary element in a much larger aggrandizement of forms, to make it vanish via dazzle. Unlike Gwathmey, Giurgola, or Anshen and Allen, Graves completely dispensed with the Stanislavskian fiction, unabashed about differences.

The intended result of both styles of camouflaging—the Method and the Dazzle—is identical—the original building is made to disappear. However, Graves, in effect, reverts to the original modernist strategy that today's wimpy "contextualism" so eschews. He simply adds his thing next door with confidence. Alas, it is a miserable shriveled thing. Yet this does seem like the only real game in town. Apologetic architecture never rises to the occasion. And—if you believe in aura—any impinging shifts. So why not go for it. The real answer, however, is to leave it be. One does not add a movement to a Beethoven symphony simply because the hall has been booked for an hour and a half. These buildings are also well enough alone.

1992

Airport 98

The young architect from Norman Foster's office who was showing me around the new Hong Kong airport wanted to talk about shopping. It was not simply that he had spent months sweating over aisle dimensions, signage control, and fire-suppression systems for doorless boutiques, it was that retail was a major driver in the project's form. Like all new airports, shopping is increasingly the financial foundation: at Hong Kong, something over 40 percent of revenues are derived from retail sales, which gives the disposition of shops a fairly compelling programmatic imperative.

In the Hong Kong terminal, the points of purchase are concentrated in an inescapable clump between the check-in facilities and the gates. Although it is possible to skirt the main mass of shops, there is an inevitable pass-by of outlying facilities, which exist in both dispersed kiosk-style outlets and in a secondary clump at the far end of the terminal. The point, of course, is to make impossible resistance to browsing. After all, air travelers often have copious time on their hands and spend it in a mental space that exists outside of quotidian routines, an intermediate, liberated place where you might as well shop (never mind the vision of guilt-inducing eyes of spouses and kids upturned with curiosity about what you brought back from your trip to the Orient).

The deep signifier of this atmosphere of the in-between is "duty-free," a term that suggests both good deals and a certain ethical liberation. Because—given its political situation—every flight out of Hong Kong is international, no traveler is without access to this culture of putative bargains, taken by quick stages into the duty-free zone beyond check-in. There is a didactic imperative behind all of this. The emporia one encounters at the airport—from Pratesi to the Body Shop—are not simply the same ones in every other airport on the global net, they are increasingly the same ones in the mall and on the street, not to mention the duty-free cart and catalog on the plane itself. Airports are thus primary sites of initiation into multinational culture and its values.

One thing to be said for that culture is that it has consistency. This is not simply a matter of its globe-girdling sameness but of a cultural aesthetic that thrives on the narcissism of small differences, demanding precise forms of connoisseurship. The traveler is therefore remorselessly schooled as a critic, most demandingly in the air. For example, while the number of airlines continues to proliferate, the number of manufacturers of aircraft continues to decline. At the moment, we are down to only two: Boeing and Airbus (I exclude the Russians, who have yet to breech the international market). All air travelers fly in planes that are fundamentally identical and in which the primary qualities of the experience—duration of trip, physical environment, systems of access, flight path, and so on—are likewise the same and beyond modification.

Distinctions in the system tend to devolve on a series of relatively tiny differences, which come to assume extravagant meaning, especially for those of us stuck in the air for the *longue durée*. These distinctions are remorselessly advertised: a few inches of space, a choice of movies, a meal served on a cloth napkin, a more nattily attired flight crew, free beer. I am always dismayed at my own willingness to fight for these miniscule perks, but I do because the larger experience tends to be so dreary (and terrifying) that these marginal privileges are crazily magnified. I have often endured routings of illogical inconvenience simply to secure my upgrade.

The same ethos of small distinctions applies to the airport emporia. To begin, everything sold is fundamentally small, and for logical reasons: it is tough to stuff a fridge or a Mercedes in the overhead compartment. Likewise, what is available tends to fall outside normal patterns of necessity: one does not *really* need two-for-one deals on Cutty Sark or a Gucci belt. And this, if anything, is the message of multinationalism. A culture predicated on the values of consumption and entertainment is centered on the temples of an activity in which the primary motive—movement—is so pared of any supplemental value (pleasure in traveling, "seeing" the world, etc.) that an experiential tabula rasa is created to receive the corroborating imprint of sheer expenditure.

How to create the architecture for such an environment? Airport design—in every celebrated recent instance from Kansai to Denver—adopts "high-tech" as its formal language. There are good, traditional, aesthetic arguments for this. An airport, after all, is the continuation of an aircraft by other means, and there is a logic to looking at the inspirational formal language of aerodynamics as precedent or point of departure. Foster, in particular, is devoted to aircraft, rhapsodizing frequently about the form of jumbos, flying his own jet, a man in the air as often as any. And like planes, airports are machines for moving people, for the orderly sorting out and distribution of very large numbers of bodies to a fixed set of destinations, the mirror image of the flight. The airport sets up the chain of contractions—from the lofty arrival hall to the departure lounge to the cabin interior—that characterize the experience of flight.

Flying is a miracle we all encounter, a kind of conquest. The metaphorical transposition of the experience of flying—our access to the largest imaginable sensation of space available to us—suggests a certain strategy of grandeur in airport design, an architectural capture of space. In the architectural dictionary of received ideas, these spaces are often described as the successors to the great spaces of railroad termini, and this is partially right. But distinctions must be made. Railroad stations traditionally offer two opportunities for dramatic enclosures. The first (and the most obvious direct precedent) is the space of the waiting areas and concourses—like in Grand Central or the old Penn Station—those dramatic antechambers to the space of the train.

The second opportunity, however, is the train shed itself—like those of the Gare du Nord or Saint Pancras. These dramatically vaulted spaces are not simply for grandeur and show but are arguably the most efficient means of covering a large number of tracks, of keeping the weather off the trains and passengers, and of dissipating the smoke from the steam engines for which they were designed—functional spaces. What is ultimately striking about these sheds—in contrast to airport terminal spaces—is that the vehicles are admitted indoors, as if the hanger had become the terminal. The pattern at the airport, though, is more like the Grand Central experience—a capacious waiting and circulation area leading to a cramped umbilicus clamped to the waiting plane.

Foster's airport comes close to transcending this distinction between the space of planes and passengers. The building is enormously long, enormously lofty, and enormously transparent. More than any other airport I know, the experience inside embraces the activity on the tarmac. Jets nose close to the high walls of windows, take-offs and landings are clearly visible, the whole technology of flight is spread out in the foreground. There are few places on earth where more planes can as easily be seen simultaneously.

The plan of the building is itself an aircraft's. A long fuselage that swoops in section like the bulge in a 747 joins a front wing that crosses it at right angles, and a rear wing, raked like a jet's. Most impressive, the whole is a single space, covered, like a train shed, by a truly heroic (if proportionally low) roof comprised of a series of metal vaults. Like a plane's, these proportions are very precise, and the experience of passing through the building produces an uncanny combination of grandeur and calm.

It also lends a fine legibility to it all. Although my guide kept pointing **163** to the decent, if unexceptional, graphics, this was no more than signage. It is the space that impels you forward through a staggering perspectival corridor that stretches nearly a kilometer and a half. The stroll (or the schlepp, depending on the amount of luggage) can be accomplished on foot, via moving sidewalks or—underground—via a little robot train (albeit at sacrifice of the view and the sense of stately progression). The only misfortune in the space is its culmination in a view of a completely homely control tower, not designed by Foster.

Like this long room, much of what is impressive about this building and about the project as a whole is a by-product of sheer magnitude. I would be remiss if I failed to rehearse a few facts. During its (incredibly rapid) six years a-building, this was the largest construction project on the planet. An adorable little island with a 345-foot-high peak was first leveled and then expanded 400 percent to an area two miles wide and three and a half long—bigger than the whole Kowloon peninsula. A total of twenty billion dollars was spent on the project, which encompassed not simply the island, the terminal, the world's largest cargo-handling facilities, and myriad out-buildings but a high-speed rail line and a highway into downtown Hong Kong, a small city for airport employees, and the world's longest rail/car suspension bridge. At the height of construction intensity, twenty-one thousand workers were on site every day.

The terminal itself is—at 550,000 square meters—the largest enclosed public space in history ("larger than London's Soho district," according to one suggestive piece of publicity, and twice the size of Renzo Piano's Kansai terminal in Osaka), contains 350,000 cubic meters of concrete, 12 hectares of granite, 400 kilometers of piping, 100,000 light fixtures, 5,500 doors (not bad for a building with a single room), took 13 million man days to build, required 11,000 drawings, has a baggage hall bigger than Wembley (or Yankee) Stadium, can receive 35 million passengers a year, expandable to 87 million, etc., etc., etc.

The issue for architecture here is how to deal gracefully with this remorseless quant. While we live in a culture that overvalues extent, this is a project that wears its enormity lightly. Part of the reason is the beautifully proportioned roof and the sheer awesome singleness of the space. The space itself seems more tractable as well because it belongs to a class of structures—stations, stadia, malls, and so on—that we know and expect to be big. And the expansiveness of the view, the fact that turning right and left always pulls the eye out the window, across the tarmac, over the water, and to the verdant hillscape beyond, integrates the experience of the indoors with the out. By *stretching* the view, this has the not-so-paradoxical effect of reducing the portion of it we inhabit to a manageable scale.

The tractability of the space is also a product of its extremely regular tectonic character. The detailing of the building, while elegant, is in many ways surprisingly austere and lacks much of the kind of in-your-face mechanical joinery that characterizes so much high-tech work. Indeed, as a collection of details, the building has a slightly flat affect, a little bland. I think this works okay in the sense that the power of the building lies in its lightness and transparency, in its resistance to clutter of any kind. Sometimes, as in the so-called binnacles—small structures dispersed at regular intervals to house AC registers, clocks, signage, advertising, and so on—the simple articulation and neutral color cross the line to dull, but generally speaking, the laid-back articulation succeeds by being crisply unobtrusive.

Although it was initially set by master planners from HOK, the airport *parti* developed by Foster stretches a standard-issue Y-shaped plan into something quite different. Conceptually speaking, most airports are understood laterally, their gates deployed in wings, either literally or conceptually parallel to the main terminal spaces, which tend to be attenuated along the roadways that provide access to them. Kansai is among the most dramatic examples, an enormously long, fingerless slab that provides access to all gates. At Hong Kong, the sensation is 90 degrees from all this. After passing through check-in and immigration, there are, to be sure, gates to the left and the right. But what one confronts above all is that kilometer-plus spine straight ahead, the finger become concourse.

Uniquely, this spine is not simply a link (think of Helmut Jahn's United terminal in Chicago, in which parallel wings are joined by an underground space) but holds a numerousness of gates along either side with their attendant jumbos lined up like so many pets. It is a superb room, and part of what makes it so is the architect's extremely canny decision not to modulate the gate spaces in any way, save with carpeting and chairs: no barriers, no walls, no interfering demarcation to interrupt the continuous reading of the spaces. It is easily the finest experience in the complex.

There are others that are very good. The sequence of arrival from a taxi or from the train leads across gently rising bridges that fly over the arrivals hall below up to the check-in area above, which then stretches out to either side under the undulant ceiling comprised of nine of the lovely low vaults. The mass of shops in the axis of the arriving passengers' line of sight forces the gaze left and right, setting up the first—and most **165** distant—interior confrontation with the complicated scene of planes and water and hills outside. By being relatively chockablock with signage, structures, activity, and movement options, the room also sets up the greater oomph and serenity to come in the great nave waiting on the other side.

The new airport is a replacement for old Kai Tak in Kowloon, which featured the most death-defying glide slope in all of aviation. Planes descended through a bristle of high-rises, and passengers looked out their windows into domestic scenes that seemed scant inches away. The airport itself was an anticlimax. The new approach is far more stately, over islands and water, past little mountains, down to the comfortingly long runway. What the new airport offers uniquely, though, is a view of itself. Those seated on the correct side of the plane see the great gray metal roof of the terminal in a superbly shifting perspective.

What a view!

1999

No Sex Please, We're British

Something over twenty-five years ago—back in my student days—Sandy Wilson came to MIT to present his scheme for the British Library in London. A certain aura sparkled around (the much younger) Wilson, the result of his having won what seemed to be the commission of a lifetime at what was—for an architect—a tender age. Wilson could scarcely have imagined then that it would also take a professional lifetime to get it built.

Finally complete after a thirty-six-year slog (the same time, as the architect likes to point out, as it took to build Saint Paul's), the construction of the library has been a nightmare of changing site and program, financial and critical assaults, foot-dragging, cultural warfare, Tory philistinism, and harassment by the egregious Charles. Through it all, Wilson—a gentle bishop's son, dedicated painter, and former Cambridge don—has remained outwardly unflappable. In a book-length apologia, his tone is remarkably gracious and unembittered. And Wilson is right to take pride in what he has built.

The huge building sits on a site that is both complex and difficult along the north side of Euston Road, a smog-clotted artery that forms the upper boundary of central London. The library's neighbors include Gilbert Scott's flamboyant red-brick freestyle gothic Saint Pancras railway station, a series of bleak but harmless post-war office buildings, and—to one side—an extremely tasty housing project from the twenties, modeled on the social housing of "Red Vienna."

The most demanding neighbor is Saint Pancras, both because of its huge size and because of its extraordinary quality. Wilson is a self-described legatee of the so-called English Free School, a nineteenth-century aesthetic movement descending from (who else?) Ruskin and committed to picturesque recombinations of Gothic forms to suit then contemporary needs for such postmedieval programs as railway stations. Saint Pancras is a founding example. Wilson sees the school as one that continues in the "organic" examples of Wright and, most especially, Aalto, the other great hunk in the Wilsonian sensibility.

The library speaks to the station most directly via its facades of beautiful handmade red brick, from the same source as Saint Pancras's. The match is impeccable, and the lovely brick fairly glows. In its massing, too, the library tithes the station in a certain reminiscent spikiness and by framing direct views in which it can be seen in combination with the station. And there is a conceptual affinity. Saint Pancras is configured in two parts, the over-the-top head house—a huge pile designed originally for a hotel—and the train shed behind, the largest such room constructed to its time. The library also deploys elaborate spaces of public use adjacent to its great room—here the iceberg of mechanized stacks below grade. It is just the orientation that shifts. At the station, the huge space for the trains sits *behind.*

The message of the red brick, however, is not purely contextual. That the national library of Great Britain—the central receptacle of the nation's intellectual accomplishments—should be built of red brick is fairly rich with the aroma of postwar policies for the democratization of education. The so-called red brick universities created as a result became the symbol of an effort to dissipate the class-based system of higher education—the Public School/Oxbridge hegemony—and replace it with a model of more universal access. The symbolic importance of red brick—that "honest," working-class material—in founding an identity for these places was inestimably consequential. The vivid red building on Euston Road surely caps this process.

Most of the critical heat the building has taken to date has been for its exterior, which—to be sure—is no great shakes. Part of the problem is the painfully long period of gestation, which has given the building a kind of fly-in-amber quality. With its picturesque massing, shed roofs, strip windows, clock tower, and brick detail, the building looks very much like something out of the sixties, the actual period of its imagination. It looks like the library at a red brick university.

Wilson began the project in collaboration with the architect Leslie Martin, a leading light in a group of British postwar architects, which also included such figures as Denys Lasdun, Basil Spence, and others and from whom Wilson's own style in part descends. Their architecture shared a thick anti-monumentality (yielding, on occasion, predictably oxymoronic results) that resulted from a collusion of modernism, the memory of the "free style," and Morrisoid ruralism, as well as a certain penchant for the Nordic. None of these architects was an outstanding talent, and their collective oeuvre shares characteristics of both simplicity and of an excess of weight combined with a poverty of detail.

Wilson, in particular, has had a long-standing interest in the synthesis of the free-style tradition with Scandinavian modernism, especially the work of Aalto, whose famous little town hall at Säynätsalo in Finland is a ubiquitous referent. That amazing ensemble in red brick, stepping down its terraced site, compounded of small shed-roofed components, is one of the gems of modern architecture. As an architectural figure, it clearly inspires Wilson's own sensibility and—by his own account—undergirds the composition of the library.

The problem with the translation is scale. Seen from its exterior, the library—with its picturesque massing and mild inflections of form— looks like a much smaller work that has received a massive injection of architectural growth hormone. This means figures that might be accessible at the small scale are when blown up to monumental size, robbed of their more intimate satisfactions. It also means that the sheer density of detail as well as the numbers of repetitions of elements are dramatically affected, if in opposite ways. Attenuation begs the question of variety, arguing for more moves and layers, and not simply for mitotic subdivision, the press of no more than more.

And the exterior detailing—while very systematic—is not terribly satisfying. The day of my visit, I circumnavigated the behemoth and found two men in a cherry picker, washing the pigeon streaks from the blockslong brise-soleil on the building's eastern wing (a little less visual poetry than the streaky manes of the Forty-second Street lions). For me, this suggested a strategy more invested in precision than nuance and a little ambivalent in the logic of its detail. For example, exterior columns have metal covers, articulated to resemble Aalto's trademark wooden column wrappers. Never mind the reduction of the function of these wrappers to pure decoration (many sit behind fences, themselves protected from whimsical dings), they are without the sort of refinement based on modest purpose that is so significant in Aalto's work. There is simply too much compensatory pressed metal—column covers, slab markers, copings, and so on— doing the work of what might have been a more tectonic articulation.

Entering the building, however, such cavils are blown away. The sequence of arrival leads first across a sequestered forecourt of comfortably generous dimensions, which helps pare away the bustle in the street. The building entrance is low and compressive and sets the visitor up for the finest space in the library, the entry foyer and main vertical circulation space. This is a wonderful, complicated room, perfectly modulated in detail, sufficiently dense, and at once elegant and relaxed. Diagrammatically, the space occupies the interior of a large A formed by the two main wings of the library, and the nonparallel framing walls both animate and "free" the space beautifully.

The room opens from the low portal into a triply, upwardly cascading section of great grace and powdery light—a distributor that organizes both program and circulation with clarity. The main stair is to the left (the humanities side of the collection), and bridges—the bar in the A—cross from the stair to the science wing on the right. In the midst of this room, just beyond the bridges, stands the building's self-described holy of holies, the King's Library—a collection amassed by George III—thousands of volumes bound in sumptuous leather and housed in a six-level glass box, which Wilson refers to as a transparent version of the Qabaa in Mecca.

While this description certainly does justice to the symbolic roles of the collection, its real source is both more recent and less spiritual. Indeed, the glass library within an opaque volume was very similarly explored by Gordon Bunshaft in his Beinecke Library at Yale, housing the university's rare book collection. Wilson—who declined the entreaties of Kingman Brewster to take up the post-Rudolph deanship of the Yale architecture school in order to work on what then appeared to be the imminent rush to produce a scheme for the library on its first site in Bloomsbury—has a long association with Yale and would have known the project well and the power of such an object in space to organize a perspectival interior landscape around it. And of course, books are the only truly suitable iconic representation of books—no chiseled names of great persons.

On the far side of the library tower lies the dining space with staff refectory beyond, facing out to far side of the A bar toward the north. At one end of the space sits a little elevator tower with a Leon Krierish "belvedere" on top. Sitting with one's lunch, facing the library tower, the winningly picturesque quality of the library becomes clear. And it is a good vantage point—amidst the clink of silver and glass—to observe that the building's acoustics are superb, simultaneously sharp and muted. Acoustics are obviously critical to the functioning of a library, and this one produces few notes of discord. Noise levels are highly controlled, with no sense that sound is being compressed. I was a bit distracted by the muffled reverberation of my footfalls on the carpeted floor-decking—hollow to provide a service chase—but otherwise extremely impressed with the calm.

The other great environmental necessity for a library is light, and here Wilson is superb. Daylighting fills the reading rooms and the public spaces, never delivered directly but bounced, skimmed across curves, poured through apertures, or grandly rolling in from big windows. Task lighting, too, is artful, from the shaded lamps on the reading room tables to the Jacobsen fixtures suspended over the dining room. In many ways, this careful modulation of light and this bending of its quality to suit a range of purposes—from low-lit exhibition spaces to the bright lobby— are a central achievement of the building. Light, after all, is the medium of architectural space.

The reading rooms—the pay dirt of the project—are also extremely successful if ever so slightly stiff. Wilson takes due cognizance of the need to create a variety of conditions to comfort the psychical and physical needs of readers. By tiering reading spaces within larger reading rooms, he creates a range of places—from dramatically high to comfortingly enclosed—to suit different tastes. All the appointments are extremely comfortable and of the highest bespoke quality, and the organization of the spaces is very good. If there is any shortcoming, it has to do with the strategy of decorative elaboration. This is pure modernist both in its lack of whimsy and in its use of repetition of both geometry and objects to amass a satisfying density of texture with a minimum of applied decoration. The incessant build-up of squares—as lights, registers, coffers, railings—is not altogether synergistic. As with the building exterior, unmodulated more becomes too much.

In the last analysis, though, the building is a triumph both of perseverance and of architecture. Wilson has had uncanny success in combining comfort, generosity, gentility, and efficiency in a highly unpolemical project. Unlike the new French National Library with its crass symbolism, tacky materials, disdain for urbanity, and Cartesian oversimplification, the British Library everywhere advertises how substantial it is. If it is a throwback, it returns to a fine sense of dignity and permanence that seems completely on the mark for the national library of the country of Shakespeare and Virginia Woolf.

On the same day I visited the library, I went to have a look at Richard Rogers's Millennium Dome on the other side of the Thames. It is an interesting comparison, not in the least for what it reveals about what a pound sterling will buy nowadays. The library tipped the scales at something just north of half a billion quid. The dome, on the other hand, is budgeted at 750 million (including extensive site improvements). The library has a planned lifetime of 250 years. The dome will wear out in 30. While these widely differing life spans do not have any intrinsic meaning for architecture, they do speak volumes about the kind of cultural politics—the political economies—that produced them.

The dome is both gigantic (One Kilometer in Circumference! Fifty   **171**

Meters High! The Air Inside Weighs More than the Structure!) and very well done. Suspended by cables from a series of tall pylons, the dome defies (my own) automatic assumption that such a membraned structure should be supported by inflation rather than suspension. The choice to do it this way is clearly part of an insistence by the architects that the more mechanical solution would produce more architecture. By making the apparatus of support legible and available (twelve—one for each hour—the building is potentially a clock—one-hundred-meter yellow masts rise through the tent and support it on cables), they have given themselves an elaborate technical palette and then made the most of it. The joinery, anchoring, proportioning, and configuring all have both that old sense of functionalist inevitability and a great deal of panache. And it is a bloody huge room.

Like the library, the dome proposes itself as a kind of encyclopedia, a container for all of the knowledge humans have collected. The collecting strategy is as clear, in its way, as that of the library. The contents of the dome (and Rogers has wisely distanced himself from any responsibility for anything beyond the enclosure) might be said to represent the world's fair way of knowing. Deployed in an Epcot *parti* within the dome are to be fourteen "zones" that, in aggregate, parse the knowable in a bizarre but familiar way. With your indulgence, the fourteen comprise: Work, Learn, Transaction, Body, Play, Mobility, Local, National Environment, Atmosphere, Communicate, Spirit, Rest, Mind, and National Identity. Each of these is corporately sponsored (Marks and Spencer for National Identity, of course . . . you surely did not expect Al Fayed's Harrods!), and they surround an enormous performance area, where the Millennium Experience will be sung and danced six times a day by two hundred performers in an extravaganza to be produced by Peter Gabriel and Mark Fisher.

All good fun, I guess, in the same way that the Disney version—for all its meretricious slobbering on culture—manages to amuse. The pavilions will certainly range from the sublime (Zaha goes for her longest cantilever) to the ridiculous (enter the huge Henry Mooreish plastic androgyne couple through her thigh, and take an incredible voyage through that same unsexed body we were too shy to actually represent). Although I was awed by the scale of the construction and the finesse of the envelope, I simply could not fathom why—with so many more interesting needs—the Brits have bothered. And there was a gnawing in my craw that Sandy Wilson had endured so much abuse in the pursuit of something so fine when this egregious piece of junk culture breezed right through. Cruel Britannia.

1999

How French Is It?

What's with the French? For many years, France seemed to have an architectural death wish. It was not simply that no work of interest was coming out of the land of Perret and Le Corbusier, it seemed an entire culture had forgotten its taste and sense of proportion. Paris was fouled with mediocrity, from the skyline-blighting Tour Montparnasse to the array of penitential projects in the *banlieue*. How to explain this incredible lapse, a country that had lost its eye?

"Premises: Invested Spaces in Visual Arts, Architecture, and Design from France: 1958–98," an enormous exhibition at New York's Guggenheim Museum SoHo (organized in conjunction with the Pompidou Center in Paris), offers some answers, many of them contained in a catalog that is even bigger than the show. This is symptomatic of a more global malady: the compulsion to account. It is hardly an original observation (and not unique to the French), but no less true, that artistic production in the past twenty-five or so years has become entwined with theory to such a degree that the theory often eclipses the objects. Part of the underlying rationale, of course, is that art and architecture are obliged to seek out strategies of resistance and criticism to avoid being caught up in the larger culture of consumption, but this is a frail justification for the emptiness of so much recent work.

If French art and architecture have been burdened by their allegiance to theory, they have also been saddled with the legacy of their dynamic predecessor: surrealism. The critical method of surrealism was essentially ironical, a stance that allowed things to be taken apart and reassembled in weird and provocative ways, turning conventional values on their head. Surrealism anticipated postmodernism, not simply in its louche skepticism and its devotion to new theoretical realms (psychoanalysis, in particular) but in its capacity for straight-faced, parodistic looniness. Surrealism must surely be responsible for that still puzzling phenomenon of postwar France—the Jerry Lewis effect—something that can be understood only as an ironic appropriation of kitsch and the re-representation of its content as critique.

Needless to say, this kind of critical position is highly fraught. Imagine   **173** the leading lights of French artistic practice, burning at the excrescences of American-led consumerism, gazing at the dancing figure of Mickey Mouse like Aristotle contemplating the bust of Homer. The frustrations of an art that relies on any such surreal mimesis are obvious. For every smugly appropriated image from Disneyland, the Mouse delivers ten billion of its own. Distinguishing the ironic from the original requires both connoisseurship of the most traditional (and lunatic) sort and the willingness to draw a very fine line between fetish and commodity.

The fascination of French artists and architects with surrealism may explain why they are so often charmed by postmodernity in its more kitsch incarnations. Take, for example, the work of one of the artists featured in "Premises," Bertrand Lavier, who contributes a suite of work called "Walt Disney Productions," life-size replicas of the phony abstract paintings and sculptures in a 1947 comic strip in which Mickey Mouse visits a modern art museum. The catalog is worth quoting for its summary of the show's own delirious critical stance:

> Rather than making a painting that was a copy of a cartoon (as a number of his contemporaries did), and rather than reclaiming some tired abstract painting under the pretext of simulation, Lavier took directly from the cartoon itself. Since the cartoon precisely simulated a body of images prevalent in Modernist art, he simultaneously succeeded in resuscitating abstract painting. Although he did so without theoretical effort and—since his short circuit was photographic—without an excessive quantity of turpentine.

It is hard to know which failure of nerve is greater, that of the artist toying with the simulacrum of the simulacrum to "resuscitate" abstraction by yoking it to an Arp-like lexicon of cartoon shapes, or the too-clever-for-words tone of the catalog and its dumb disdain for turpentine and technique. Not only is the art dopey—and this is a show about dopey art if ever there was one—the feeble character of its critique is revealed in its slavish replication of the original image. Disney is simply too much loved by all concerned for this kind of work to pose a threat to the battalions of imagineers who blanket the world with what can only be described as the real thing.

At the entrance to the show there is a series of photographs of the French-built landscape. Commissioned by the French government as part of a WPA-like project to document changes in the environment, the images are at once tragic and bleak. Perhaps the most striking is a 1984 work of Robert Doisneau, *Villejust.* In the sky above a ravaged and alienated landscape dominated by high-voltage wires, an airliner descends, landing gear down. In the left foreground, two men wearing yellow gloves bend over what appears to be a cultivated field; on the right, a small industrial building is under construction.

The French not only have a weakness for kitsch, they also have an affinity for the technocratic space evoked in these photographs, which recall early Antonioni films, where refineries belch flames to the punctuating sound of jets overhead. If anything describes the character of most postwar French architecture, in fact, it is this technocratic style, which can also be seen in the alienating, undetailed architecture so deftly skewered by Jacques Tati and Jean-Luc Godard in films like *Playtime* and *Alphaville.*

Most of the art and architecture in "Premises" shows an affection for these grimscapes that—like the obsession with pop culture—is thinly disguised by irony or parody. This seems both a form of commentary (Paul Virilio documents the horrifying but bold tectonics of the bunkers in Hitler's Atlantic wall and then builds a church that looks just like one) and of co-optation, but it amounts to a version of the Stockholm Syndrome, falling in love with one's captor. There is a high banality that suffuses the work, a love of ugliness and silliness.

One notable exception is the Pompidou Center. If any strictly architectural event had a galvanizing impact on French postwar architecture, it was this building in the heart of Paris, designed in 1970 by Renzo Piano and Richard Rogers, an Italian and a Brit. (Filled with work by Piano, Rogers, Koolhaas, Kroll, and the Smithsons, the show does take a somewhat expansive view of what exactly it is to be French.) Drawing on an expressive "high-tech" vocabulary, the building simultaneously celebrated the technical character of its architecture and offered—in its vast open floors—a new take on the undifferentiated spaces that were so idealized in the architecture of the time. The Pompidou infused the bare-bones rationality of technical construction with a sense of joy, reconnecting with the tradition of Viollet-le-Duc, Labrouste, Eiffel, Perret, and Prouvé. (The best recent French work follows this example, particularly that of Jean Nouvel, easily the leading architectural talent in France today.)

For the most part, though, the show reflects the fact that the French architecture machine has been working overtime in the past thirty years without any compelling idea about its future. The so-called *grands projets,* with which Mitterrand sought to leave his mark, were all characterized by Modernism at its most geometrically reductive: the pyramid, the triumphal arch, the point grid—projects in which magnitude simply supersedes the necessity of detail.

175

This megalomaniac tradition in French planning and architecture has a fine lineage, from the monarchy, through Haussmann, and down to Le Corbusier, whose superb work from the fifties and sixties forms a point of departure for the show. The curators propose Peter and Alison Smithson (the British team widely acknowledged to be the parents of the New Brutalism) and French architect Yona Friedman as anti-Corbs, erstwhile "humanizers" of his "formalist hegemony." Never mind the soul-deadening character of their work and the intellectual hoop-leaping necessary to describe their functionalism redux as anything but brutal—their real effect was to reestablish the endless grid as the default of urban planning. Friedman is best known for a series of sketches of a mega-structure floating fifteen meters over Paris on enormous columns, an aerial interpretation of the Plan Voisin, Corb's project to replace a vast quadrant of the city with slab blocks. Friedman's fantasy returns periodically, in, for example, the form of the Florence-based Superstudio's famous globe-girdling grid or, in a more domesticated version, in Bernard Tschumi's art school in Le Fresnoy, where a metal roof containing various technical installations floats over the tiled roofs of older buildings on the site.

This tradition of grandiosity produced a series of grotesques, most strikingly in the hyperscaled projects of the Spaniard Ricardo Bofill, who delivered what must surely be a conceptual deathblow to the large-scale housing project with buildings in Paris, Montpelier, and elsewhere, styled in a witlessly inflated classicism, in which monster precast concrete Corinthian columns enclose bathrooms or kitchens. Crossing the line between surrealism and megalomania, this work was bizarrely influential. The result was not simply a bending of the rules but an obviation of them. In the right hands, this might have been pleasingly anarchical, but in those of so many practitioners, it simply led to incoherence. The voyage of Christian de Portzamparc is exemplary. Although he is an architect of obvious talent, I have never found his compositional sensibility persuasive—klutzy is the word that springs to mind, probably because he collages hackneyed forms (the architectural equivalent of those "Walt Disney Productions"—wavy roofs, angled windows, standard-issue curtain wall) into ensembles that do not transcend their origins.

I am not altogether sure why I found "Premises" so annoying. It is not the pedestrian installation or any single piece of art or architecture, although the percentage of winners does attain a historic low. I suppose it is because the show—in its immensity, the sheer weight of accumulation—is actually so successful in reproducing the style and the mood of its subject. It becomes another installment in the ongoing story of the *grands projets,* size before content, amalgamating weak ideas and unappealing forms into something that trivializes art and architecture. Why can't these people get over themselves, lighten up, and get serious?

1999

Upstairs, Downstairs

Elvis' family and friends recall his always saying to others "Come to Memphis, I want to show you Graceland." Elvis is thus regarded as Graceland's original tour guide.

Elvis Presley's Graceland: The Official Guidebook

It gives us great pleasure to invite you to visit the house, to enjoy the ambiance of its rooms, and to experience for yourself this national treasure.

Hillary Rodham Clinton, *The White House: An Historic Guide*

On the covers of the official guidebooks, Graceland and the White House look pretty much the same. Tight shots on white porticoes—four classical columns each—evoke the big house, our standard-issue national icon of gracious living. And, of course, I am writing this piece because we are *all* invited for a visit. Indeed, more people visit these two houses than any others in the United States, over a million to the White House annually, three quarters of that number to Graceland (no numbers are available for drive-bys at Rockingham).

Which brings me to the first big difference: nobody *lives* at Graceland. It is different in D.C. According the White House guide book, the presidential residence is the "only residence of a head of state open to the public on a regular basis free of charge." Is this not exactly what we have been fighting Saddam about? Putting global resonances aside, this is an extraordinary piece of information. Indeed, in today's Did-Bill-Kiss-Monica atmosphere, such national visitation rights suggest that we hold our presidents' privacy to a pure celebrity standard—inquiring minds need to know.

The open-door policy relegates the president to shopkeeper status, living above the store, a tourist attraction in his own home. This is a hallmark of the contemporary presidency: we all want to get up close and personal with the man in the White House. Even I receive a Christmas card from the First Family and, having gotten a couple, feel that I am entitled to receive them forever. We expect hospitality from the president— at least a look around the pad—and we can get it just by showing up at the door. Such simultaneous free access to both the press-hyped presidential peccadilloes and to the president's space begs the current questions: what did the president do, and where did he do it?

This surveillability of the presidency has become increasingly optical and architectural. I lifted a page from an airline copy of *U.S. News & World Report* during my recent swing to Washington and Memphis to get an axonometric drawing of the president's inner sanctum, otherwise "off-limits" (like the upstairs bedrooms) to the public. Actually, this is a somewhat elastic situation: upstairs is the area of the residence that *is* open to the public on payment of a (fairly substantial) fee. The magazine image maps the Oval Office, study, dining room, bathroom, pantry, patio, and secretarial office. More interestingly, the drawing also shows the location of several peepholes, which allow a calculation of precisely the optic surveillability of the space, even when it remains behind closed doors. Unshown in the image (but alluded to in the text) are a photoelectric sensor system for keeping tabs on the president's movements and a "secret" tunnel joining the office and the family quarters.

It is a map of the invisible, of the few gaze-free zones in the White House, not necessarily the scene of the crime but scenes in which the commission of the hoped-for-crimes *might* be undertaken. Elvis was himself no slouch in the peccadilloes department, and like the White House's, the Graceland tour is structured to both reveal and conceal, to create a forbidden region where forbidden pleasures (the pill popping and the girleen bacchanals) might have taken place. Like the White House, Graceland puts upstairs off-limits out of respect for the privacy of the King. And it is off-limits: the flack who took me around had been in Graceland's employ for ten years and had never mounted those fateful stairs. Canny management. The unknown is the most fertile ground for fantasy, and everyone, it seems, who comes to Graceland is interested in the fundamental mysteries of the cult. Half of the country claims to have seen Elvis in the past six months, after all. This makes him strangely visible, which, in turn, makes the preservation of his privacy a thoroughly reasonable idea.

We have come to accept a standard-issue version of celebrity. Ours is the culture that invented attention deficit disorder, and we like our icons as succinct and empty as possible, no nuance please. By such shorthand, Graceland and the White House produce the aura of celebrity very similarly. Both offer the spatialized mysteries of the second floor and the secret ceremonies of the Oval Office or the Rec Room, sites where we can attach our own conclusions about the most interesting aspect of the private **179** lives of celebrity, its appetites and follies. There is also the rock-steady neoclass, homes-of-the-stars architecture, one of America's signal contributions to world culture. I remember a trip to Karachi some years ago, during the days of the Afghan war. The city was awash with tremendous wealth accumulated by arms and drug smugglers. A beachfront quarter of the city was filled with their mansions, and the most magnificent of them was a preternaturally white replica of the White House at the correct ⅝ Disney scale.

"America's White House bears the stamp of every president" reads the guidebook. Some, of course, leave a greater imprint than others, and decorating does not seem to be a particular passion of the current occupants. Elvis—after buying it from some local patricians—moved into Graceland and really *redid* the place. If the White House is a shrine to the genteel styles of the early Republic, Graceland is a Mecca of High-Tack, just the decor to go with sequined jumpsuits and pink Cadillacs. Never mind the mirrored walls and carpeted ceilings, though, the effect was very much like my White House visit, at least structurally. Whatever one's decorative sensibilities, these are both places deeply invested in *period*. While the one may be done in Empire Bleu and the other in Avocado Green and Harvest Gold, this is taste that is definitely not of our time.

But that is not exactly true either. I was recently at the Getty Museum in Los Angeles, another fine example of the architecture of power. Like the presidential mansion, the Getty is an enormous white (and, er, beige) house stuffed with period decor. The familiar formula is less successful here than at either Graceland or the White House because the aura of J. Paul Getty—deceased long before the realization of his institution—is simply too spare to inflect the result in the direction of either dignity or kitsch. One grasps at straws: standing in front of van Gogh's irises, the best I could do was to put myself in mind of the fate of Getty's grandson's ear.

Elvis and the president (Elvis is the not surprising Secret Service handle for Clinton) enjoy(ed) the same perks, beginning with the relatively modest mansion (Graceland is *small*!) and continuing with Air Force One and the fleets of armor-plated cars, the ubiquitous retainers, and especially that man in the crowd carrying the "football" with its hot line to Armageddon. On the side of purer pleasure, the standard scenes of the American presidency include the White House pool (think JFK skinny-dipping with Fiddle and Faddle) and the private screening room (think of Nixon and Kissinger watching *Patton* for the umpteenth time). Elvis's screening room—done in delicious mod-squad style by Memphis decorator Bill Eubanks—even incorporates presidential technology, the triple TVs that Elvis had admired in the LBJ White House (although Elvis used his to watch not the three networks' news but a simultaneity of football games). Elvis had just what the president does (and it is all on display at Graceland, including the jet), and he lived the style to the hilt, a wiggling dervish of sociability wading through a crowd of sycophants and hangers-on.

One of our national myths is that anyone can grow up to occupy the White House. As Graceland makes abundantly clear, you do not even need to be president to do it.

1998

part iii

Misfits

Container Riff

I have a bad reaction to the idea of "containers."

It seems a despairing word, a link in a dispiriting etymological chain: containers, containment, contamination. . . . The word problematizes content and privileges the membrane and its impermeability, raising anxiety about leakage, about the uncontained, about too spontaneous events.

The word also seems to belong to a critical lexicon that has come to overcharacterize the discourse of urbanism. We are eager to describe the city with a certain fatality. To be sure, our urbanism is out of control, driven by globalizing systems and exponential leaps in scale. The metropolis becomes the megacity becomes the continuous urbanization of the planet. We revert to the convenience of systems, defining cities in the technocratic language that is the death of the accidents and differences that make the city beautiful, democratic, and productive.

A few associations.

First Chernobyl, its containment vessel breached by explosion, releasing its invisible poisons to waft around the world. The failure of the container resulted not simply in thousands of lingering deaths but in the invidious destruction of an enormous territory, removed from the possibility of habitation or production for an age. The failure of the system to keep its harmful by-product in its place is the ruin of its surroundings. A ghetto for strontium, the reactor functions like any other ghetto. Its force—constantly marked as dangerous—is useful only if it is contained. Released, its potency pollutes.

The failure of Chernobyl—which took place at the moment of the collapse of the Soviet system—was a vindicating inversion of the success of another container, that of postwar American foreign policy. This was long predicated on the idea of "containment," the erection of an impermeable membrane designed to thwart Soviet expansionism, the growth of the "evil empire." Chernobyl provided a chillingly telling metaphor for this enterprise. Schooled since the war to believe that the iron (though lead might have been more suitable) curtain concealed the manufactory of insidious demo-toxins, Westerners could plainly see that when the

Soviet system crumbled (of course our nukes—products of a different system—posed no such threat), there was an inevitable leakage of the poisons that had constituted the very substrate of Soviet power.

Let us withdraw from the fulsomeness of this metaphor for a moment to consider a system of containers of even more directly architectural character. I am thinking, of course, of shipping containers, of the system of modularized containerization that is one of the great enablers of the global economy. This impressive system, designed to efficiently integrate road, rail, ocean-going, and (in another modularization) air transport is the quintessential model of modernity. *Existenzminimums* for goods, the stackable, hoistable boxes—which, jettisoned, often become housing for the desperately poor—fulfill a historic dream of democracy. Predicated on a meticulous fidelity to an outward sameness, they define the territory of difference with inviolable exactitude. "Any color at all as long as it's black" went the early motto of the Ford Motor Company. Any contents at all, as long as it fits.

Urbanism—at least its currently sanctioned discourse—is in recovery from this same fantasy. There is a little distinction though. In the dreams of Corbusier or Hilbesheimer, the sameness simply reproduced itself everywhere: the transmission of ideas resulted in the transformation of culture, resulting in an inevitability of construction. The container system goes this one better by collapsing at least two of the terms. The creation of a universal spatial particle that can itself be freely transmitted imparts a kind of physics to the system. The circuit of ideas, the circuit of capital, and the circuit of space become homologous in a great reverie of globalized consumption, a vindication of the module.

I may somewhat overstate the originality of this system and must refer to a familiar production on the cusp of postmodernity. In the sixties and seventies particularly, many of us collaborated in various guises on inventing images of pod housing, chopped from L.A. to Marseilles for insertion in the voided maws of waiting megastructures. That fantasy broke up on the shoals of its banal formal vision, the economics of transferring so much weight, and a market unready for real property to be so unfixed—although the idea that property could have a life independent of land has a charm that will be much revisited. One of its more suggestive contemporary reincarnations is the model of the time-share condominium. Here the mobility of capital is paired not with the mobility of space but with that of ownership. Space is shared through the medium of time in a magic formula of real estate relativity that puts us in the condo in Boca during March
and in the chalet in Vail late in May (no snow, alas, but really cheap).

Certainly, the notion of the container sits athwart a staggering increase in personal mobility. As we flow faster and faster across the globe, how are we to be organized in relation to events and activities? One possibility—suggested by the shipping container—is that we become attached to a kind of universal space particle that we bear—turtlelike—with us, ready to be inserted in some available slot at our destination. The logic of this system must flow either from the availability of some meaningful set of differences at that destination or a religion of pure mobility—perhaps an expansion of that current totem of self-importance, frequent flier miles, to frequent mover miles—or on a physics of aggregation that allows these mobile particles to be assembled into space molecules of meaningfully variable form and purpose.

Which brings me to another container, a container of milk in the cooler of the American supermarket. Poignantly, for the past several years, these containers have often been printed with photographs of missing children, accompanied by further description and the particulars of their disappearances. These containers harbinger what will surely become a characteristic crime in this future of circulating containers and trackable particles, the loss of a subject in space. Such crimes can cut both ways. Kidnapping and rebellion both result in a disappearance from the sight of the system, a losing track. The container (with its bar-coded rune) is an instrument for assuring that things and people are in their place. Postmodernity, in its panoply of simulations, its eviscerations of difference, its confusions of geography, has created a titanic vexation of place. Containers are to be the medium for sorting this out, substituting a unifunctional science of activity for the unsurveillable leakiness of traditional places. We know you are at the Mall because you used your MasterCard to buy those size 34 jeans at the Gap. And weren't you a 32 last month? How much space do you think you are entitled to?

If anyone ever tested that particular limit, it was Walter Hudson. At the time of his death three years ago, Hudson weighed close to 1,200 pounds, somewhat down from the 1,400 pounds that established his Guinness-certified record as the world's fattest person. Hudson was so large that when he died, a wall of his house had to be torn down and a forklift brought in to remove his corpse.

Hudson is the paradigmatic citizen of containerized postmodernity. What makes him exemplary, however, is not so much his bulk as his immobility: except for a tragically brief period of slimming, Hudson was unable for years to leave his house, unable even to leave his bed. He was sustained in this stasis by a kind of minimum apparatus of contemporary personhood: flanking his specially constructed bed were refrigerator and toilet, computer and television set. With a Big Mac in one hand and the TV remote control in the other, Hudson led his contracted life.

For me, Walter Hudson represents the next step in the culture of containerization. In a sense, his bulk is coincidental, merely relic. He was, to be sure, "as large as a house" (indeed, he occupied more space than anyone in history), but this is merely an irony. In his enormity Hudson simply makes visible a containerization to which we are all susceptible, the idea that the body, positioned at a nexus of surveillability, immobilized by the possibility of continuous observation and regulation, becomes the modularized degree-zero of architecture.

We are everywhere beamed encouragements to the immobility for which Walter Hudson was poster child: tribalism, fear of epidemics and criminality, uncontrolled population growth and diminution of resources, and especially the continuous assertion of the equivalence of life on the Net to the old experiences of spatiality, all suggest a reduction of the territories of freedom to the confines of the skin, a neutralization of the idea of the city that threatens—should the technical resources become available—to make even bodies irrelevant. Our intimacy with the Net, our willingness to submit to the constant vetting of the global electronic system, harbingers a day in which the line between the last bastion of private space—the body—and the public sphere is finally obliterated.

Perhaps I run a bit ahead of the story. Walter Hudson's immobilization by excess spatiality is, for the moment (more irony), reflected in our own enormous mobility. Here we sit in Barcelona, gathered from the corners of the world, to issue cautions to one another about the generic mechanisms of the world city. As members of the class that enjoys the privileges of both the old Newtonian style of mobility and the new, electronic, virtual mode, we experience this condition of intermediacy as a kind of pleasure, as a supplement, not a constraint. However, the zero-sum character of the equation seems unmistakable. As the persuasiveness and convenience of virtual relations rise, there is a corollary decline in the meaningfulness of differences in physical space. The trope of placelessness (we watch CNN both on the airplane *and* at the Hilton) is too much with us late and soon.

As I suggested before, a container is defined by the character of its membrane. There are those designed to keep things out and those to keep them in. If I seem to be carried away with the panoptic, carceral model, it is because that is the model that is closest to my own experience. The

reemergence of a culture of national, ethnic, and sectarian separatism is surely a projection of this idea of the container onto political space. The breakup of Yugoslavia into ethnic enclaves and the parallel efforts of the United Nations to create a series of "Safe Zones" impermeable to the violence (if not the hatred) all suggest that paranoid conflation of separateness and difference on a notion of the container sufficiently large (and the idea of "bigness" is precisely one of the tools of this paranoia) to assure that a fixed pattern of differences will be retained, that the possibility of "sameness" is avoided, but, equally, so also is the unconfined possibility of splicings and mutations, enlargements of the catalog of differences.

The convolutions of such strategies of containment can be fascinating. One of the historic—and tragic—geopolitical containers in the American experience is the Indian reservation. Within these territories, Native Americans continue to possess a certain degree of legal sovereignty. This limited autonomy allows, among other things, Indians to operate gambling casinos on their lands in many states where such establishments are not otherwise legally permissible. Recently, the city of Detroit, a metropolis in dire financial straits, has begun the process of transferring a piece of its downtown to the Chippewa tribe, creating a tiny reservation on which a casino might be built. The municipality envisions this resulting in the creation of a large number of jobs as well as a considerable tax return on the gambling revenues.

A fair number of inversions are entailed here. Whereas the container of the Indian reservation historically erected a membrane that systematically devalued the territory contained, the Detroit strategy relies on the notion that the new Indian reservation would become so radically valorized that it would dramatically transform the economy at its periphery. This is a clear distillation of the public logic of so-called containers more generally. The inscription of football stadia, shopping malls, multiplex theaters, and so on in existing urban and—more frequently—suburban tissue is predicated on the creation of territories that are cauterized from the continuous fabric of urbanity. These places—like Indian reservations—are conceptually hermetic, distanciated environments whose peripheral logics are not spatial—like any good urban architecture—but financial. The flow of capital they generate is bodiless and conceptual, unlikely to stick, unbound by the niceties of physical adjacency, by the kinds of incremental, reciprocal, influencing growth that is crucial to health of the city.

Signs on the New York City subways enjoin the carrying of open containers of alcohol. The traditional strategy for circumventing this injunction has been to carry your bottle in a brown paper bag, placing the container within a container, camouflaging its character and thereby **189** legitimating—via a kind of discretion—its decanting. The subway signs—one step ahead of this old ruse—are explicit in pointing out that drinking from a bottle in a bag is likewise prohibited. But there is a lesson for urbanity here, and it lies exactly in the condition the system seeks to forbid: the open container.

The genius of the city—as opposed to the genius of a discrete piece of architecture—lies in the tractability of its edges, in its permeability, in its support of accident. As a compound of territories and enclosures, a boundary-making and measuring system, a labyrinth of spaces, the city relies on a certain illegibility, on the possibility that it can be read beyond the particulars of any single—or even complex of—containers. The places so described are, of course, sometimes physical, sometimes conventional, sometimes imaginary, and such zones depend as much on precedent and habit as they do on the instigations of construction. The nuances of such urban definition—of boundary making—are and must be rich, as rich as possible.

The city is not simply a phenomenon of extent, it is an ecology, a locus both of fixity and of complex and shifting relations. Talk of urban containers participates in a functionalist fantasy of rationalized relations in which a set of predictabilities is offered as a hedge against dysfunction. During the recent outbreak of the Ebola virus in Zaire, health workers imposed a system of "barrier nursing" to try to contain the deadly disease. Functionalist urbanism—still our default discourse—imposes a similar fantasy of prophylaxis, a kind of germ theory of urban subjectivity. This dovetails efficiently with the monadic system of global consumption, the disciplines of uniformity that create subjects as particles, victims of an evermore circumscribed field of choices.

It is time to stop thinking and speaking this way. Both the urbanism of blind traditionalism and the acquiescent urbanism of bigness and replicable containers are out of date. If the container is a hedge against accidental or uncontrolled contamination, a medium of manipulation and control, the redress against such a degrading notion of space is in the fight for intimate, plural, and malleable spaces, spaces in which differences are invented and celebrated. The city should be the hothouse of both accident and consent, the zone of experiment, and the site of an infinite variety of consensus.

1996

Family Values

The upcoming millennium could hardly be better timed. Unlike the last one, much anticipated but finally a nonevent, things really are about to change. Not to put too fine a point on it, the world as we know it (and I use this phrase advisedly) may soon be gone. Should this happen, architecture will be affected. Indeed, unless we are prepared to do something about it, architecture as we know it may soon be gone. I mean it, and the threat that concerns me is this: space, the palpable and dimensioned territory of architecture, is rapidly ceasing to be its reliable measure.

We are everywhere confronted with a mendacious, unreliable architecture, an unreal architecture, an out-of-space architecture, an antidemocratic architecture. Relations of space that once mapped our relations and rights are being blown away by a gale of simulations, an architecture of the ersatz, an indistinguishable, globalized, mendacious, disenfranchising architecture of festive shopping malls and Disneylands, of atrium hotels and high-security suburbs, of airport lounges and hermetic offices in the middle of an endless nowhere. How did we get into this mess?

Culture certainly had something to do with it. I draw my first example from a figure I regard as synthetic culture's highest achievement to date, from a cultural performance of unalloyed simulation totally untainted by the fey self-defensive ironies we all so desperately cling to to justify our love-hate with the course of events that sweeps us so breathlessly along. I miss Reagan. Odious as he was and optimistic as I am about the new administration, I admit a certain ugly nostalgia for the easy clarities of Republican culture: we knew the enemy and it wasn't us.

During his years in office, Ronald Reagan came to be nicknamed the "Teflon President." Teflon, as you know, is a plastic coating used on pots and pans to prevent food from sticking to them during cooking. Reagan acquired this sobriquet because no matter how deceitful his behavior, no matter how many transparent lies he uttered, no accusation seemed to stick to him. However often they were reported in the press, proofs of his mendacity were never persuasive to his adoring public.

Over time, Reagan became a kind of sublime epistemological conundrum, a riddling sphinx. It was impossible to confront his ubiquitous **191** face without worrying about the very origins and reliability of knowledge itself. From his dyed hair, to his genial hypocrisy, to his bald-faced lies, every aspect of Reagan seemed to beg the question of the nature of truth. By the time of the still-playing Iran-Contra scandal near the end of his second term, the inquiry had come to be embodied in a pithy incantation repeated over and over by virtually all who cared: "What did the President know? And when did he know it?"

This proved the crucial formulation of Reaganism. By introducing the aspect of temporality—the "when did he know it"—the media arrived at a summary of the Reagan riddle that took into account both the fact of his monumental dishonesty and the incredibly abiding love that the American people persisted in harboring for him, a love that simply refused to see his lies as lies. The new construction solved the puzzle by moving the site of the question from the terrain of ethics to the territory of memory. Reagan's actions could thereby be dismissed as merely the difficulties of senility, the innocent failures of an old man, a medical problem. Tacitly acquiescing to this, Reagan developed a mirror refrain of his own, repeated at every press conference, deposition, and photo op: "I can't recall."

The great metacultural irony in all of this is that Reagan rose as the first true postmodernist politician: his politics was symbolized precisely by his own longevity. Reagan came to power as the apostle of memory, promising Americans a return to a golden age, a time to which his years allegedly gave him special access. This mock vision of Elysium infected all of culture, including architecture. During the Reagan years, memory emerged as the most powerful complicit value in architectural discourse. From historicist theories of the city to the revolting classical reminiscences of endless neo-con building projects to the Disneyfication of most of material culture, the reek of a decomposed "past" crowded out the sweet perfume of invention and experiment.

Architecture's crisis today is a crisis of authenticity—if I might use that disreputable concept—a crisis about locating value in an age of simulation, the same crisis that produced Reagan, the simulated president. Under this phony regime, everything is thrown into undecideability, removed from the territory of consent. The commercial asks, "Is it real or is it Memorex," as the recording of Ella Fitzgerald shatters the glass. Or consider the following. One of my favorite artifacts of the Reagan era is an American television program called "Puttin' On the Hits." The show is, in effect, a lip-synching competition. Participants dress up as some venerated pop star and proceed to simulate one of Madonna's or—more to the point—Milli Vanilli's greatest hits. In format, "Puttin' On the Hits" simulates the kind of simulations one sees on shows like "American Bandstand" or "Soul Train," shows on which actual pop stars lip-synch to their own recorded performances, imitating themselves performing. Of course the situation is really even more complicated because the "authentic" performance at the source of this great chain of simulations has no actual autonomous existence, being something that was elaborately constructed from various tracks laid down in the sound studio. The whole thing is further complicated nowadays that the show is in reruns.

At the end of these simulated simulated simulated performances, a panel of judges—marshalling an incredible array of completely spurious expertise—numerically rates the contestants in categories like . . . "originality." Here we are getting close to the heart of the matter. The problem with "Puttin' On the Hits" as a cultural model is not the lip-synch: the real problem is with those judges, with the way in which they naturalize the fakery in terms of familiar routines of authority, some standard beyond whim or taste meant to assure us that the ersatz is just like the "real" thing. The field of consumption is dominated by such assurances, the claim that the petrochemical slime purveyed at McDonald's really is nutritious, "natural," or—as Peter Eisenman would say—"strong" food.

We acquiesce in this unreality to cover our inability to obtain better or simply to obtain the sanction to get our little rocks off. Jessica Hahn's late-night TV ads for her 900 stroke line parade sultry babes clasping phone receivers as different numbers flash over. Sultry Jessica successively intones, "Redheads—yeah. Blonde girls—woow. Brunettes—ummm. Black girls—awright!" She codas with the tag, "Different styles, different desires." It is an interesting, completely supportable principle, this democratic yoking of rights and pleasure. But of course it is a shuck. Vile sexism aside, the point is that the differentiation is a fraud, the blonde number is as likely to yield a brunette. In a culture of simulation, plurality is the main mode of homogenization.

As if further evidence of the weird cultural construction of our political, aesthetic, and moral discourses were needed, the ocean of bullshit proffered during last year's presidential race on the subject of so-called family values certainly serves. The nadir was reached shortly before the election, as *Murphy Brown*—watched by half the TV viewers in America—responded to Dan Quayle's earlier assault. The news shows that followed, reporting on this bizarre event, cut between the image of Candace Bergen, acting in the imaginary space of the show, surrounded by a group of "real" single parents, and Quayle, sitting in someone's living **193** room, surrounded by his own group of "real" single parents. Like "Puttin' On the Hits," here was another discourse validated by the adjacency of some agreed on but unverifiable reality while diametric meanings were simultaneously adduced. The regress was infinite: even the hapless Bush piped in, helpfully adding that the American Family should be more like the Waltons and less like the Simpsons. Thus are all images—aura stripped—reduced to a condition of meaninglessness.

Let me elaborate. I cannot seem to get through a lecture without recourse to my favorite metaphor for the apparatus of contemporaneity, that good old surrealist entertainment, the exquisite corpse. You know the one. Breton described it as "a game of folded paper played by several people who compose a sentence or drawing without anyone seeing the preceding collaboration or collaborations." The now classic example, which gave the game its name, was drawn from the first sentence obtained this way: "The exquisite corpse will drink new wine." The surrealists held this game in high esteem. "Finally," wrote Breton, "we had at our command an infallible way of holding the critical intellect in abeyance, and of fully liberating the mind's metaphorical activity."

The exquisite corpse is a primitive juxtaposition machine, a means of literary or artistic gene-splicing. It aims to break down conventional structures of meaning by declaring that anything goes with anything. Television is a sophisticated juxtaposition machine. Contemplate for a moment the actual experience of television. Whether it is produced by the remote control zap or the *flânerie* of the daily schedule, the cut is television's main event, producing an unbelievable miasma of ever more miniscule bits, fragment after fragment after fragment. Like the playing of the exquisite corpse, every watching of television yields an astonishing, totally original artifact, a fresh freak. That characteristic jump from the rotting bodies in Bosnia to the douche commercial ought to be ludicrous, but it is not. And that juxtaposition reveals the power of modern culture, the power to make true and false obsolete.

For consumerism—which seeks simply to maximize the available number of things—this system for eroding the inflexibilities of meaning is amazingly economical. After all, if any juxtaposition makes sense, no combination is lost. It is just like those infinite monkeys sitting at their typewriters, pecking away until one of them finally produces *Hamlet*. The only problem with that system is the implied waste of manuscripts before the Bard is successfully aped. Television resolves this difficulty with bold economy. Since there can be no illegible artifacts, every chimp is a Shakespeare. By extension, any accident can be president . . . or architecture. Indeed, the freak is the characteristic reconciliation of simulation and authority.

Don't get me wrong, I love the abundance, and there is nothing wrong with being a freak. What is missing here—what the TV system (and the architecture and urbanism that grow out of it) prefers you not to have—is a useful, truly meaningful means for distinguishing, for working through it all. The surrealists, of course, had surrealism: they wanted their images to be screwy and presumably examined the products of their juxtaposition machine for traces of familiarity. But what are we to do? Take a look at this Hollywood image, the very latest in the constructed subject! Michael Jackson and E.T. are—along with Ronald Reagan, Mickey Mouse, and Chairman Mao—easily the most mediated images of the age. Michael and E.T. belong together not simply as embodiments of the cuddly Other but due precisely to the degree of their mediation: they are neighbors in the same conceptual space. Fabulous, furry, freak brothers. They belong together precisely because anything belongs together on their planet. This is a recipe for inertia, for sitting there and changing the channel again and again and again and again.

But let us take a slightly more serious look at the probable character of human subjectivity should this regime prevail at the millennium. Last Christmas eve Walter Hudson died. At the time of his death Hudson weighed 1,125 pounds, slightly down from the 1,200 to 1,400 pounds (he kept breaking scales, the exact figure is unknown) that established his Guinness-certified record as the world's fattest man. Indeed, his body was so huge, a section of the wall of his house had to be torn down and a forklift brought in to remove it. His enormous coffin was towed behind a hearse to the cemetery, where he was buried in a double plot.

Walter Hudson is, for me, the paradigmatic millennial man, an ideal subject for the postelectronic age. His quintessence, however, lies not in his bulk but his immobility: except for a tragically brief period of slimming, Hudson was unable to leave his house. Indeed, for years he was unable to get out of bed. He was sustained by surrounding himself with a kind of minimum apparatus of personhood: flanking his specially constructed bed were refrigerator and toilet, computer and television set.

His bulk, however, is not entirely irrelevant to his exemplary condition. To be sure, it was the medium of his immobility. But it was also the reason for his celebrity, for his visibility. Hudson is such a superb emblem for our current condition precisely because of the transitional nature of his situation, its simultaneous evocations of old and new strategies of visuality. On the one hand, his baroque corpulence—his   **195** achievement, the nominal reason for his celebrity—speaks of historic routines of spatiality. Hudson's distinction was, after all, precisely to occupy more space at a given moment than anyone in history.

But if his initiating condition was to apotheosize an antique, volumetric condition of space, a rhapsodization of excess, his celebrity came via a new, televisual condition of spatiality. We knew Walter Hudson via his endless presence on the evening news as he battled his bulk, ran his business (couture for fat gals), and strove to survive. He was a citizen of that virtual world of images that is coming to so dominate consciousness with its infinite, recombinant, mendacious mobility. Hudson's heft always argued for his pre-virtuality, but his mobility was entirely virtual. When Hudson entered a million living rooms at seven o'clock around the globe, he entered via TV because that was precisely the only way he could get in the door.

I sincerely believe that we are among the last generations that will enjoy or suffer (depending on your point of view) non-virtual subjectivity. More, I believe that this divide between an artificial, electronically or chemically conjured reality and that which is more directly apprehended by the senses is the dominant issue that we confront as architects. The postmillennial struggle will surely be about space and autonomy, about the politics of limits to mind—and more relevantly—body. The bottom line here is that if the virtual reality jockeys prove themselves able to conjure sensations of physicality that are either indistinguishable or better than the quotidian version, it may be time to move along, to chill out, to fire up the CAD and design the fleshy ergonomic toggles to switch the Holo to Virtual.

The site for these struggles or investigations or resignations—at least in the near term—is likely to occur along the seam between virtuality and physicality. A vast new discourse of the prosthetics of translation is already arising, yielding a class of objects that bridge between the spatial, nondimensional world of virtual space and the body-bound world of antique reality. These will range from stereoptic laser scanning glasses able to beam virtual images straight onto the retina, to a myriad of stimulating implants, to a million shrinking appliances, bringing numberless images into our shrinking homes, rendering us all unmoved movers, aswim with fantasies of total mobility even as we sit paralyzed in our chairs. Already, children learn to hold the TV remote control before a fork.

For me, the totemic, if primitive, nowadays example of this site is the
cash machine, a translation device par excellence bridging between the

material and the ethereal realms. The existence of these machines is predicated, obviously, on the need for cash, on our condition of not-quite-readiness to relinquish the reliability and palpability of paper notes to a more completely abstracted, electronic relationship to money. Here is also architecture degree, if not quite zero, let us say, at least .01. In its minimal way, the cash machine links this transaction with the electronic beyond to a tiny ordering of actual space.

In ancient Egypt, gateways to the afterlife were included in funerary architecture, depicted as narrow stone slits. The cash machine is also such a portal, a point of entry into the virtual, electronic global city. Activating the system by the insertion of a plastic "identity" card into a slim orifice, the citizen attempts to "log on." This is a moment of great tension, the pause as the invisible police test you, examine your account, decide whether to let you have what you want. It is the primal test of citizenship in the new world order: the only qualifications for admission are a balance and a number.

In many American cities, certain nonelectronic realities intrude on this transaction. For security's sake (increasingly architecture and design's most absolute rationale), cash machines are often located in glazed antechambers to bank branches, places, in theory, of adequate public visibility to deter robberies on the spot. To be admitted, one sticks one's card in an external slot, the computer runs a check, and an automatic door buzzes you in. To penetrate this first circle of security, low-level qualifications are adequate: one merely needs a card, not a balance. In practice, even a card is unnecessary to get in. At most banks in New York, homeless people are stationed at these doors, opening and closing them in circumvention of the security system, cups in hand, self-designated door persons.

The scene is in many ways a perfect rendering of the degeneration of the physical space of public activity in the millennial, postelectronic city. Efficiently, it deploys a compact apparatus of privilege, ranging from the untouchable at the door, demeaning him or herself in the hopes of some trickle-down from those admitted to the inner circle, to the Brahmans secure in their secret code numbers and reliable balances, Reaganism made flesh. What they share, though, is not simply the meanly designed physical environment of the little cash piazza: all participate in a culture in which surveillance has come to stand in for public space.

It is an irony of this essentially paranoid condition that the most enfranchised members of this electronic public are those willing to submit to the most draconian forms of observation. To fully participate in the electronic city is to have virtually all of one's activities recorded, correlated, and made available to an enormous invisible government of shadowy credit agencies, back-office computer banks, and endless media connections. To exist in the public realm of the electronic system means to be wired in. The ultimate consequence is that the body, the person, no longer simply exists in public space but actually becomes it. This is the heart of the threat to architecture, that it shrink to the dimensions of the body.

As with the cash machine's bridging position along the seam between physical object and immaterial network, the intermediate character of the present is also reflected in the vast increase in mobility that the global citizenship is currently experiencing. For the moment, we are obsessed with an old, Newtonian vision of mobility. Status among multinational mental proletarians such as ourselves is calculated in frequent flier miles. But the global corridor is also a direct physical analogue to the space of virtuality. It is increasingly, to begin, everywhere the same. But it is also a condition of intense surveillability. The endless credit card transactions, security checks, car reservations, seat assignments, and special meals speak of a condition in which one's position is constantly fixed. Over a billion people pass through this system annually in a state of flat mobility.

In the end, though, literal mobility matters almost not at all. In a world of exponential population growth, we are constantly receiving (mixed) signals to take up less space. Keep your cigarette smoke out of my eyes, become an anorexic, sit still and watch television. Here is the message: I believe we are all at risk of becoming so many Walter Hudsons, well-wired lumps of protoplasm, free to enjoy our virtual pleasures, mind-moving and disembodied, unable to get out of bed. For such subjects, architecture will not be necessary. On the other hand, though, there are lots of mornings when not getting out of bed seems like a pretty appealing alternative to me.

The real question, though, is whether we will have the choice. Architects must decide on the degree of complicity they wish to share with this enterprise, whether they wish simply to be the fixative on the body politic or whether they will join the struggle for space. Clearly, if we are going to avoid having this rammed down our throats, we need some standards for judging, however personal. This is the challenge of a culture dominated by television, the medium that begs the most fundamental questions for architecture.

Architecture must somehow account for this unruly realm or die. As I have suggested, the anything-goes space of simulation has the power to overwhelm architecture in two fundamental ways. First, by the creation of a so-called virtual reality that is as persuasive and mesmerizing in its sensory effects as anything we are able to produce at the drawing board. We must quickly decide whether this electronic, hallucinogenic space is to be the new space of architecture. More immediately serious is the promiscuous pluralism of the consumer juxtaposition machine, the fearsome repression of absolute tolerance that makes ludicrous virtually any decision that we make short of total surrender. Classicism today, deconstructivism tomorrow—who cares, it is only images.

What resources do we architects have against this? Obviously a critical stance is crucial. To paraphrase Lenin, patience and irony are the chief virtues of a true architect. But beyond critique, I think it is crucial for each of us to ask the kiddie's first question: where do buildings come from? Every architect, in his or her formation, must invent architecture afresh: we all need our primal scenes. Beyond the requirements of good citizenship and respect for the planet, this obliges the organization of some system of preferences, some serious self-emboldening as to the sources of the answer.

Nowadays, there is a struggle over the organization of these preferences into doctrines, an impulse to arrogate the authority of other systems to give an absolute account for taste. Like the man on TV testifying about the weight-loss formula that allowed him to lose two hundred pounds, architects everywhere give endless accounts of their procedures. . . . I drew a line from the AA to the Albert Memorial, I read Calvino, I rotated the grid the same number of degrees as it was Celsius on the afternoon that I met you, I spat on the drawing, I traced the outline of last night's pizza, etc., etc. Such slavish dedication to the empty authority of procedures is especially rife in the schools.

This kind of daffy, postfunctionalist methodology (form follows . . . anything!) is probably as good a place to begin as there is. I like the talk just fine—it is the piety that is disturbing. For me, sources give no special authority to forms, however much they may veneer a layer of curiosity or provide fodder for graduate students and psychoanalysts. Still, where else can you begin? What, finally, is there really to talk about other than intentions and whims. So, as my contribution to the coupling of architecture and culture, I would like to offer you a series of theses, my own intentions and whims, this week's nineteen most immutable points. But *theses* is too overbearing a word. Rather, let me offer some slogans or mantras or—even better—homilies—to use in confronting the ever looming crisis of beginnings.

These homilies lead nowhere in particular: I do not think this is the moment for prescription, exactly, certainly not at the formal level. We scarcely need to assert the universal necessity of pilotis and a free ground plane, the superiority of regionalism, the importance for architecture to express in its every beam and joist the destabilized character of modern social relations. My homilies are simply sites, spots where architecture seems especially fluid to me, the places where I am thinking about architecture, the advice I give myself, my family values. As someone who sees himself in a condition of just starting, I choose also to give them a swelling millennial tone, in the expectation that a decade will carry me somewhere. These slogans are both hopeful and cautionary.

Just Do It

To begin the game, you do have to put the signifier into play. Fold paper, close your eyes, stab the dictionary, pick your nose, and examine the product carefully, watch TV day and night, make rubbings of your beloved's backside. Although we all crawl before we fly, architecture is no universal language, not for long at any rate. It is true, though, that useful beginnings comfortingly tend to be on all fours, the most modest statical condition. Later we learn to boogie.

Space Is the Place

As I suggested earlier, if architecture as we know it is threatened by millennial technical change, it is because the gremlins of DNA and silicon and the wizards of aerospace and entertainment—the military-industrial-biological-theme-park complex—are increasingly able to provide experiences of simulated spatiality that are ever more indistinguishable from the "real thing." Walter Wriston, ex-CEO of Citibank, recently remarked on television, "the 800 telephone number and the piece of plastic have made time and space obsolete." Or as Don DeLillo has a character in his novel *White Noise* say, "For most people there are only two places in the world, where they live and their TV set. If something happens on TV, they have the right to find it fascinating, whatever it is." Who needs Ronchamp when you have *The Cosby Show*? I do not mean to sound the Luddite, but I must repeat that I do believe that the retention of literal physicality will be the great crisis for architecture in the coming century. Many will argue that if virtual reality turns out to be better, more useful, more under our control, more profoundly connected to the Lebenswelt, architecture might as well wither. Allow me to remain a skeptic. Propinquity is democracy's engine; the chains of mediation with which we must increasingly live are no friends of our rights or our art.

The Name of That Place Is I Like It Like That

Speaking of the simulacrum, isn't architecture getting a tad onanistic? There is a narcissism abroad, a tightening gyre of self-simulation. Our feeble, co-opted avant-garde—caught up completely in the routines of the gallery system—takes itself much too seriously, obsessed with pedigree, giving endless fawning declarations of tattooed seriousness as vaccine against further Nagasakis and Treblinkas. Let's stop this. The hermeneutics of nothingness can only yield the architecture of despair.

It is another millennial symptom, though, an issue of family values, a crisis of authority striking a class of production nervous about its own irrelevance. Recent Frankenstein attempts to graft the purloined authority of theory and history onto the comatose body of unexamined architecture has—to date—not even managed to produce many particularly stimulating freaks, merely pretty baubles foaming about how true they are. Slathered with decon mascara or regional rouge, the content does not change, despite the claim. The result: an architecture obsessed with buggering flies and telling the rest of us not to get it on. Why this nervousness in front of the teacher when it would be better just to have fun? Here is a good formula for judging architectural results: that's the way—uh-huh uh-huh—that's the way I like it. Or how about this one, paraphrased from the great Duke Ellington: "If it looks good, it is good."

All You Need Is Love

A few sights that interest me: the strange conjoined expressionistic planes of the stealth fighter; the weird attenuated snout, darting long tongue, and push-me, pull-you body of the anteater; the billowing of clouds; the way navigation devices are grafted to the sides of airplanes like goiters; crepuscular blue skies; almost any construction site; the little knobs on brioche; extremely long flights of stairs; dinosaurs, especially stegosaurus; the heliotropic bending of trees in the city; long hairs that sprout from little bumps on the cheeks of dogs; the bristle of cranes at harborside; bits of plywood stuck to concrete when formwork is removed; steam-rise from cappuccino machines; the dimples at the small of the back. Why shouldn't mimesis be free? Why shouldn't function follow form?

You Can't Dance to a Lousy Beat

Naturally, though, function should not follow form anywhere. Taste is not an absolute substitute for thinking, never mind how elaborately it is rationalized. After all, the waltz is only one beat away from the march. Is

201

it possible to love both? Only with some changes: all fantasies of cooperation are not the same, there is good sex and bad. My own deepest
pornographic fascination—as you may have gathered—is with aircraft,
with needle-nosed fighters, swing-winged bombers, and hulking, bul-
bous transports. Such aesthetic fancies are mighty troubled. After all,
these are implements with no good uses, murder weapons. While gener-
alissimos at the Pentagon may stare with untroubled satisfaction at velvet
paintings of sunsets streaked with B-52 contrails, slavering with the same
unalloyed scopophilia as the teen boy crouched over the centerfold of
Miss October, the rest of us—neither futurists not fascists—encounter
greater difficulty with these images. The answer is what the Situationists
called the *détournement*—the twist—dancing to the march, turning the
sergeant major into Sgt. Pepper, wearing their clothes on our bodies.
Functionalism begins with fun.

No More Secondhand Superego

I do not exactly know why your unconscious should become my folklore. Why should anyone be bothered by the return of someone else's repressed? Once we are adults, we can try to be clear about the engines
that regulate us, we can fight to make a choice. If you would rather have
Einstein than the Brothers Grimm at bedtime, so be it! If you prefer
Chaka Khan to Jacques Lacan, let's disco! Some caution, however, seems
prudent. There is somebody under that Mickey Mouse costume, and it is
not clear that he is friendly. Whenever we dance, I think I feel his grip on
my wallet. Go to hell Mickey! An architect needs sharp teeth, ready to
bite the invisible hand.

Don't Let Gravity Get You Down

Ah, yes. One of the glories of the age is that—for the first time—architecture is about to be loosed from its most primary and historic constraint:
gravity. The vast project of extraterrestrial construction, already begun,
proceeds almost entirely without us. Aren't we foolish to be missing out?
I, for one, want to participate, to go to this place where up and down
cease to constrain, where our own motion can assume any angle at all.
Let's build that damned space station! Let's go to Mars! Creating an
earthbound architecture decorated with signifiers of this possibility—
hanging columns and wiggly walls are not enough, just nostalgia avant la
lettre. Free coordinates—an architecture able to find any geometry it can
imagine and striving for none—beckon off the horizon. The tyranny of
the grid—that great totem of the right of all modern citizens to surren-

der their differences—is about to be breakable. The plan has ceased to be the generator. I speak here simply of form. The suspension of gravity, after all, is not the same as the suspension of memory.

Hack, Hack, Hack

Architecture exercises its morality by its scrupulous choice of means. The brick does not choose what it wishes it to be, we tell it and we do not have to tell it the same thing twice. Of course, our choice has influences— culture, religion, diet, drugs, psychosis, jet lag—the usual conspiracy against the unexpected. Technology is simply more culture, it is not received or inevitable: science is what we make it. Every technology useful to architecture must be vigorously questioned with every single use, if only to keep up with the breathy pace of change. Our prejudice must always be for better or more fun solutions: let culture play the conservative while we swing out over the void. The weight of a billion bricks laid up through history ought not deny the billowing strong gossamer film, the tensile metallic sinews, or the solar-powered electronic thermal regulator being born today in the labs of invention. We must make extravagant demands of technology, not simply take it off the shelf. Hackers, those happy Robin Hoods of appropriated technology, whizzing down the wireprint byways of the Web, are models for us: in control, critical, ready to crash bad systems, out for good times, independent yet happy to network for what is right, for freedom and sound choices. Let us adopt the motto of the hacker as he or she penetrates to the next circle of shrouded mystery: "Further!"

Do What Comes Naturally

Every day is earth day for architecture. A planetary view demands an architecture that knows both how to assert and how to recede. Terrestrial architecture, after all, is different from what we will make off earth. Down here, the goal must be inclusion: the fantasy of regulation is unhealthy, father of pesticides and panopticons and grids without end, amen. Architecture must be green, must open its windows to let things in and out, must collaborate in the cycles that would happen without us. It is time to vet every aspect of construction for sustainability. I sing a song of fuzzy buildings, happy to blur the edges between themselves and the woods, bored of the old arguments about distinction. I sing a song of ecology, of buildings certain of their roots, of their rejection of that zero-sum game where any building's rise has a companion depletion someplace unseen by those who have always kept their eyes pressed tight against such **203** thoughts. Why should we be still be scarring the earth?—architecture wants to be about renewal. Let it blossom. Let us soon grow our buildings from seeds.

If It's Broke, Fix It

What are buildings for, if not use? Architecture for architecture's sake is just narcissism, no closer to the matter than a novel or a smooth stone. However inspirational a grain of sand can be, it is only a goad, not an answer: the world is just not in there. Today, especially around the schools, there is a grim daft reticence about architecture's utility. Beleaguered by a threatening technical supersession, architecture's true defense is not to diffuse itself into an ever expanding field, conflating with sculpture or cinema or philosophy or gardening, surrendering the brilliant abiding fact that it really is useful, that it keeps us warm, dry, curious, hidden, wet, in, out, safe, and at risk, to vague formulations about poetry or cosmology. Don't get me wrong—the whole thing works only if form has real autonomy, if it is born free, if all fantasies can be points of departure. But to suppress the million happinesses of inhabitation is suicide. Architecture is strong medicine, and we are the doctor. Why take the dose if you don't feel better afterwards?

Less Is Less

Are you as bored with minimalism as I am, with these tired old men flogging their empty boxes as if they were the containment vessels of profundity? There comes a time when that little square ceases to look like nothingness and begins to look like . . . a little square, when we grow tired of staring at the naked emperor's dick, however big. What is wanted now is what engineers—our ridiculously successful sibling rivals—call elegance. There is a fine and abiding idea about minimalism here. Not the dumb, meaning-pared, limbo minimalism of the art world—that how low can you go, paranoid about complexity, minimalism—but the isomorphic minimalism of aerospace or machine tools. The point is to find purpose that abets form, form that abets purpose, the complexity that comes from demanding that architecture do everything that we want it to do even as strange new complexities invite us to want more and more. If it is complicated, let us have complication, fusion, not fission, more analogies, an endless game of egging on and I dare you. Let us have an architecture of raised expectations and ceaseless elaboration. Architecture cannot escape the complexities of the world.

Back to the City

The city invents architecture. It is the engine and laboratory of human relationships, a pattern computer, a Rosetta stone. The city is the source of architecture's meaning. Over the past twenty years there has been a shift in architecture's understanding of the city. Nowadays, the city is too much mere mnemonic, not enough terrain of invention and art. We love Borges but do not see the city as he does, convolute and mysterious. We merely see Borges, looking at the city, and we shut our eyes in imitation of the blind man's gaze. Designing cities has become little more than the pseudo-psychoanalysis of elderly forms. We arrive at the office. The corpse is on the coach. After fifty minutes we say, "I'm afraid your time is up." But the analysand is no Lazarus. He just lies there, and the stink gets worse and worse.

Enough of this. It is time for architecture to reembolden itself in the face of the city, to reengage the act of imagining new cities, invented from scratch, the vast possibilities for new relationships liberated by fresh technologies of juxtaposition, by happier visions. We did not live through Woodstock, May '68, Tiananmen Square, just to go back to living with our parents in the suburbs. Modern urbanism has provided the world with a vast legacy of diminished expectations, both physical and social. If architecture has a single duty, it is precisely to raise as many of them as we can, and keep raising them, even when Daddy and Mommy say no. The new city, invented by induction, growing just out of control, needs as many centers as there are citizens. Electronic media, economic globalization, and ecologized production need not be the enemies of the urban but an opportunity for reinventing urban form according to the tests of freedom and pleasure. Invidious zoning—the oppressive deployment of class and use—dies in the space where anything can go. We must rise to reinvent a new galaxy of the particular. The greatest architectural crisis of the millennium is precisely to retain the city as the premier site of optimistic physicality and real difference. To repeat, without propinquity, there is no democracy.

Tail Wags Dog

Raising hopes may be the whole game. One of architecture's historic poignancies—and one of its charms—has been that its reach so often exceeds its grasp. I am a Lamarckian about this. I think that overreaching—like the giraffe straining to nibble the tender leaves at the treetop—is the only way to grow tall. Try as it will, architecture has never been able to truly invent human relations, however brilliantly it maps or wraps them. No, the most we can really do through building is to everywhere inlay a multitude of canny little distortions, provoking insights and twists, flea-bites on the doggy politic that cause it to shift and wiggle, and scratch like a mad dog. Enough of such excitement makes a new hound. Once he has heard Chubby Checker, Fido wants to twist again. Fortunately, much of this activity will appear to be funny. Terrific, I say. Let us have lots of hilarious architecture. Let us blow away the awful burdens of seriousness in gales of laughter. Architecture is getting too lugubrious nowadays. Hemmed by piety on one side and a wink and a nudge on the other, we need perplexity, belly laughs, and amazement.

Embody the Body

The human subject is architecture's center. This is literally true, no metaphor. Architecture is not designed around a recollection or an image but to serve a fact, two-legged and vertical, air-breathing and susceptible to colds, happy and afraid, full of moods. Nonhabitable architecture is a perfect oxymoron. This means that all building (and unbuilding) is finally prosthetic, about extension, about extra eyes and ears, big new noses, long sinewy legs, vast foliate lungs. If architecture provides no enhancement to experience, who needs it! Otherwise, let its tasks be taken up by other arts. The only trouble with architecture prosthetically imagined is that it does open the path to a certain monstrosity. We do not want our architecture making us into robots, shrinking our possibilities by leeching out space and leaving us narcoleptic, Walkmen in our ears and remote control TV zappers in our hands. The answer is to keep working, priming our pumps: more will always be more. But I repeat: let us not spend too much time in front of the mirror. Architecture wants to be anthropomorphic in content but not always form—people are not the only measure, just the only reason.

Enough Is Enough

As culture's complexity burgeons, we need a hedge against too much order. Architecture ought to be fallible and richly flawed. We should always imagine architecture and our ways of making it with a boundary of apraxia, a place beyond which it breaks down, ceases to work, a point of failure where the system reaches a complexity beyond which it can no longer perform coordinated movements. There is such a thing as too much architecture: buildings and cities that overreach should crash and burn, lie on their backs like crabs overturned, all flailing legs and vulnerability, anxious frustration, easy prey. Every home should have a memento of some foolish collapsed tower, some bauble from Babel.

Just Say No

Can we have stimulus without addiction? Can architecture be more like a sweater than a syringe? Not an ordinary sweater, of course, but an exceptional sweater, a thrilling sweater, cozy, useful, glamorous, and unexpected. A sweater beyond sweaters, from a closet full of fabulous sweaters. The best pleasures are chosen, not obliged. Tyranny is at bay only so long as we can freely remember or not remember. There will, after all, be many days when we will want no sweater at all. On these days, we may lie naked in the sun, tanning nicely as the VR Helmet transports us to tea with Nanook, among the ice floes.

Ugly Architecture

Ugly is what the fearful call the new. This being the case, let us not shrink from the occasional act of reasoned terror. The main tyranny in the world is the conspiracy to save us from every unpredictability. Genetic screening allows us to abort the fetus that hasn't the brainpower for Harvard or the reflexes for a goalie. The shopping mall makes sure all our choices are equivalent, everywhere. Yeltsin guarantees a Pepsi for everyone. Let architecture rise in the defense of unreasonable fantasy: too much Pepsi or none! Architects should be sex fiends, coupling with whatever is willing, climaxing like crazy. To be a great architect is to love all your kids, especially for their differences. Let us make grotesque, Rabelaisian, crazy architecture. As Bakhtin reminds us, this is the mode of regeneration and utopia, a gay parody of the official styles of reason. I like an architecture that thumbs its nose.

Everyone Architect

Why do we guard our prerogatives so jealously? Why not surrender them instead. Architecture, after all, is common property. How can it be then that we are so white, so male, so nicely dressed?

Who needs a license to make art? And why do so few people really know us at our best?

Space Is the Place

I reiterate the message by way of conclusion. Against the onslaught of virtuality and simulation, architecture—if it wants to survive—must counterpose the space of reality and the reality of space. Against the antidemocratic assault on the physicality of space, architects must insist on a millennium of concrete fantasies of construction, inhabitation, and pleasure.

And those are some of the values in my family.

1991

The Second Greatest Generation

Never Trust Anyone over . . . ?

For the past twenty years I have been over thirty, the actual milestone having occurred slightly before the lapsing of the seventies (which was when much of the sixties actually occurred). And I am not the only one. As the boomer bulge in the bell curve grinds toward oblivion, we are driven to ask: what has the aging of youth culture meant for architecture?

Youth, of course, is strictly a cultural matter. My generation is by self-definition—the only one that counted for us—young. Architecture, the "old man's profession," has never been congenial to us (among others). We certainly returned the favor: bridling at the "man," many of us re-belled, abandoning architecture, heading for the woods, hand building, advocating for communities, drawing, making trouble, laying the ground-work for the cultural revolution.

This did not really work out as we planned: the world seems not to have changed along the lines of the image we had for it. Somehow the "liberating" mantra of sex, drugs, and rock and roll changed into the nightmare of AIDS, Prozac, and MTV. How much of a hand did we have in this cultural devolution?

The Clinton Library

Limiting politics to resistance or selling out has not served us entirely well. Our own first president illustrates the sheer porousness, the cor-ruptibility of these categories. Clinton is not exactly one of us, in the same way any member of student government during the late sixties was not exactly one of us, but rather something between a quisling and a geek (depending on whether one focused on politics or style). Now we are witnessing the spectacle of two co-generationalists running for the presidency. These—the eternal frat boy and the sell-out student govern-ment type—give the lie to certain fantasies about the triumph of the countercultural. Sixty percent of Bush's class at Yale—the class of '68!—voted for either Nixon or Wallace. Gore elected to go to Vietnam. Patrician universities, with their solid ruling-class values and their various schools of social architecture, have a way of countering countercultural agendas, it seems.

And they have a way of promoting the middle of the road. When the time came for Clinton to build his shrine in Little Rock, did he turn to an architect his own age? Did he seek to radicalize the repository via form or effect? Not at all. He made his choice from the slightly older generation, choosing an architect not quite old enough to be his (absent) father but certainly enough to Wally his Beaver. The first boomer administration runs from its roots, affecting the same brain-dead Hollywood style that answers the question "Rock and Roll Museum?" with the answer "I. M. Pei " (author of the first "modern" presidential library). And we have not seen the presidential sax since he was trying to persuade us he shared our values (we will keep our pain to ourselves, thanks).

Blah, Blah, Blah

The political rebellion of the sixties announced itself in the characteristic speech of the late twentieth century: first person. But the self-promoting, self-conscious "I" of our generation has been hobbled by the awareness of the unconscious, which has hovered over us like a specter. This unconscious has not only promised the possibility of a "liberation of desire" from social constraint, it has also rallied skepticism of our best intentions. The unconscious, after all, *always* trumps the conscious as a cause of action and, thus, of political striving. Beneath the desire to do good lurks a neglected child. Behind the orderliness of minimalism lies crap in the pants. Politics itself has been reduced to just another symptom; it dare not promise a cure for fear of being labeled the dupe of its own neuroses.

Whether this is a proper reading of Freud is really not the issue; it is the one that undermined our sense of the world's reliability and of our own political will, producing a special generational uncertainty principle. We all have our styles of superego, and this combination of license and guilt has distinguished us, on the one hand, from the "greatest generation" of our parents, who—dammit—had something unequivocal to fight for, and on the other, from the gen X'ers and Y'ers, the Reagan *Jugend,* whose traumas seem so *fifties,* inflicted by the pressures of consumption, rather than rebellion. Thus, questions of influence acquire for us a special anxiety. The unflagging hegemony of the sixty-something and seventy-something cadre that rules, that formulated the parameters of the depoliticized, desocialized postmodernity that swept architecture in the seventies and eighties, needs a violent shaking from the left.

No More Secondhand Dad

What to do when the parents in your own family romance are the avant-garde? We received ours twice handed down, which somewhat diminished our sense of its originality. Avant-gardism is about rupture, overthrow, the father-murderous rage of art. Classic early-twentieth-century avant-gardism wanted a radical reworking of the visual aspect of architecture, *and* a reinvention of the process of production.

The postmodern "avant-garde" is a somewhat different creature. Compromised by a sense of having inherited both its credentials and its topics, its intellectual agenda was caught in the avant-garde dream of its ancestors. It thus recovered much of the ground explored fifty years before, redoubling the critical discourse it had inherited with its own meta-critical commentary, interpolating another layer of interpretation between the "primary" investigation and its own. *October* magazine, for example, bible of postmodernity (and exemplar for our own theorizing), continues to be held hostage by its obsession with surrealism, as with some lost idyll. And architecture carries on with fresh formalisms of the broken (or the perfect) square.

Try as we might, we have not been able to get Oedipus out of our edifices; inherited property still defines us. A false patriarchy continues to structure the discipline and practice of architecture, where a fraternal order of equals is presided over by a simultaneously dead and obscenely alive father, father Philip in this instance.

Life in the Past Lane

This stalled fascination with former revolutions is the result of a failure of nerve and of invention. It is also evidence of the ideological and psychological trauma that has beset our attempts to formulate an avant-garde in rebellion against an avant-garde to which it desperately desires to remain faithful. The result has been a kind of fission. One by-product is the hyperconservatism of our melancholy historicists. The other side—while it has produced visually novel buildings and has begun to build bridges to the new world of the virtual—still clings to dusty desires for legitimacy.

The lesson we have been unable to learn is that it takes a lot more rebellion than we have been able to muster to remain faithful to the heritage of the avant-garde.

Market Share

I am not sure the *New York Times* did us any favors with its gossipy, prurient cover story on Rem Koolhaas, our momentary laureate. Depicting him as a kind of edgy Martha Stewart, refusing to pronounce "it's a good thing" on any endeavor, effectively depicting his as the "mission of no mission," the *Times* tried to inscribe his fundamental cynicism into the format of the hero architect, *Fountainhead*-style. Of course, they went for the Hollywood version. Gary Cooper may have behaved like Frank Lloyd Wright, but the model buildings in the background were strictly Gordon Bunshaft.

Sound familiar? The challenge of collapsing the ideologue and the tastemaker is sure to test one side or the other dramatically. Is it possible to be Paul Auster, Sam Walton, and Kim Il Sung at the same time? Will Rem succeed in branding the generic?

Africa Shops at Prada

Jetting in to Harvard to administer his shopping seminar, Rem snags a job designing Prada stores. The press praises his strategy of branding: no design "identity" but *a space where things happen*, "an exciting urban environment that creates a unique Prada experience." A TV camera in the dressing room will permit you (and CBS ["Big Brother" is another Dutch import]) to see yourself from all sides at once. Will thousand-dollar shoes move faster when surveilled from all angles? Will there be an algorithm to airbrush our worst feature away? Must we buy this privatization of culture? Does the postmodern critique of the museum, the call for tearing down its walls, do anything but free art for the shopping mall? I will take Bilbao, thanks.

The trouble with an age of scholasticism is that you can talk yourself into the idea that *anything* is politics. By the time it has devolved from direct action to propaganda, to critical theory, to the appropriation of theory, to the ironic appropriation of theory, to the branding of theory, to the rejection of theory, something is lost. Critique stokes its own fantasy of participation. On the one hand, this produces boutique design as social practice, and on the other, it segues into the more rarefied reaches of recombination. My Russian partner, Andrei, has been smoking cheap cigarettes that someone recently brought him from back home. The bright red pack is emblazoned with a picture of Lenin in high-sixties graphic style. The maker is "Prima," the brand "Nostalgia," the smell appalling. What next? Lenin Lites and Trotsky 100's? Must we succumb to the speed of this? Can't we slow the thing down?

Nostalgie de la Boue

This new nostalgia (the nostalgia for packaged nostalgia) is everywhere. Now that my generation rules the media, part of us keeps busy looting our experience for the rudest forms of exploitation. If you have turned on your TV lately, you have seen *That Seventies Show,* a slick package of affects, the decade as a set of tics and styles. The expropriation continues to the limits of corporate memory. Advertising nowadays is lush with sixties themes, as fiftyish account executives preside over the wholesale trashing of the culture that nourished them. "I Feel Good"—a laxative. "Forever Young"—invidious irony—incontinence diapers. On *Survivor* flaming torches turn the game-show paradise island into Trader Vic's.

Nostalgic for fifties and sixties forms, yet too hip not to be troubled by the accumulated political baggage of the project, this cadre offers a stance of almost pure cynicism: "I am saying this, but I don't actually believe it; in fact, I don't actually believe anything, because it is no longer possible to do so." With Niemayer or Lapidus or Harrison serving as sound tracks (and the Stones, perhaps, playing on the answering machine), they seem to want to suspend indefinitely the moment when they would be obliged to take a position.

A microgenerational conflict now exists among those for whom the sixties represent a source of anxiety, those for whom they still represent possibility, and those for whom they are simply ancient history. Most invested in the middle alternative, I grapple with this legacy, but the particulars grow vague (the feeling stays evergreen).

That Vision Thing

Our fantasies did have vision, the product, mainly, of the working out of certain congruent themes of prior modernisms. Those domes and inflatables and garbage housing were not just technologically and environmentally prescient, they also figured—whether in their civil rights or Woodstock variants—in political ideas about the extension, openness, and spontaneity of spaces of assembly. And, the canny melding of technological control with an "anti"-technological ideology gave birth to appropriate technology.

The alternative visuality of the sixties, however, has had only the most marginal impact on architecture. (Many breathe a sigh of relief.) The psychedelic style that included Fillmore posters, the Merry Pranksters bus, and Sgt. Pepperesque couture, required a certain lag before becoming appropriable by architecture. We liberated the seventies supreme soviet—Venturi, Stern, Moore, Graves, et al.—from the kitsch closet and **213** made it permissible for them to love Vegas and the roadside. But always they had to rationalize it, to capture it for their outmoded agendas and fantasies of control. We responded with disengagement and irony as usual.

The "appropriated" art of so many artists of my generation was a typically limp response, immediately gobbled up by the art machine and offering not a hint of what to do about it. Having bought into a critical history that denigrated intentions, we then bought into our own ironical reappropriation of intentionality via obsessive proceduralisms and poetic trances. Too late! Narcissism is not the same as self-confidence. Even Seinfeld has been canceled.

Vive la Différence!

The Whole Earth Catalogue and *Our Bodies, Ourselves* are our holy books, good news for a political body and a contested environment both. These really were milestones: we are all a little more gay now, a little closer to the earth, a little more skeptical about the system's "choices." The politicization of the personal (as the formula *should* have been) demands idiosyncrasy beyond the tonsorial and sartorial. Pity about our architecture. So many interesting sites wasted.

It Isn't Easy Being Green

We always hear that green architecture "looks bad," and most of it does. At the end of the day, though, separating your trash is probably a greater contribution to world architecture than Bilbao.

Well, maybe not Bilbao.

2000

214

War Is Swell

I was born after the war, a boomer. "My" war was Vietnam, which I experienced as a resistor. For me, the Second World War is history, pure mediation, and my primary visual source an engineer father who worked virtually all of his professional life at the Defense Department. I recall visits to his office on the Mall, where I was entranced by the display of remarkably accurate model ships, a sight that still inspires my work. I remember the blue copies of *Jane's All the World's Aircraft* and *Jane's Fighting Ships* that my father brought home every year, with their mesmerizing photos, performance data, and elegant line drawings. And I remember childhood war games and fantasies, enacted either outdoors in roaming bands or indoors at the side of a paralyzed friend, where the action consisted in narration, the dying of heroic deaths, he lying in his dystrophied bed, me in a chair alongside. I remember sitting at the back of my grade school class, drawing aircraft in my notebook, their bomb loads dropping to the bottom of the page.

The image of the war was ubiquitous then, and I approached it with both fascination and embarrassment. Forbidden war toys by a liberal-minded mother, my consumption of the war took a covert turn, part of a larger family drama. War games were fought with the toy guns of neighbor children, my reading done in bookshops and libraries, the *Sands of Iwo Jima* switched off at the sound of parental footfalls. Thus enjoined, the war and its images assumed the fascinations of the forbidden, an erotogenic turn. And not just the puerile phallomorphism of bombers and subs but florid irresistible death. Images of bodies dismembered and still were the unspoken object of the war research that absorbed much of my childhood—of the childhoods of so many boys, turning the pages of old *Life* magazines for photographs of Marines mangled on Tarawa beach, of Chinese civilians with bodies blown naked by Japanese bombs at Nanking, of the corpses stacked at Birkenau.

This furtive, varnished pleasure stimulated broad inquiry, and I amassed an astonishing breadth of knowledge. Even now, I can identify hundreds of aircraft, ships, tanks, guns, uniforms. I know the battles and the strategies, still experience the anxiety of a series of might have beens— **215** had the cloud cover held above the Ardennes, had the bomb killed Hitler, had the radar signals been correctly interpreted at Pearl Harbor, had the U-boat buildup been begun a year or two earlier, had the rail lines to the camps been bombed.

The war was my first big body of knowledge, with its vast classifications of things, masses of narrative, and its endless style. Every schoolboy of my generation had a complex lexicon of favorite war machines based on a careful connoisseurship. For many of us, the war provided the grist for our first real systems of objects. However, unlike those other great taxonomic reveries of American boyhood—motorcars and athletes—the hobbying of war objects begged an ethics, some engagement with the question of why. Indeed, it is in the space defined by this gap between the consumability of these images and the lassitude of the constraints on their enjoyment that a characteristic American consciousness is constructed.

Simply put, the message America received in the forties and fifties was that the war had been beneficial, a war unlike other wars, the "good" war. For us, it had been good in many ways. Between 1939 and 1945, the GNP increased from 88 billion dollars to 135 billion. Real compensation of industrial workers rose 22 percent. Net farm income doubled. Corporate profits had an after-tax growth of 57 percent in 1943 alone. Average plant utilization went from forty hours a week to ninety hours. The number of skilled black workers doubled. The percentage of women in the workforce grew dramatically. By the end of the war the United States was responsible for over 50 percent of the world's industrial production, including 40 percent of its production of arms. The war rescued America from its economic and psychic depression, thrust us to the forefront of global power, established us as the dominant national culture of the twentieth century.

In *Wars I Have Seen,* Gertrude Stein describes the Second World War as a cultural equivalent of the "dark and dreadful days of adolescence," marking a moment of transition from the childhood of the nineteenth century to the adulthood of the twentieth. For Stein, the war represents modernity, a modernity situated in a condition of uncertainty, of strangeness. She sees the war as a kind of epistemological break, a juncture after which the certainties bred of positivistic, nineteenth-century science were ruptured, destabilized, throwing the idea of progress, with its secure relations of means and ends, into radical doubt. For Stein, too, the war marked the end of the possibilities for the realist text, its supersession by the more disjunctive relations of modernism. Bring on the hounds of hyperreality.

Indeed, can there be any doubt that those hydra-horrors, the Holocaust and Hiroshima, yielded a level and character of anxiety that was entirely fresh? Here the Clausewitzean means are attenuated beyond comprehension. Yet postwar America—birthplace of the Strangelovean theory of Mutually Assured Destruction—bankrupted itself precisely to enable this straining antipathy between means and ends (freedom guaranteed by looming global Holocaust) to be resisted. Of course realism had to die. The language we were forced to use was so unreliable, so fundamentally mendacious, that such a literature was impossible.

My own adolescence was marked by that ripest of postwar graphics, the encircled black on yellow trigram of the fallout shelter/radiation logo. It is a symbol that cuts two ways, a certification of its own impossibility, trying to mean opposites (radiation and safety from radiation) at once. The most readily available summer design jobs during my college days—a brilliant piece of co-opting make-work—were assisting in a nationwide fallout shelter survey, an invitation to read every building in America with the eyes of a paranoid.

Not that the feeling was strange to me, I had been brought up on it. I remember—during the late-fifties mania—going to the familial backyard and beginning to dig. I was afraid, of course, horrified by the flood of images the media were whipping up in those days, but also angry, disappointed that my parents showed no interest in this latest consumer (it was hoped) durable, not keeping up with the Joneses, another sign that my parents were simply inattentive to the needs of the (post)nuclear family.

The fallout shelter was a malignant inversion of the historic modernist housing fantasy, the notion of a guaranteed *Existenzminimum* for every worker, a fantasy played out on the bright side of planning for the war in those sunny and cooperative communities that so aptly merged sensibility and purpose. Indeed, if one were to parse the descent of the inter-war urban ideal, one stream leads from the planned communities of the war down to the enfeebled New Towns (like Reston and Columbia) of the sixties and seventies. Another crests at Levittown, the egalitarian automobile suburb. And a third—the ultimate revenge of the windowless monad—leads to the shelter craze, the ultimate one-family home with its global hearth. The shift was very rapid. If the image of sheltering during the war was collective, of civilians huddled together in the London subways (as depicted, for example, in those remarkable Henry Moore sketches), the standard issue equipment for the A-bomb shelter always included a rifle, to keep everyone else out.

Reporting on the trial of Adolf Eichmann in Jerusalem, Hannah Arendt remarked—indelible phrase—on the "banality of evil." In postwar America, our embrace of the evils of war as a national project resulted in a discourse that was not so much banal as bizarre. The happy techno-talk, the cults of euphemism, the very insistence on describing nuclear war in the antique terms of military tactics and strategy were not simply an instance of "generals always preparing to fight the last war" but of postmodernity itself. The postmodern environment is one in which old notions of combination and sequence have broken down. Indeed, the fetishization of the implements of the Second World War is surely a nostalgia for the "conventional" in both senses, for pre-apocalyptic means and for the immemorial master narratives of conflict.

The notion that the war was something to be looked back upon sanctified its artifacts. Such reverence for raw instrumentality is very American. We romance handguns as "equalizers," conferring a democratic aura on a thing, converting it to a right. The six-gun, symbol of the frontier, allegedly enshrined in constitutionality, serves simultaneously as instrument of the romance of self-individuation and citizen power and of the manifest destiny of the American imperium. In the Second World War, we had myriad good and undeniable reasons for taking up the gun. But can the satisfied pursuit of national violence, however just, fail to expand the envelope of individual propensity?

I have never written expressly about the war, and—not being a historian—I write about its effects on the territory of my own interests, on architecture, urbanism, and design, on the transformation of their contexts of possibility. I agree with Gertrude Stein that the war was a highwater mark of modernism, one that enshrined its dominant construct—functionalism—as a virtual national aesthetic. Functionalism, enamored of the "objectivity" of industrial objects, argued for a theory of absolute accountability, for the singular legibility of every aspect of the artifacts under its view. Although functionalism was a theory of pure purposiveness, its investment was always in means rather than ends. This led to its characteristic myopia, its focus only on the efficient elegance of the bomber's design, celebrating its capacity for maneuver and flight, ignoring its lethality, or, rather, translating it into pure allure.

Functionalism is an aesthetic of adolescence, sustainable only due to the narrowness of its preoccupations, its immaturity vis-à-vis any larger notion of consequences, whether in use or in expression. In the postnuclear, postmodern, postwar climate, this functional reading of objects—no longer undergirded by a national consensus about their meaning and purpose—unraveled. Forms were easily wrested from their original contexts and endlessly recombined, destabilizing original meanings with profuse substitutions and modifications. Emptied, the objects of war became mere insignia. For consumer culture, the result was an avalanche of metonymy, of things that looked like things. In the art world, functionalist efficiency devolved into minimalism, a last gasp run on the proprietorship of meaning, an attempt to keep the faith with the idea of pure, unassailable expressiveness, by a deliberate evisceration of all scope for nuance, the optimism of pessimism.

But let's get down to cases.

P-38

One of the preferred aircraft in my adolescent war fantasies was the Lockheed P-38. Legendarily a "hot" fighter, it still commands the enthusiasm of buffs and collectors. In part, this is because of its functional pedigree: the P-38 was a fast, agile, technologically advanced aircraft, appreciated by its pilots. It was also extremely distinctive visually, with twin engines and twin fuselages, its cockpit suspended between the two fuselage booms. P-38 was the aircraft that Frank Sinatra flew (and crashed) in *Von Ryan's Express,* an apt technical haberdashery for old blue eyes, an American plane, big, throbbing, powerful.

As symbolic postwar object, though, the P-38 reentered the culture in transmuted form. The aircraft was the favorite of Harley Earl, the legendary General Motors styling chief and father of the automotive tail fin. The P-38 first crossed over in the 1948 Cadillac, whose pubescent fin buds were direct emulations of the rounded twin tails of the P-38. That appropriation was already nostalgic—jets were flying by then—but Detroit quickly caught up with the jet age and then the rocket age via the styling medium, converting tragedy into farce in a familiar process.

For aircraft, form does follow function: visual differences enjoy a direct translation into differences in capability, performance, or mode of control. The automotive system—and the entire system of consumer machinery, in which it sits at the apex—flattens the legibility of such readings by surrounding them with a set of signifiers that sit at greater and greater distance from their practical points of origin. The tail fins of the Caddy—growing yearly topsy-like larger—may have originated in the memory of the control surfaces of one of the machines that contributed to the winning of the war, but in their descent into the rococo stylings of the early sixties, their meaning became ever more purely engaged with **219** the signification of mere, sheer excess. We simply believed that the cycle of prosperity would never cease.

Eisenhower

It is no coincidence that the election of Dwight Eisenhower to the American presidency coincided with the germination of the tail fin. The human and material instrumentalities of victory in a war regarded with great positive feeling by Americans were thus doubly celebrated. The reassuring Eisenhower, architect of victory and, by imputation, of the great prosperity it engendered, was a logical choice to continue and expand those very values.

In his way, Eisenhower was also an avatar of fashion. As general, he was known for the short "Eisenhower jacket," which was his preferred uniform. This outfit signified a senior staff officer dressed with an attitude both sufficiently casual to evoke a disdain for rigid hierarchy and sufficiently practical to take the field (all those photos of Ike getting out of the jeep driven by Kay Sommersby, another unspoken subtext). In studied contrast to the buffoonery of the uniforms of Goering and the Germans, the anachronistic cutaways and toppers of the Japanese government or the jackboots and swords of its generalship, Eisenhower, Patton—even the aviator-shaded MacArthur—conveyed the image of men at work, differing in appearance only in degree from workers on the factory floor—or ordinary soldiers.

In his postwar, presidential incarnation, Eisenhower continued to set the tone. Here, a double image prevails. The first is the Brooks Brothers, narrow-lapelled haberdashery of the organization man. The simple suits of the "conformist" society of the fifties offer up a mufti analogue to the GI drag, drab and regimented but with an acute slippage of purpose. Madison Avenue, after all, was the emblematic locus of fifties employment. For the consumer leviathan, advertising was the extension of war by other means. The sacrifice of war rotated around the axis of prosperity to become the leisure of peace.

Which brings us to the second classic postwar Eisenhowerian image: the golfer. Like some invert Cincinnatus, Ike forsook carbine for niblick, launching his spheroid missiles toward the halcyon green of American happiness. This image of Eisenhower offered copious sanction for a new sort of national enterprise, the conversion of the ethics of work and struggle into the project of recreation and leisure time. Ike, after all, was carpingly accused of being a president whose mind was too much on his golf game. Yet in this he displayed a remarkable prescience about the real nature of postwar America, about the true quality of private time in an era of abundance. What, after all, were we to do with our prosperity, with the fruits of our victory, if not enjoy them?

But Ike was no mindless duffer. He recognized not simply the product of war but the means of its achievement. In what was possibly the most important cultural observation to be made by an American president, Eisenhower left office with a warning. The "conjunction of an immense military establishment and large arms industry is new in the American experience," Ike cautioned. And continued, "we must not fail to comprehend its grave implications. . . . In the councils of government, we must guard against the acquisition of unwarranted influence, whether sought or unsought, by the military-industrial complex. The potential for the disastrous rise of misplaced power exists and will persist." No clearer statement of the dangerous basis of our war-won prosperity was ever uttered.

The Interstates

If there is a single physical legacy of the Eisenhower era, it is the enormous national highway system initiated during his presidency, 41,000 miles at completion, joining every joinable state. Indeed, the largest "thing" bequeathed on the nation by the war was the Interstate Highway System, easily the biggest single artifact ever built, ever imagined. The Hitlerian antecedent (". . . but he did build the autobahn") is not irrelevant. The Nazi road system responded to two imperatives: the stitching together of the nation and the creation of a transport infrastructure for the movement of armies. Our system—enabled by legislation calling for a National Defense Highway—did the same. The war had begged the question of the purposive coordination of the entire nation, and it was in the physical movement of people and goods that this integration found its highest expression.

The Interstates, however, were built after the fact of the war.

They expedited not the movement of war matériel but the dissemination of a single form of national prosperity. The Interstates were the venous system that infused a vast network of cultural homogeneity, the consumer version of the univalent apparatus of war. At every interchange rose an identical McDonald's, Roy Rogers, Holiday Inn, Mobil Station, Seven-Eleven. Down the exit ramp were the FHA-stimulated suburbs, the shopping centers, and the boomer schools. On the roadway itself, tens of millions of new cars tooled across the nation, finned like fighters. As Charles Wilson, Ike's secretary of defense, famously remarked, "What's good for General Motors is good for the country." The Interstates brought the happy ethos and methodology—victory and prosperity through the mass production of mobile machines—of the war back home.

In many ways, the Interstate system and its effects represent the high-water mark of American federalism. Funded at 90 percent, they were lusted at by the states, eager not simply for the almost free money but to be included in the new American system of prosperity. Their construction also coincided with that other great war-stimulated effort at integration: the extension of civil rights of black Americans. It was Eisenhower who called out the troops to defend the desegregation of the schools of Little Rock. Ike was clearly fixed on a vision of the spreading good.

Of course, there was a down side. What was good for General Motors was not uniformly good for the country, and the concrete ties that bound could also destroy. The Interstates foundered precisely where they encountered the complexities of the urban, where form and the deployments of class were not the sparse and regular monotone of rural and suburban America. Spilling the clot of cars into spaces that could not accommodate them, bulldozing neighborhoods for efficient passage through them, the highway program became a kind of carpet bombing, warring on hapless civilians who simply happened to find themselves in the way of some higher aspiration to order and efficiency.

Opened Cities

In many American cities today, buildings have their addresses painted in enormous numerals on their roofs. This is intended to increase the efficiency of aerial surveillance by the police, to make the order of the city more visible. Rendered surveillable by the universal possibility of over-flight, the city was suddenly exposed, vulnerable not simply to attack but to new modes of comprehension. Cities were reunderstood from the point of view of the bomber. The Second World War, after all, was the first great "war of the cities." Even the insane carnage of the First World War had been largely a phenomenon of the battlefield. Total war—directed against civilian populations with the same vigor as against armies—was the strategic contribution of the Second World War.

An immediate effect of this visibility was the proliferation of strategies of camouflage: the war recast the very idea of the landscape. On the vast roofs of western aircraft factories mock landscapes were constructed, complete with roads, houses, and foliage. To frustrate the bombers, urban installations were made to disappear, suburbanized. Although the United States was never under serious threat of aerial attack, the fear remained and gave the efforts at camouflage their compelling logic. The logic of camouflage also extended to a logic of dispersal. Great wartime facilities were often located outside of cities—at Oak Ridge, Hanford, Los Alamos in the case of the atomic program—both to protect them from attack and to bring the entire American landscape within the orderly regimen of the war effort.

The scopic mentality of the bomber system became that of the planner as well. No need to rehearse the tribulations of urban renewal, the careful wantonness with which "dangerous" parts of towns were measured and destroyed, made safe for another vision, for the modernist rationalities of cars and commerce. The perishability of the metropolis was reseen in light of the experience of war, both physically and conceptually. The blazing cities of Europe and Asia and the dissipated motor archipelago of America both gave the project of postwar urbanism confidence.

The war made the world safe for Disneyland. For the first time in history, a global vision of cities had truly emerged. Habituated to the single comprehension of the world by the speed and scope of the war, to the possibility for truly enormous cycles of destruction and reconstruction, to the loosing of the project of urbanism from its basis in traditional centers, and to the logics of camouflage and re-representation, the plannerly imagination was free for unprecedented acts of recombination and reinvention. The complex against which Eisenhower cautioned in his valedictory address was, after all, multinational, and—at the apex of the American Century—it was only logical that an acquisitive, commercial, quickly depreciated, image-saturated urbanism should flourish.

Disneyland (opened in 1955, now physically incarnate on three continents, virtually ubiquitous on TV) is both the leading fact and the dominant metaphor for this transformation. Its creative geographical practices—which allow the free juxtaposition of the elements within the park as well as the free juxtaposition of the parks within host cultures—participate in the great war-bred spatial departicularization of the postmodern city. But Disney finds its resonance not simply in the familiar mendacities of its counterfeit architecture but in its project of pure consumption, its vision of the city as a factory for leisure. In this, it perfectly parallels Ike's own passage from the trenches to the links, afflicted equally by the narrow dimensions of its recast purpose.

Hollin Hills

I grew up in a fantasy of a suburb. Hollin Hills was begun in 1949 and constructed in two major phases through the early 1970s. The project of **223** developer Charles Davenport and architect Charles Goodman with a landscape scheme by Dan Kiley, it stood out among its Fairfax County, Virginia, neighbors for the candor of its modernity, legendarily different from the colonialoid carpet of its surroundings. After tooling through red-brick Alexandria in both its authentic and ersatz incarnations (the Georgian Gulf station . . . the Federalesque dry cleaner) and passing a legion of more typical suburban constructions, the split-levels and mini-Taras of the standard-issue American dream, one arrived at an unexpected Arden of the new. Glass-walled and crisply lined, the houses were of the same materials—wood and brick—as the neighboring burbs but were radically unlike them in expression.

Although the basic plan types were limited, each house was inflected cosmetically or in configuration to produce a satisfyingly individual character for each. Variations in cladding and finish, orientation, elevation, roof type (flat, pitched, or "butterfly"), layout, and detail made up a brilliant and satisfying system of customization and variety. This sense of expression and elaboration within a consistent modern idiom was extended over the years by an amazing proliferation of additions (each vetted by a community architectural board) that served to house the growing families and prosperity of residents, who thought themselves virtual citizens of the place.

Hollin Hills's modernity strongly predicted the character of its inhabitants. First settled by a cadre of civil servants and others drawn to Washington by the New Deal and the war, its politics were strongly liberal from the outset, reinforced by an infusion of New Frontierspersons after the Kennedy election. In this it stood out strongly from its surroundings—still in the Jim Crow throes—a tiny demographic blip. In the early days, the subdivision's liberalism imparted a fine sense of reciprocal beleaguerment and hostility: the roads were notoriously unplowed after snowstorms, icy for days after the surrounding streets were running free. Residents felt dramatically unrepresented at all levels of government. Adlai Stevenson was surely the post-Rooseveltian politician who most succinctly embodied the (frustrated) political dreams of Hollin Hillers.

In many ways, Hollin Hills was the postwar variation and resting place of the territorial imagination of the New Deal and the war, the extension of Radburn or Greenbelt by other means, transformed by a new postwar attitude toward collectivity and prosperity. Hollin Hills was the new town as suburb. It retained the organic site planning, the reverence for landscape, and the collective green spaces of the Greenbelt towns but replaced their apartment and attached architectural typologies with the single-family house. The collective activities of the new town were (in a familiar paring) reduced to recreation—community open spaces, swimming pool, and tennis courts. An interesting side debate about the mutual definition of community character came in the early sixties, when a proposal was floated to augment the sports facilities with a squash court. The initiative was defeated because squash was considered to be too "elitist" a game. Similarly, efforts to install curbs, sidewalks, and streetlights were consistently rejected as inimical to the Arcadian character of the community.

Although the hyperdevelopment of Fairfax County has now flattened the demographic anomaly of Hollin Hills, it strongly retains the character of its architectural and planning intentions. One might argue that mass suburbanization is the result of the war, of the simple calculus of prosperity plus automobilization plus the GI loan, but Hollin Hills is clearly a special case. If the war redeemed functionalism as the national mode of design, Hollin Hills retained the purity of this intention and carried on the collective fantasy of both prewar new town planning and the wartime collective housing. Like the experience of the Greenbelt towns, it thrived on its sense of experimental anomaly.

Mushroom Cloud

Observing the first blast at Alamogordo, Oppenheimer spake, following Shiva, "I am become death, destroyer of worlds." For the first time, global annihilation had a form: the mushroom cloud was death's placenta. My own first memories of the nuclear age are somewhat more benign, via Walt Disney's production "Our Friend the Atom," which I consumed both on television and in the tie-in book. The atom was civilized by being reduced to its most minute, benign, and stable form. Its principal signifier in the early postwar era was the nucleus with its happy surrounding of elliptical orbits, the Trinity Site of proton, neutron, and electron.

The atom's invisibility suggested exactly that it could not hurt you. Unlike microbes, which (in contrast to the abundantly foregrounded images of the atom) were never presented as having any discernible form, the atom was made to seem harmless by its very representability. The image of the atom thus proliferated as a symbol of science and progress, visible everywhere from home appliance logos to drive-in restaurant marquees. The decor of the fifties is all bursts and orbits, nuclei and energetic spheres. The atom was fully relegated to the class of things, isolated from life.

The most familiar depictions of the bomb's effects were strictly taken from the cosmos of objects, images of the old warships sunk at Bikini, of the test houses blown apart at the desert site. Of the bomb's effects on humans, the image was of troops watching the blast through sunglasses or simply turning away. We were spared the site of the hapless livestock vaporized in New Mexico or of the Hiroshima maidens. The paranoia (and the cancers) came a little later.

That the atom so readily became a chipper symbol of American modernity in the immediate aftermath of its use as the greatest instrument of mass death in human history speaks volumes about the relationship of the accomplishments of war to the formal culture of peace. The bomb is simply the extreme case of the necessary modifications. Of course, part of the agenda behind all of this was not just retrospective redemption but foundation laying for the prodigies of military expenditure to come and for the great, failed buildup of the atomic power industry. But beyond that, the representations of the atomic, its breakneck passage into commercial folklore describes a crucial mechanism of American understanding of the war: nothing bad could come of something so good.

Manzanar

War made America a monoculture. It encouraged us to "put aside our differences" in order to unite in the common purpose of victory. This unity had many happy consequences, including widespread prosperity, increased racial integration, and an opening of the workforce to women. It also accelerated a pervasive discourse of visuality, a corporate identity for the nation, a commingling of the notions of sacrifice, virtue, and purpose. The message was not simply that we were fighting in defense of our values, but that the order and means by which we defended them *were* our values.

The war was—inter alia—a remarkable feat of urbanization, an era of instant cities. From military camps to huge projects for armaments workers, millions were newly housed in the most unprecedented construction surge in the nation's history. At one level, this effort was a titanic success. Quantitatively, the sheer orderly enclosure of space, the provision of infrastructure, the organization of production was peerless. At another level, though, this was qualitatively an urbanism of total failure, a setup for failures to come.

These new cities were company towns raised to the nth power. Consecrated to a single function—housing troops, aircraft, or atomic workers—they were conceived and valued in terms of the efficiency of their hermetic arrangements. Even those towns most generally singled out for praise—Oak Ridge, Linda Vista, and so on—are striking not for any special contribution to the richness of urban social life but rather for their relative sensitivity to the landscape, for their confirmation of the principles of the Garden City/Greenbelt movement, or for their prototypical suburban-style shopping centers.

The most extreme examples of these wartime single-purpose towns were to be found in America's own gulag, the internment camps into which Americans of Japanese origin were forced, beginning in 1942. Here, in effect, was the dark side of Radburn and Greenbelt, preemptive prisons for a part of our citizenship that, while having committed no crime, was nonetheless viewed—for racial reasons—as harboring such a propensity. Modeled on military camps, these towns included none of the garden city or architectural niceties of the better-designed war-work communities that were built concurrently with them. Like military camps and company towns, the internment camps were essays in the limits of architecture, the edges of elaboration and comfort necessary to insure the disciplined and self-conscious behavior of their inhabitants.

The Janus of the monofunctional, monocultural settlement pervades the dominant settlement types of the postwar American landscape. The suburbs—company towns for the project of consumption—owe their failures exactly to their incompleteness, to the invisibility of the workplaces necessary to sustain them. The animating fantasy of the suburbs is a rising and universal prosperity to which they, however, make no contribution, save as reward. In their own way, the suburbs require a discipline as sacrificial and exacting as any factory town, hemmed by a set of possibilities that forces the production of variety entirely into the domestic sphere.

The other great postwar phenomenon of American urbanism is the housing project of "urban renewal." The standard understanding surely overemphasizes the role of architectural and urbanistic modernism in propagating the ethos that led to the construction of the drear archipelago of American public housing. To be sure, modernism, with its Cartesian, Enlightenment roots, was predicated on the notion of a universal subject, a new everyman, prepared to sacrifice his or her individuality to the melting pot of the new culture of rationality. The war with its ideas of common purpose, universal service, and uniform(ed) expression was the high-water mark of an optimistic vision for possibilities of such difference obliteration as a strategy for happiness.

Manzanar represents the means for the oppressive imposition of a virtuously rationalized sameness. The imprisonment of the Japanese "aliens" was but a modest experiment in comparison with the vast undertaking that was to transform so much of the American "inner city" after the war. The new subject was not Japanese Americans, of course, but African Americans. The war had provided the rationale for the mono-functional order of the spaces of production and culture. Such organiza-tion was both necessary and beneficial because the aims of warring were so self-evidently good. So too, in general, were the results: America was restored both to prosperity and to world leadership. The result was a sanctification of the forms that had produced the victory. On the one hand, this lead to the proliferation of consumer machinery, and on the other, to a rampantly univalent view of the environment. Unfortunately, the means of waging war, the kinds of social organization inspired by emergency, proved to be an equally adept means of waging a kind of in-ternal warfare, of subjugating a home population that was the object of both fear and revulsion. The argument for Manzanar—so easily accepted at the time—was brought, under the banner of therapy and optimism, to every city in America.

John Wayne

One of the premier media spectacles of the 1993–94 season was the twin trials of Lorena and John Wayne Bobbitt in Manassas, Virginia. As you may recall, both Bobbitts were acquitted, she of assault (the charge was cutting off her husband's penis), and he of rape. Although the spectacle was global, the trials took place in a town that was itself the object of con-troversy as the proposed site for a new Disneyland. That project also faced great trials: instead of the usual deployment of Tomorrowland, Fantasyland, Frontierland, and so on, the new theme park was to be based on the re-creation of scenes from American history, including the battles of Bull Run, themselves fought nearby. As with any act of media-tion, both struggles were over what was to be believed, what versions were to be included and which excluded. As the media produced show trials for the Bobbitts, so Disney proposed to convert history into show.

The trial mesmerized the world for its mythic—almost Greek—char-acter, dominating both local and global media for weeks. It especially resonated as the desperate rising of a woman against a historic routine of domination, against a familiar imperial ordering of the world. The names (Bobbitt = Babbitt plus the Hobbit?) were crucial and inescapable and served to enlarge and mediate the event. The emasculation of a former Marine named John Wayne by his Latin American wife thus also marks a cutoff of an axis of penetration of the image of the Second World War into American life. As Disney's effort to make Civil War carnage into an afternoon's fun was an inevitable aura sapper, so Bobbitt's bad behavior (like that of his nominal brother John Wayne Gacy) only rewrote their eponymic make-believe war hero as a brute.

America exited the war with a sense of exhilaration. As a child, this was conveyed to me in the countless World War II films, which were a staple of Hollywood production until the endless, rivening folly of Vietnam made the bloodless optimism of these films impossible to sustain. No figure better embodied the blithe one-dimensionality of this perspective than John Wayne. In role after role, he portrayed the laconic heroism of America, fighting and cosmetically dying for a purpose that was simply beyond disputing, continuous with the democratic project of America itself. Emblematically, Wayne's *Green Berets,* a final attempt to make a boosterish World War II–style film on the subject of Vietnam, itself marked the last gasp of the genre.

Wayne's minimalist politics found their way into the actual corridors of power in the person of Ronald Reagan. Reagan was the end of the line for the conversion of the war into an empty aspect of the national fantasy, the complete adolescent's version of the war made policy. As an actor, Reagan had sat out the war in Hollywood, making films, parading around town in an impressive uniform. Although he lived through it, Reagan had—in an officially sanctioned version—the same relationship to the war that I had as a boy, rat-a-tat-tatting with a pretend machine gun, consumed with hardware, with the sheer weight of gadgetry, with the astounding adventures of secret weapons and international intrigues.

Indeed, the centerpiece of the Reagan presidency was his promotion of that incredible fantasy of cinema bellicosity: Star Wars. This program to spend our way to ultimate security was aptly named: George Lucas's films recuperate the Waynesque war movie via genre bending. Those aliens marked for annihilation by their storm-trooper-style headgear collaborate in a project to reduce warfare to a matter of style and decor, to further inscribe the experience of the war into the realm of boyish play-acting and the sphere of the cartoon. With Star Wars, Reagan refined the postwar *propter* war fallacy to the ultimate degree: he completely identified prosperity with warfare. This was the delusion of Reaganomics, the supply-siders' inability to distinguish between spending and prosperity with the result that we simply waged economic warfare on ourselves in a potlatch of mutually assured bankruptcy.

As real memories of the war fade, its artifacts become more and more important, unattached mnemonics awaiting the valence of culture. The P-38 becomes the '52 Caddy becomes the Millennium Falcon becomes . . . John Wayne becomes John Wayne Gacy becomes John Wayne Bobbitt becomes . . . With each successive iteration, meaning is both lost and replaced, and we more and more pass into the Disneyland of distorted recall. Fifty years after its end, the effects of the war are everywhere, just less and less visible as they dissolve with a hiss and a rush into the memory of the nation.

1995

Genius Loco: A Success Story

Over and over, the memory recurs. Lobsters, muckling in grandmama's tub, awaiting the pot. Motley green, moving slow-mo round the perimeter of the bath, invulnerably carapaced. Or so I thought.

Later, chucked into the boil, battering their death tattoo against the tin, pockmarking the sealed cylinder of their doom.

Then the emergence, the miracle: masque of the red death. Bright babies. And delicious.

Chow down, little Lobster, my gramma would tell me, tail cracking and butter dipping, handing over lumps of meat so delectable it was not possible to have enough.

Afterward, shells in a heap, soaped and washed, handed to me. I had collected a multitude. And (the dream begins) built amazing houses, bound with tape and Duco Cement. Here happy little shell-less lobsters lived, plump, fleshy, cherubic, tended by me. I mopped their little crustacean brows, still fevered from the pot. Why always penance for pleasure?

I was actually born here. Grew up in Hollywoodland, in the valley of the shadow of the original sign, before our premiere symbol collapsed into inaccuracy. My parents had emigrated from Detroit shortly after their marriage. According to a favored family account, yours truly was conceived on the Twentieth Century Limited on the way out. To this day, I am unable to hear the cadence of a train's clickety-clack without summoning up an image of rhythmic humping, pa athwart ma. I dream of the interruption of the porter's knock but know well the consequences for myself.

I do not get my artistic propensities from my father. He was an accomplished accountant of great arithmetic acumen (this gene was transmitted to me) and self-defeating honesty. His life crisis came when he was working at MGM and was approached by no less than Irving Thalberg to make some modest culinary modifications to the company's books. After brief but intense agonies, he left their employ and was from that moment a bitter and broken man. To the end of his days, he held Thalberg responsible for his misfortune. He was unable to forgive Scott Fitzgerald for the flattering portrait of "that Jew Mephistopheles" in *The Last Tycoon*.

My mother was for many years under contract at Paramount. Although her roles were never large, they were numerous, and she moved gracefully from pert maids to bloated dowagers. She once—in the otherwise forgettable *Mongoose Serenade*—even received a kiss from John Barrymore. This became the cause of considerable friction between my parents. After his debacle at MGM, my father took an even more jaundiced view of Hollywood morality and increasingly saw my mother's continued employment in the industry as an affront to the memory of his own scrupulosity.

My childhood was spent in a stucco bungalow in what my mother referred to—with considerable latitude—as Hancock Park Adjacent. My boyish fascination with the liquid death of lower life forms turned to the faint primeval prurience of the nearby—if vastly more viscous—tar pits of La Brea. Mind, this was long before the civic weal, in its wisdom, scenogrified the place with the current heart-rending elephantine statuary. On the banks of the pits stands little mammoth Dumbo, trunk extended in amazing poignancy and despair toward the perpetually sinking figure of Mama Jumbo, about to slip beneath the slime.

Angelino emotions crest in such moments: we are all cartoon characters out here. The place incites us. In my nursing dreams, the figure ministering to the lobsters is drawn in plain, if deft, strokes, a troubled-looking baby Huey, topknotted like a samurai and swaddled in diapers like a tiny Mahatma. My reveries at the pits were like. Endless hours imagining the way different persons and things would sink. My mother, Donald Duck, the house, the car, the Griffith Observatory. In my head ran Warner Brothers Technicolor reveries of slow death . . . tha . . . tha . . . tha . . . that's all folks! Thus passed many happy hours.

I sometimes think that this rhapsody of displacement was what lead me to architecture. As I stood beside the pits wondering if the sinking of the Pan Pacific auditorium would cause the scum to rise enough to envelope my frail self, I became a whiz at the mental calculation of volumes. My speed at such math certainly contributed to my indispensability during my early office career. I could make an idea, however fraudulent, substantial. Where would the world be without men like me?

A sensitive but indolent young man with vague literary ambitions, my parents had sent me to the University of Southern California to polish my tennis and acquire other rudimentary trappings of higher education. After four years of beer, blondes, and bathos, I had decided to be a poet. Duly, I established myself in a noirish flat on Bunker Hill, Angel's Flight out my window. Alas, the flight was inclined, but I was not. Daily, I would set out fresh bond and fill my Schaeffer for the labors I hoped would come. Mind you, though I may have drawn a writerly blank, my pages were nonetheless filled. I was a demon doodler. Reams of inked skeins and cryptographic variations on my name were balled and trashed on the way to a conclusion that accumulated weight with my waste. Finally it dawned on me: I preferred to draw.

Architecture was only natural. It is pointless to be a painter out here. The struggle is precisely to resist the two dimensions, against illusion. How, after all, could even Vermeer, even Picasso begin to compete with Walt Disney. What is *Les Demoiselles d'Avignon* next to *Bambi* or *Snow White*? However many thousands of paintings the balding satyr may have produced, they are as nothing against the gels oiled for Walt, tens, hundreds of thousands of paintings framed and sent to dance in the dark before the rapturous eyes of millions!

These thoughts were not exactly on my mind when I took the decision to pursue architecture. Maybe some weeny germs, but nothing specific. My tenure among the beleaguered citizens of Bunker Hill as a sniveling would-be writer had also awakened a certain John Reedesque sense of hubris vis-à-vis my own credentials as proletarian slug. And my personal colossus—architecture-wise—was Frank Lloyd Wright, mediated via Ayn Rand and Gary Cooper, whom I loved for *Beau Geste* and *For Whom the Bell Tolls*. Needless to say, this conflation of freedom fighter, leading man, and architect was bound to appeal to an asthmatic twenty-two-year-old on the cusp of an uncertain career commitment.

I went to work for old Lawn Johnson, the builder (a neighbor of my parents), shirtlessly framing spec houses in Las Feliz. Apt name! Happy I was. Burnt penitentially red like a lobster, blessed with incipient musculature, I joyfully nailed my way through a cloudless summer. Johnson, as you may know, was not simply g.c. for those stick rancheros, he was contractor to the stars of the L.A. architectural firmament for close to forty years, the man who brought the work of three generations to being. Johnson built them all, from Schindler to Soriano, Eames to Ellwood, Wright père down to Wright fils. I was aware of none of this at the time I started out.

Lawn knew more about the work of those architects than they did themselves. After all—as he never tired of repeating—he had designed most of it, converting "piece of shit details" into the elegant economy of the building trades. We soon developed a nice rapport based on flattery and gin, and he began to take me around to the job sites of his more interesting projects, showing me exactly how he had "saved that Heinie's **233** ass." This was my education in wood and steel, stucco and glass, then as now the favored Southland building materials. It was also on these tours—me at the wheel of Johnson's Packard convertible—that I first began to learn of the powers I had acquired on the banks of the pits.

It seems that I could walk into a room—barely framed out—and estimate at a glance its dimensions and volume to the inch. Johnson pretty quickly realized the utility of this particular knack and put me in charge of cost estimating. I was a wizard here. Once I got up to speed on a few basics, I found I could ballpark a four-thousand-foot house in ten minutes and come up with really accurate figures in under an hour. I rapidly became, for the first time in my life, indispensable, the measurer of all things.

When war broke out, though, the work dried up. Asthma kept me from the army (fear my wheezing would betray our position to enemy troops, I presume), and I wound up with time on my hands. I had a nisei friend, Ted Fujitsu, who was studying architecture at USC when the authorities put it to him that he could either go sit in a concentration camp in the desert or head inland to some place where he would be unable to signal Jap subs from the Santa Monica pier. Ted wound up at the Armour Institute in Chicago, and I decided to join him.

Mies himself greeted us from behind a cloud of Havana smoke as we strode in disheveled from the Super Chief. His greeting was perfunctory: "Gott iss in ze details. Now, go draw bricks. Flemish bond, ja?" And so we passed two years, drafting elevations for our *Liebermeister,* passing from brick to steel, from houses to skyscrapers. My thesis project was a shoe-box-shaped glass and white steel house, up on little stilts, which I was somewhat chagrined to see several years later standing in Plano, Illinois.

There still was not a lot of construction going on in 1943 when I got back—mansion building was a little sluggish—so I was obliged to look elsewhere for work. I also felt a tad ambivalent about my noncontribution to the war effort and looked for some assuaging employment. I wound up as a draftsman at Douglas Aircraft in Santa Monica. It was a perfect situation, really. I was working nights, which left the day for the beach and my own artistic endeavors. These, despite my initial thinking on the subject, took the form of paintings.

I began to paint Los Angeles. I figured that since the subject matter was itself surreal enough, there was no need to dress it up with any fresh distortion, although I did—more often than not—manage to work a bright red lobster or two into the view somewhere. I rapidly became enamored of the horizontal format: my reading of the town was all lateral, long cruises down Wilshire with the rangy hills following to the right or left. And I loved the palms, especially the tall royals, rising like skyrockets to burst a hundred feet above the street.

At war's end, I demobilized myself and went back to Lawn Johnson. Armed with Uncle Sam's credit, the Southland was aswarm with vets chasing mortgages. The mortgages were chasing houses, and business was booming, split-levels hatching like lobsters in the springtime. Johnson was getting on in years and had come to prefer nine holes of golf in Brentwood in the morning to screaming at his carpenters in the valley. This left me at the end of a lot of phone calls that the old man would otherwise have taken. One day, a Dr. Bricklmeier called up and wondered whether there was anyone at Johnson's who could design him a house. Said he could not understand why he should have to hire both an architect and a contractor. I said, why sure there was somebody and set to work.

The result is pretty well known today, in all the guidebooks. Less well known is the fact that the neighbors used to call it "Bricklmeier's Shit House" when it first went up. Chicago had paid off. The house is not altogether unrelated to one of Mies's for a brick villa (turnabout is fair play!). His never got built. Mine did. As did my next house, for Dr. Schutz (why these doctors?), which I decided to do in steel. I do believe the first crisp-cornered I-beamed house (outgrowth of my thesis) was mine for Schutz. There are others who agree with me on this.

Unfortunately for the historical record, Schutz was a quack: he had been selling various suckers (and we are the capital of credulity here) some piss that he claimed to be the secret of eternal youth. He was shot to death by one of his marks barely hours after taking possession, and the house passed to his nephew Cerwin, who could not stand the place and had it done over in pastels and fake timbering, obliterating the evidence. There was some justice, though. About six months later Cerwin was apparently smoking in bed, and the whole thing (including Cerwin) burned to a crisp.

This pretty much jinxed my career as an independent operator in the field. The potential client base just dried up. I had already abandoned Johnson to strike out on my own, and was not about to go crawling back. Having established that I could turn out houses just as good as the next modern architect, I was loathe to go to work for anyone. But, a boy's gotta eat, and my enforced indolence was not putting too many lobsters on the table. What to do?

For the first time in my life I responded to the waking dream of every

Angelino and headed for Hollywood. Celeste, my then girlfriend, had a friend who was a middling-level "creative" type at Disney. He had been over to visit (I was living at this point in the High Tower apartments at the end of Hightower—the one with the Bolognese elevator), had admired my paintings and my hapless houses, and had suggested that there might be a place for me in the organization. He had especially admired, unsurprisingly enough, the work I had been doing on crustacean themes.

I did not know exactly what awaited me at the studio—I had imagined a job as a set decorator or painting forest (and sea) creatures in the animation mill. Things turned out differently. I had—like Philby or Blunt—been plucked from my sincere obscurity to serve a higher purpose. It was 1952, and the greatest imaginative undertaking of the era had, under cover of secrecy, begun to rapidly emerge from the realm of ideas into the world of forms. I had been recruited to become one of Walt's Imagineers, the brain trust that delivered Disneyland.

I moved up fast. I flatter myself with thinking that I became the Oppie on this particular (anti-)Manhattan project.

You see, I could do everything. I could conjure an image fast. I could manage the technical drawings—my years at Douglas had given me a pretty good grip on machinery. In no time flat, I could tell how much it was going to cost. And as a designer, I soon discovered I had no scruples. If only Mies had been able to see me sketching the papier-mâché bricks for Mr. Toad's Wild Ride or drafting up the chomping mechanism on the fiberglass hippo that has scared so many millions on the Jungle Cruise.

Walt and Mies are the yin-yangs of twentieth-century visual culture. I have often imagined what their meeting might have been like. Perhaps, like matter and antimatter, they would have simply annihilated each other. To be sure, I did not see much of Walt myself. He mainly communicated with me as if from the beyond, mysteriously, notes appearing on my desk overnight, doodles on my drafting board. The comments were often minor, but that was not exactly the point. If Walt understood one thing, it was that the appearance of authority was inseparable from its substance. The man was a metaphysician.

Conventional wisdom had it that Walt knew just what he wanted at Disneyland. Well, he did and he didn't. Walt's imagination was L.A. incarnate, just fragments. It was me who gave it some kind of logic. Walt's vision was really just of an incredibly clean amusement park with really good rides enshrining the members of what he cloyingly called his "family." Every time the man would get dewy-eyed over Dumbo, my mind would waft back to the tar pits. I could see dozens of Dumbos, trunk to tail to trunk to tail—an elephantine daisy chain—marching down Wilshire Boulevard with glazed eyes, gigantic lemmings, longing for the tar. And in they would go, each with a comforting slurp of suction as he sank beneath the mire. Many was the night this happy narcotic saw me safely to sleep.

One of the keys to my power over the situation was the fact that Walt was not simply a terrible draftsman but was filled with secret anxieties over it. I, of course, am a splendid draftsman, a fact that has been one of the keys to both the successes and failures of my career, such as it is. Walt's charm and his genius were both linked to his—you should forgive the phrase—retention of his capacity for childlike wonder. There was always an undercurrent of weirdness around the studio, prompted by the fact that there we were, nominal adults, educated and talented, whisky drinkers and womanizers, spending our days creating the cult of a talking mouse.

As I was saying, the keys to my manipulation were draftsmanship, *Mauskultur,* whiskey (of which, more later), and that faint pornography that undergirded so much of the operation. If I had an idea for the park that I wanted to put over, I would draw up a magnificent perspective, vanishing points galore, ink washes, fiendish detail. At the bottom, I would draw a little winking Dumbo, pen in trunk, nominal auteur, surrounded by a dozen tinkerbelloid nymphs, anatomically correct under gossamer. This, I would leave on my desk, caught in the beam of my drafting lamp. Mornings, on my return, the drawing would be gone, the lamp shut off, and faint fumes of Chivas Regal suspended in the room. Inevitably, next day, a drawing of a leering, winking mouse with a hard-on would turn up on my desk, captioned in Walt's unmistakable calligraphy, "Mickey likes it."

Walt and I did occasionally pass time together. There were meetings, naturally, but these were perfunctory, rituals at which we assented to foregone conclusions. But Walt and I had a secret life. It began one evening when I was at my board, working late on a rendering of the Cinderella's Castle. I remember the warm smell of Chivas drifting over my shoulder and turned to find Walt. I was prepared for this and produced a bottle and a couple of glasses. Walt was all maudlin volubility, and we talked about his life and dreams for the better part of an hour, me, as ever, artfully inserting the concepts and phrases I thought were key, embedding them for future retrieval.

Suddenly, Walt said to me, "Let's go someplace." It was clear he had someplace in mind. We drove in Walt's big Chrysler convertible out toward the desert along the Vegas road, top down, whiskey-serious, silent under the dome of stars. Around Palmdale, we turned off and roared down dirt to what was, in those days, described as a roadhouse. Walt parked and reaching under the seat, produced the most ridiculous-looking red rug imaginable. He gave me a wink, put it on, and in we went. It was a dark bar, a crowd of a dozen or so in their desultory cups, evidently waiting for something to take place on a small stage. The barman asked "Mr. Smith" if he wanted the usual, and at Walt's nod, brought the Chivas bottle over to the table and poured us each a stiff one.

A spot lit the tiny stage as the piano man began "When You Wish upon a Star." From behind the curtain, a little girl—no more than eleven or twelve years old—in a tutu emerged, dancing on pointe, a star-topped wand in her hand. Walt sat bolt upright, transfixed as she pirouetted and pliéd to the music. As the now attentive clientele shuffled their chairs in for a closer view, she peeled one and then the other of her straps and slowly slipped out of her costume to stand prepubescent naked, except for her toe shoes. Walt was quivering with excitement, his eyes swimming with tears. The girl pirouetted round and round, ever so slowly, irradiated by leering stares. Then, she stopped, turned her back, grabbed her cheeks, and threw Walt a lingering moon before prancing offstage. Walt stared and stared in silence at the place she had been, finally murmuring, "innocence."

Now I am not a person to deny a man his proclivities. Indeed, as a premiere devotee of L.A., the holy terrain of dumb preference, the free-fire zone of anything goes, where every man's castle is his home, I can hardly regard myself as anything other than staunch, ACLU-firm in defense of whatever he harmlessly pleases to do within. But—call it a weakness, call it conventional—I have just never cottoned to that kind of short-eyed entertainment. Now, the astute among you may well observe that my activities on behalf of the Mausmeister were themselves no more than the same. Ah, but there is a difference. This place, this hallowed pueblo site, this Angelus, this sump of hopes, this last resort, this testament to the banality of freedom, this shrine to physical health without mental . . . isn't it about childhood? About life forever? Why is Walt presently a nitrogen ice cube, daily converting his senescence into youth on the lengthening span of his time? But there is the point! It is one thing to be a child, another to take advantage.

After that evening in Palmdale, I drifted away from Walt and his works. In truth, the thing, the degenerate utopian park was done. Unbeknownst to Walt and his sycophants, I had patterned the whole thing on Los Angeles, twisted with craven irony. In the self-congratulatory palaver of the office, we had persuaded ourselves that we created an enclave in the city of the automobile, a sea of pedestrianized tranquility in the motorcar's very maw. Ha! What had we really made? A shrine to the car. After all, what was there to do in Disneyland? Ride on cars of all descriptions, ride them outdoors, ride them indoors! We had conquered the last zone to be free of them. Imagine the sight. Millions of meso-Americans sweltering on lines, overpriced ice cream dripping down their fat credulous faces, as they awaited their three minutes of bliss on a teacup car or submarine bus. And the lines! After inching for hours on the freeway to Anaheim, they got it again: the ultimate traffic jam, waiting carless to ride.

I took my leave of Walt in the midst of what we now call the fifties, an era I had in no small measure already helped to shape. Although I had served Walt well—better than he would ever know—I felt a little sullied by it all. I resented his having exposed my aptitude for mendacity. Oh the sow's ears I plucked from the fire for him! Who was it who benignified that trashy Main Street by reducing its scale to ⅝ths of "reality"? Like those giant cars that marked the era, I empowered millions of citizens by enlarging them, scaling up their presence in the world. I was the Harley Earl of the built environment.

My next job was only apt: I went to work for the architect Owen Wister, the mad dog of the Arts and Architecture crowd. Wister—late-blooming Marinetti—had been making noises about architecture's aspiration to be "as good as a fin-fun Caddy Eldorado" for some time. Infelicity of language notwithstanding, I figured I was the man to help him make good on his promise. The first thing he gave me to do was to work on the original Chee-Chee's drive-in on Sunset. Torn down now but remains forever amber in the eyes of partisans of the higher kitsch. And god knows, there are plenty of them. Hell, I have talked to dozens of graduate students—pimply semioticians from the land grants—writing their dissertations on the sign alone.

I take full credit (or blame, if you prefer to see it like that). Of course, we would never have done the sign the same way today. At the time it seemed a stroke of genius. After the thing made the cover of *Life* magazine, Wister made me partner on the spot. The sign's origins are not exactly shrouded in mists of confusion. I had just seen *The Seven Year Itch*, and of course, there is the scene where Marilyn's skirt just will not stay down. A cinch in neon. And those, needless to say, were the days when a hamburger could not be sold without at least a whiff of musk. A more innocent time, as I believe it is often referred to.

The genius of the sign, as these whelps never seem to figure out, was not the idiotic bottom-baring carhop, it was the whole spatial thing. The shapes were different obviously, but the perspectival relationship between the sign and the triple doors (skaters in, skaters out, and customers) was borrowed from the proportions of the Duomo and the Baptistery in Florence. I tried to persuade the management to include a Giotto Burger on the menu as a little joke, but the philistines balked. Not that it would have stood out exactly, sandwiched between the Fonda Burger ("Young Mr. Burger") and the Hayworth Burger ("coated in a sweater of melted all-American cheese"). Then again, maybe it would have. At least they didn't question the lobster in the carhop's hand. Universal symbol of fine eating.

The other big deal I worked on at Wister's was the so-called Flying House, which we built for that schmuck producer from Paramount. Little did we know how that moniker, all poetry and line, would come back to haunt us. As the litigation demonstrated, the fault lay with the soils engineer and the subcontractor for the footings. But that was seven years after the fact. Too late to save Wister's career.

Still, the concept was a piece of brilliance. The massive, spread-winged bird form, soaring out from the hillside, supported by those two skinny steel columns. Wister was just so enamored of reinforced concrete (who wasn't in those days) that the thing was too damn heavy for a structure we had no idea we had underdesigned. But the idea, all that weight almost magically airborne, was pure Wister. Unfortunately, 2.1 on the Richter was enough to send it halfway to Hollywood Boulevard, and six houses with it, not to mention the little mogul. The thing that really broke Wister up, though, was that it pulverized that old Lincoln of his, the one he had bought off Mister Wright. Only time I ever saw the old man show the slightest emotion.

For my money, Owen Wister was the best architect of his generation in L.A. That was not his real name, of course. Alois Winkelmann. From Graz, Austria. To hear Wister tell it, half the architects in L.A. before the war spoke German. Wister started out with Van Nest Polglase at RKO. The way he remembers it, the white telephone was his idea to begin with, the whole damn big white set. "Like Christmas in Obersalzberg." There are those who dispute the specifics, but there is no doubt that Wister (he loved cowboys, he learned English from Tom Mix, reading his lips, which must account for his strange accent. It certainly accounts for the Stetson) got his flair for the dramatic from the movies. The rest of the expatriate crowd—Schindler, Neutra, and that bunch—always smirked at him a bit, at all the taffeta and colored lights and such—but it was only the envy of lesser men. Wister thought that they were a bunch of "Teutonic stiff-boys," a category that also included Mies and Gropius. Even after the war, he never tired of telling Neutra to lighten up. I remember how he used to talk about them: "Vat do I need vit all zis Apollonian shit ven I am Dionysus playing on his flutes."

After I left Wister, I went to Herrera. Personality-wise, Chuck Herrera was everything Owen Wister was not: agreeable, smooth-talking, well-connected, patrician, eager to please, crazy to be rich. His office stood in comparable counterpoise. Where Wister's place in an old building on Vine was tumbledown, ink-stained, and casual, Herrera's shiny tower on Wilshire was Barcelona chairs, neckties, the whole corporate culture (you'll pardon the oxymoron) package. Adaptive as I am, an afternoon in Bullock's had me fit to fit in. I can work with anyone.

Although, I will never be given the credit, it was I who steered the firm into the phase that nobody disputes was its greatest glory. Since the early fifties, bread and butter at Herrera had been shopping centers. Basically, they had all been the same. A vastness of cars fronting a long, undistinguished, porticoed enfilade of shops. Just a pituitary version of a Western town, the parched parking lot standing in for the street. Clearly, this would not do. It was boring. And it was replicable. Any hack could throw one up: the Herrera formula lacked sufficient signature.

Now I was a man who knew a thing or two about signature. Disneyland hardly slouches in the John Hancock department. And this is what I told Herrera was wanted, a little reach to go with the grasp. I had another insight that was pretty key, a notion I had glommed from Walt. It was a southward view, down-coastal, the Orange County strategy. The insight was not simply over the axis of development: any boob could see that the lust for lebensraum would ultimately lead that way. No, what I recognized (and reproduced in Anaheim) was that there was culture aborning, that there was hygiene and homogeneity undreamed of in the relative liveliness, the melting pottery of El Lay.

So I put it to Herrera, if shopping is culture, our job was to invent the culture of shopping. And as Disneyland was the greatest architectural implement ever devised for separating fools and their money, this was the road we should follow. Chuck took all of this with a certain amount of circumspection. The man still harbored dreams of becoming a modern master, a stylist, a Mies. But I hammered home my point, that style was stiff and dead, irretrievable victim of styling. I declined to suggest that Chuck had about as much talent as a lobster (no offense meant, life form

241

of my dreams), despite his great and distinguished silver head of hair and matched Porsche. But there he actually had the point. The silver hair and the Porsche were what mattered, we were after appearances.

But let's not talk philosophy. The result of my persuasion was what was initially known as United Nations Plaza. You may not recognize the name. That was pretty quickly changed by the developer to U.S. Mall after a flurry of pressure from the John Birch society. For us, it just meant a change of flags in the central mall. But I am getting ahead of myself. U.S. Mall has earned its evergreen status, its Ezra Stoller photo in every standard work by being no more than the apotheosis of what I had begun chez Diz: bringing it all indoors. Before me, there were shopping centers, linear jobs, mere intensifications of the strip. After me, the city had a fresh form. Changed forever. My gift to the race: civitas for sale.

Herrera loved it, which should come as no surprise since I had turned him into even more of a Croesus than he had ever dreamed. I had clever-ly copped another page from Diz by animating U.S. Mall with marching bands, baton twirlers, teen folk-singing shows, and every manner of rank amateur talent that passes for culture in Orange County (and by exten-sion, the whole U.S. of A.). Chuck took no end of delight in telling civic groups, newspaper reporters, anybody who would listen, that he had brought Main Street back to America, given our communities a heart. For architectural audiences, there would be slides of the Stoa of Attalos and the Piazza San Marco and a raft of other self-serving, entirely irrele-vant examples. In front of merchandising groups, preening Chuck let the fat cat out of the bag. Our malls were moving merchandise at blinding speed, leaving the old shopping centers in the dust.

I stuck with it for a couple of years, drawing up endless riffs on the *parti*. But the formula—with its anchor stores and specialty shops, its Adolf Eichmann glass-box elevators, its shiny, crib-stimulus mobiles, and its playfully gurgling fountains, into which the shopper drones mindless-ly chucked endless coins, propitiations of the shopping gods, grim re-hearsal of the day's activity—charged America. Whatever. To the sleazy magnates of the industry, though, it was just another profit center. When Herrera was a few gimlets to the wind, he liked to boast that his (his!) ar-chitecture was of such sublimity and popular appeal that people could not resist throwing money at it. The hubris of the jerk.

Not that I wasn't making money myself. I was. But Herrera had per-suaded me to invest it in the development corporation he had set up to build the malls, a sure-looking thing. It was a con, of course. To Herrera, the corporation was no more than his own private wishing well, and he looted its capital accordingly. Fortunately, poetry and justice coincided for once. Herrera had devoted considerable of his ill-gotten gains to the construction of the *Mall Deuce,* a grotesque yacht of ocean-liner proportions. I had often wished that Herrera might simply turn into the Los Angeles version of the Flying Dutchman, endlessly cruising on his monster boat, unable to find anyplace to park. What happened was perhaps more sublime. Sailing near Santa Barbara in a fog, *Mall Deuce* struck an oil rig and went down with all hands, including Herrera's, which I might note were grown sleek and slack from not having touched a pencil or drafting implement in many, many a year. The resulting slick killed half the marine bird and mammal life, every hapless abalone, pelican, and clam, on a hundred-mile stretch of coast, an aquatic La Brea such as I had never dreamed. The delicious irony is simply this: this was the big spill that galvanized local antidevelopment forces into cogency, the death dong for many a mall.

What was I then to do? I repaired to Tuscany, thinking I would paint, a perfect transition for an incipient retiree sinking into his cups. But I could not. How could I spend my sunset years away from the sunset? I had been spoiled by L.A. Every cypress reminded me of home. Every whitewashed villa and farmhouse conjured up Holmby Hills. Had I spent too much time with Walt? All of Italy seemed to be Los Angeles in a bad state of repair. I had come to prefer "Tuscany" to Tuscany. I had been the Svengali of surface so long that I preferred an orderly fabric of lies to the unpredictabilities of what passes for "real life." Indeed, I had gone to Italy for a dose of same but could only think how much more I enjoyed the costumed version, those teen-aged Swiss Guards and pumped-up Buckaroos at the real Magic Kingdom.

The fates, as was their wont, found me undone, and took a hand: mine, as usual. While I was at Herrera's, we had had a designer named Gary Lonigan (known to one and all as "Studs"). He was a bright boy, and clearly destined for better things. Predictably, after a few years, he had left the firm to strike out on his own. The lad was talented but confused, lacked the instinct for organization that is necessary for propulsion to the stars. Still, he was doing something that interested me, and when he asked me to come into his office, I said yes. Is it too grand for me to say that I smelled redemption. You see, Lonigan was about everything I no longer was. He was young. He was a mess. His friends were artists. He was endlessly talking about his psychoanalysis.

Still, his work stank. Gary exuded potential, but his projects remained on the stiff side. I thought I could help him. And I thought I knew how. **243**

L.A. was bubbling, a happening time, America's then version of the city of the future. It was time for an architecture that would capture the town, say it all. I would be Svengali, here, or Victor Frankenstein, and Gary would be my Trilby, my creature. It would be all skewed newness and dazzle, the reproduction in form of every subterranean current running through the town.

Where to begin? Daily I sent Gary off to his shrink with some rummy concept to chew over while I worked out the labyrinthine thing. I began below, tectonically, with the primal latency, the unstable earth. Our architecture, I thought, must not merely quiver but shake, readily fall, freeze-frame the disaster of the perpetual perhaps. And burn. Parched earth. Maddening Santa Ana's shoving conflagration down hillsides, flames tonguing at smug suburbanoid arcadias, desperately trying to keep green and safe, resisting apocalypse with lawn sprinklers. Ha! Ha! And Slide.

Those prayed-for fire-time rain torrents never do come. But yes, they do. Months later. Disasters never cancel each other, they multiply. Now, the earth is saturated beyond bearing, and the slanting gray shower loosens denuded mountainsides, which cascade like thunder, reducing prideful architecture before their fall. Retaining walls, relief pits, and barriers are as nothing before the onslaught. I would make an architecture as mesmerizing, as random, as frightening as this heap of ruin, this terminating moraine, an architecture of the downside.

Excuse this enthusiasm. But I realized that I was on to something. Beneath the glitz, the roil. I would be—like Nathanael West or James M. Cain—amanuensis to the whole town, exposing its demons, ventilating its innermost, most repressed fears and desires. It was time to cash in, and I became an old fellow aflame, and Gary bent like a twig before my kindling enthusiasm. He had just bought himself a house, a smug little hispanico in Mar Vista, and I persuaded him to modify it to conform to the new vision. I knew that the change had to be dramatic and—I have spent my life in this town—that the transformative event should be just that, an event. I hired klieg lights and a wrecking ball and got the media down to cover my stroke of genius.

One drop of the ball accomplished it—total demolition of the front of the house. We made all three local networks and the national broadcast of CBS. We then spent two weeks stabilizing the rubble exactly as it fell and covering it with an artful quilt of glass, inside and out. The effect was fabulous. Equally successful was the ensuing trial in Municipal Court. Gary was charged with conducting demolition without a permit. Well, canny me managed to turn this into some kind of a cause célèbre. We argued that the charges were no less than an assault on artistic freedom, the response of narrow-minded philistines to genuine innovation, the paranoid response of little minds to a confrontation with genius.

We were fined $50. The publicity was priceless. None of this could have been any comfort to the neighbors, whose happy complacency and sense of the familiar was irrevocably dislodged by the daily sight of the glittery ruin. In a pathetic act of revenge, several of them attacked the alteration with sledgehammers late one night. It took a week and a half to notice that the addition had been damaged. The more they assaulted it, the more they improved it. Stud's wife, initially sympathetic, was herself displeased with the mastic-covered (Oh La Brea!) mobile home we had installed in the backyard to compensate for the space lost to the primary alteration.

The mobile home completed the basis for this new, this *LArchitecture,* as some slavering art-critic logoed it for us. That establishment fell rapidly in line. I cannot begin to enumerate the number of articles praising Gary for his cunning synthesis of vernacular expression with inspired, rarefied artistry. "The seismograph of contemporaneity," as one magazine had it so felicitously, so usefully. My needle was certainly wiggling.

Converting this capital to commissions was a cinch. That, after all, is where Hollywood comes in. Once I had—with one masterstroke—established Lonigan as the ne plus ultra of hip, we practically had to beat the producers and the ham actors from our door. We did twenty houses in the first year (about ten of them were demolitions, and ten from scratch). The best, I think was the so-called Casa Montalban, constructed primarily of baled Chryslers. We signed a novel contract with the client that holds us harmless in the event that a quake or other "natural or artificial" disaster results in the "rearrangement" of the house. It surely offers the client an important sense of artistic empowerment to share so explicitly in the risk of the new.

Work came in from everywhere, and we were especially popular in the Land of the Rising Sum. We were deluged. Art Museums, Corporate Headquarters, Apartment Houses, the works. At first, our relentless skewings seemed right and resonant, but soon our imitators grew legion. It was time for something new. We had been having some difficulty organizing the plan for a golf club in Fukuoka, and Lonigan and I were sitting in Gladstone's for Fish, desultorily doodling on napkins one day, when the waitron arrived to bib us up for the coming repast. I upended my Margarita, gazed out to sea and back, and my eyes fell on Lonigan's newly protected chest, where I saw not the object of my endless reveries printed on plastic but a fully realized, if artless, perspective drawing of a red and bloody wonderful building. Visions of brick arches in sinuous curves, dark interiors, waving antennae!

It was not immediately easy to sell to Gary. This was a fairly considerable change in direction, inimical to what we had so assiduously hyped as inevitable. But I had an answer. It went to the heart of the Angelene inner methodology. Our tumbledown constructions were the fossils of abstraction, too arcane for a town that thrived on, exulted in, the very surface of surfaces. The world, I told Gary, fervently cracking a claw in perfect twain and sucking out the dripping meat with a violent cyclonic slurp, was ready for the restoration of representation! When Disney drew a duck, was it some Rorschachian inkblot (I said, manipulating the pathetic dweeb)? No, no, a thousand times, no. It was palpably duck, beak and tail, webbed feet and by god a quack!

Our buildings (of course, I said *his* buildings, the story of my life) could no longer afford to be less. In theory, I had allayed his fears about killing the goose that laid the golden egg (representation, what would mythic life be sans?), but he remained troubled by the particular. "Why lobsters?" he wondered, briskly unaware of the personal categorical imperative behind the creatures. I decided to argue in the Angelene mode: no particular logic, just an irresistible tsunami of images. There was Nerval's originating lobster, strolling down the Boul' Miche, mascot of surrealism, father and mother of anything goes. The lobster quadrille, the Disney version of course, happy square-dancing arthropods. Red Lobster, for the seafood lover in you. And then, how I embroidered on the immigrant status of the pure succulence that we were, even as we spoke, polishing off. An abalone, that overtough indigenous mollusk was altogether too modernist: one curve, however compound, and it's done. No, like all the best in town, lobsters were migrants and scavengers. Indeed, every lobster in Los Angeles was an outsider, flown in, resituated, recontextualized, like the Schwarzwald bungalows in boys town or those Dryvit Taras in Brentwood, old fish transformed by stimulating new water. It had to be lobsters.

He bought it. We built Fukuoka. It was the right thing. The age fawned, and before long we were invited to recross the Pacific in triumph, our way to the top clawed at last. Studs had been offered the commission of a lifetime. In 1984, eager to bleed off surfeit capital, Michael Milken approached us to build an enormous cultural center in the San Fernando valley, a zone into which culture had barely impinged, save, perhaps, in the Ruth Benedictine sense. The office spent two years working on the project, which was fiendish in its complications. The same tilers who heat-shielded the space shuttles would have toiled for us, sheathing the endless red carapace curves (perfect acoustic shapes) covering the numerous auditoria.

One day in 1987 it all belly-upped. Damn junk bonds! Damn the SEC! Damn Drexel Burnham!

The day after Milken bagged us, I left Lonigan, who had, in truth, matured into the role himself. I spent long days at Zuma beach, just walking. I stared into the eyes of wiggling, pegged, and rubber-banded green lobsters in the cooler at Ralph's, wondering what they would tell me were they unimprisoned by evolutionary destiny in tank and phylum. I wondered why they could not thrive on their own out here, what Lotusland withheld from them. Gradually, I came to see the expressiveness in their crusty physiognomies, detected, I thought, a wisp of a smile on their sea-colored carafaces. And I thought I knew why. They had what I wanted. Little lobster babies, wearing of the green, always at home, where the tough part is. Looking at the eyes of a three-pounder one day the meaning came clear.

Ladies and gents. I am that lobster.

1992

Publication Information

"Eleven Tasks for Urban Design" originally appeared as "Michael Sorkin: Future Zones [and] Eleven Tasks for Urban Design," *Perspecta,* no. 29 (1998): 20–27.

"Branding Space" originally appeared as "The Big Peep Show: The Media Have Invented a New Kind of Pornography for Times Square," *New York Times Magazine* (December 26, 1999): 9–10.

"Times Square: Status Quo Vadis" appeared in *Harvard Design Magazine* (Winter/Spring 1998): 29.

"Round and Round" appeared in *Metropolis* 18, no. 3 (November 1998): 45–47.

"Cranes over TriBeCa" originally appeared as "Letter from New York," *The Architectural Review* 206, no. 1233 (November 1999): 36–37.

"Big Deal" originally appeared as "Six Degrees of Phyllis Lambert," *Metropolis* 19, no. 3 (November 1999): 82–84.

"A Passage through India" originally appeared as "Chandigarh after Corbusier," *Architectural Record* 186, no. 2 (February 1998): 68–73.

"Instrumental Cities" originally appeared as "Hyper Growth in South China: From the Pearl River Delta to Shanghai," *Architectural Record* 185, no. 7 (July 1997): 72–77, 151.

"Containing Cairo" appeared in *Architectural Record* 189, no. 4 (April 2000): 82–90.

"Second Nature" appeared in *Metropolis* 17, no. 8 (May 1998): 33–35.

"Millennium in Vegas" originally appeared as "Crap Shoot: Gambling on the Triumph of 'Taste' in Las Vegas," *Metropolis* 18, no. 7 (April 1999): 59–61.

"Acting Urban" originally appeared as "Acting Urban: Can New Urbanism Learn from Modernism's Mistakes?" *Metropolis* 18, no. 1 (August–September 1998): 37, 39; and as "Acting Urban: New Urbanism Is Becoming the Acceptable Face of Sprawl," *Urban Land* 57, no. 10 (October 1998): 10, 111.

"Notes on Vibe" originally appeared as "The Urban Vibe," *Architectural Record* 186, no. 6 (June 1998): 68–71, 218.

"Phoenix Rising" originally appeared as "Can Williams and Tsien's Phoenix Art Museum Help This Sprawling Desert City Find Its Edge?" *Architectural Record* 185, no. 1 (January 1997): 84–97.

"Remembering the Future" appeared in *Architectural Record* 187, no. 6 (June 1999): 96–101.

"Animating Space" originally appeared as "Frozen Light" in *Gehry Talks,* edited by Mildred Friedman (New York: Rizzoli, 1999).

"Siza the Day" originally appeared as "Siza Day," *Metropolis* 18, no. 10 (July 1999): 73–75.

"The Borders of Islamic Architecture" appeared in *Metropolis* 18, no. 4 (December 1998): 33, 35.

"Filming Wright" originally appeared as "Documenting Wright," *Metropolis* 18, no. 2 (October 1998): 75–77.

"Inside the Biosphere" originally appeared as "Utopia under Glass," *I.D.* (September/October 1993): 58.

"Come and Getty" originally appeared as "Come and Getty: Archmodernist Meier's Work Takes an Unexpected Turn toward Kitsch," *Metropolis* 17, no. 9 (June 1998): 45–47.

"Habitat and After" appeared as the introduction to *Moshe Safdie,* edited by Wendy Kohn (London: Academy Editions, 1998).

"MOR Is Less" appeared in *Metropolis* 17, no. 10 (July 1998): 45–47.

"Far, Far AwAIA" originally appeared as "American Institute of Architects: 1997 Honors and Awards," *Architectural Record* 185, no. 5 (May 1997): 67–89, 262.

"Amazing Archigram" appeared in *Metropolis* 17, no. 7 (April 1998): 39, 41.

"Admitting the Fold" originally appeared as "When to Fold: A Mass-Market Version of Deleuze," *Metropolis* 19, no. 4 (December 1999): 96–98.

"Forms of Attachment" originally appeared as "Forms of Attachment: Additions to Modern American Monuments," *Lotus International,* no. 72 (1992): 90–95.

"Airport 98" originally appeared as "In Plane View: Norman Foster's Hong Kong Airport Brings the Tarmac into the Terminal," *Metropolis* 18, no. 6 (February–March 1999): 51, 53.

"No Sex Please, We're British" originally appeared as "Overdue" in *Metropolis* 19, no. 2 (October 1999): 97–99.

"How French Is It?" originally appeared as "Empty Premises: What Is It about the French?" an exhibition review in *Metropolis* 18, no. 5 (January 1999): 41, 43.

"Upstairs, Downstairs" originally appeared as "America's Most Visited Houses," *Architectural Record* 186, no. 4 (April 1998): 77, 192.

"Container Riff" appeared in *Present and Futures: Architecture in Cities,* produced by the Collegi D'Arquitectes de Catalunya (Barcelona: Comité d'Organitació del Congres, 1996).

"Family Values" originally appeared as "Neunzehn tausendjahrige Mantras" in *Architektur im AufBruch,* edited by Peter Noever (Munich: Prestel, 1991).

"The Second Greatest Generation" appeared in *Harvard Design Magazine* (Fall 2000): 44–45.

"War Is Swell" appeared in *World War II and the American Dream,* edited by Donald Albrecht (Cambridge, Mass.: MIT Press; Washington, D.C.: National Building Museum, 1995).

"Genius Loco" is published here for the first time.

Michael Sorkin is the principal of the Michael Sorkin Studio in New York City, a design practice devoted to practical and theoretical projects at all scales with a special interest in the city. He is professor of architecture and director of the graduate urban design program at New York's City College. He has written for numerous publications, including *Architectural Record*, *I.D.*, and *Metropolis*, and for ten years he was the architectural critic for the *Village Voice*. He is the author of *Variations on a Theme Park*, *Exquisite Corpse*, *Local Code*, *Giving Ground* (edited with Joan Copjec), and *Wiggle*, a monograph of his studio's work.